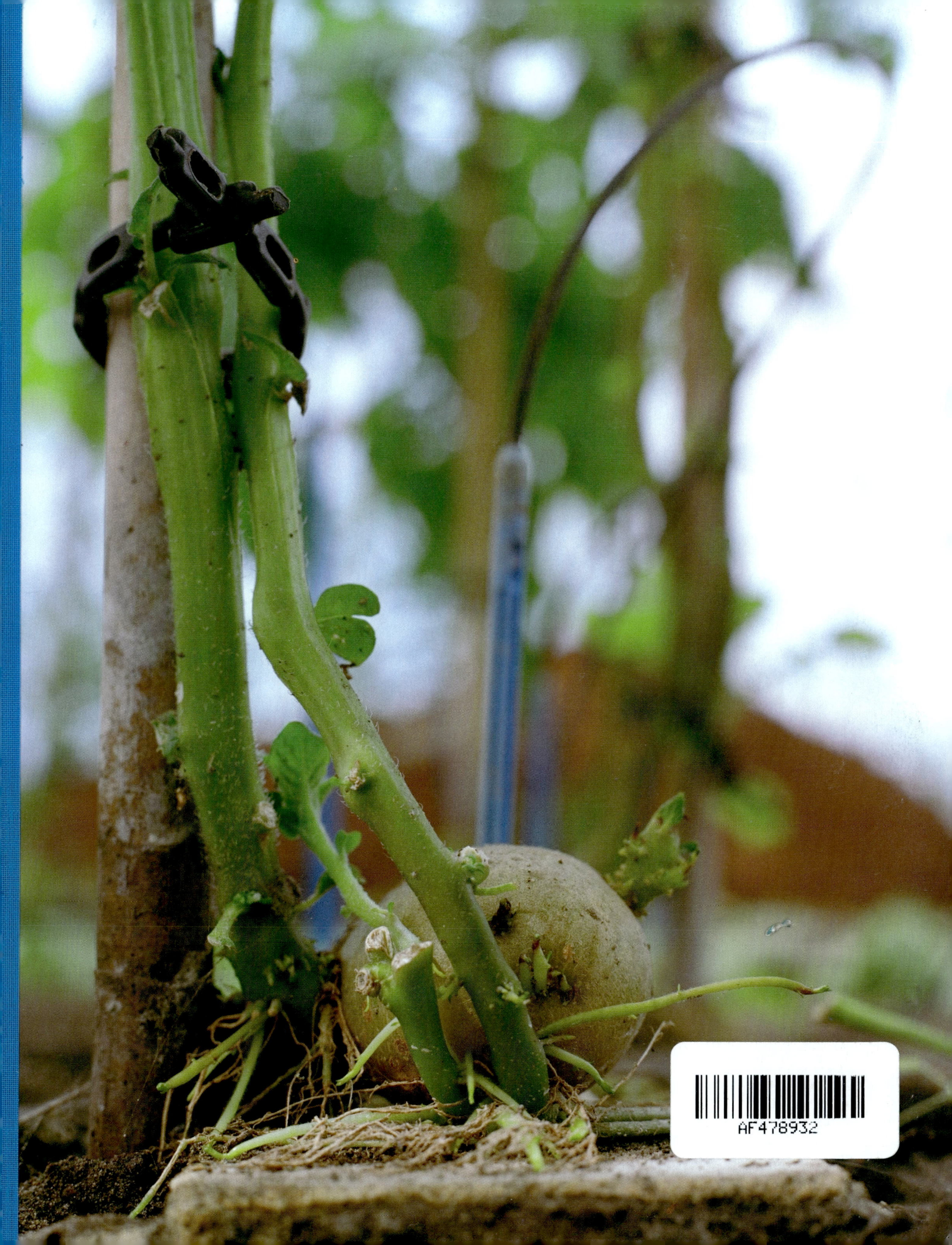
AF478932

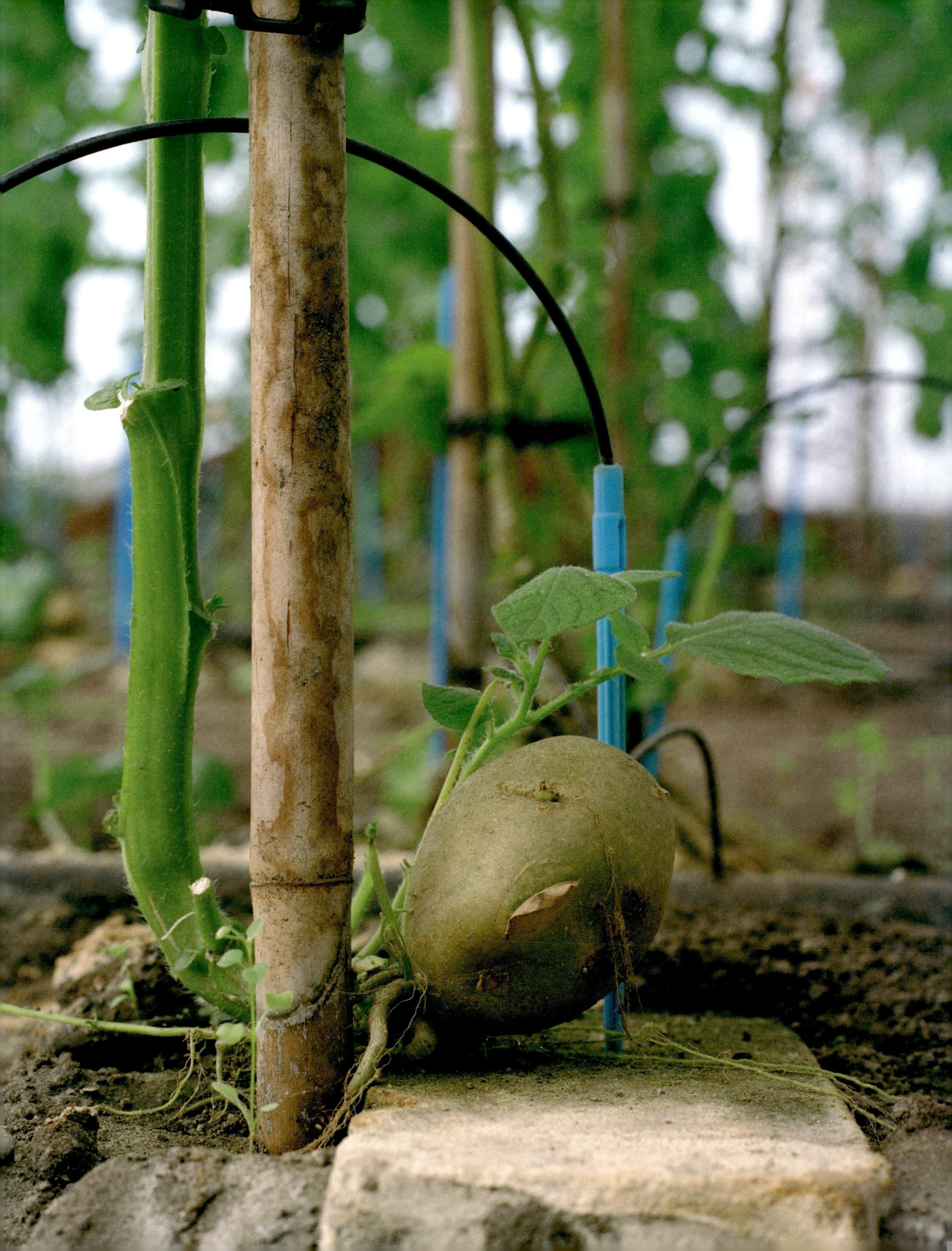

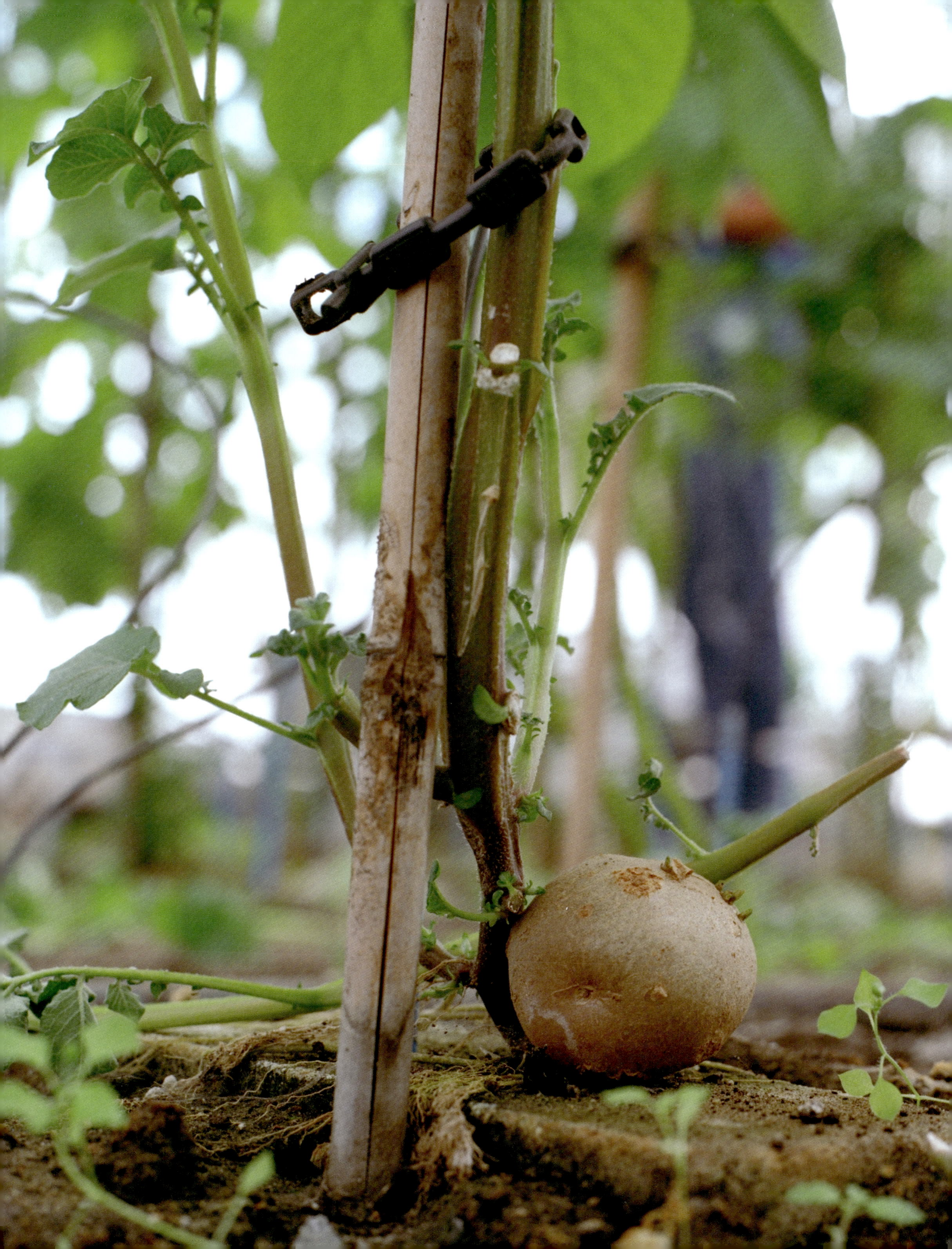

211	4340 K	5-6	
	4980	~~loofrijgoed~~ ziek bladrol
212	48167 K	8-9	
	IJsselster	Mooi loof type
213		6-6	
		loof slecht
214		6-7	
		loofmatig
215		7-7	
		loof goed
216		6-7	
		loofmatig

218   7-7
loof slecht

219   7-8
loof matig

220   6-6
loof matig

221   8-9
loof erij goed

222   7-7
loof matig

223   7-8
loof matig

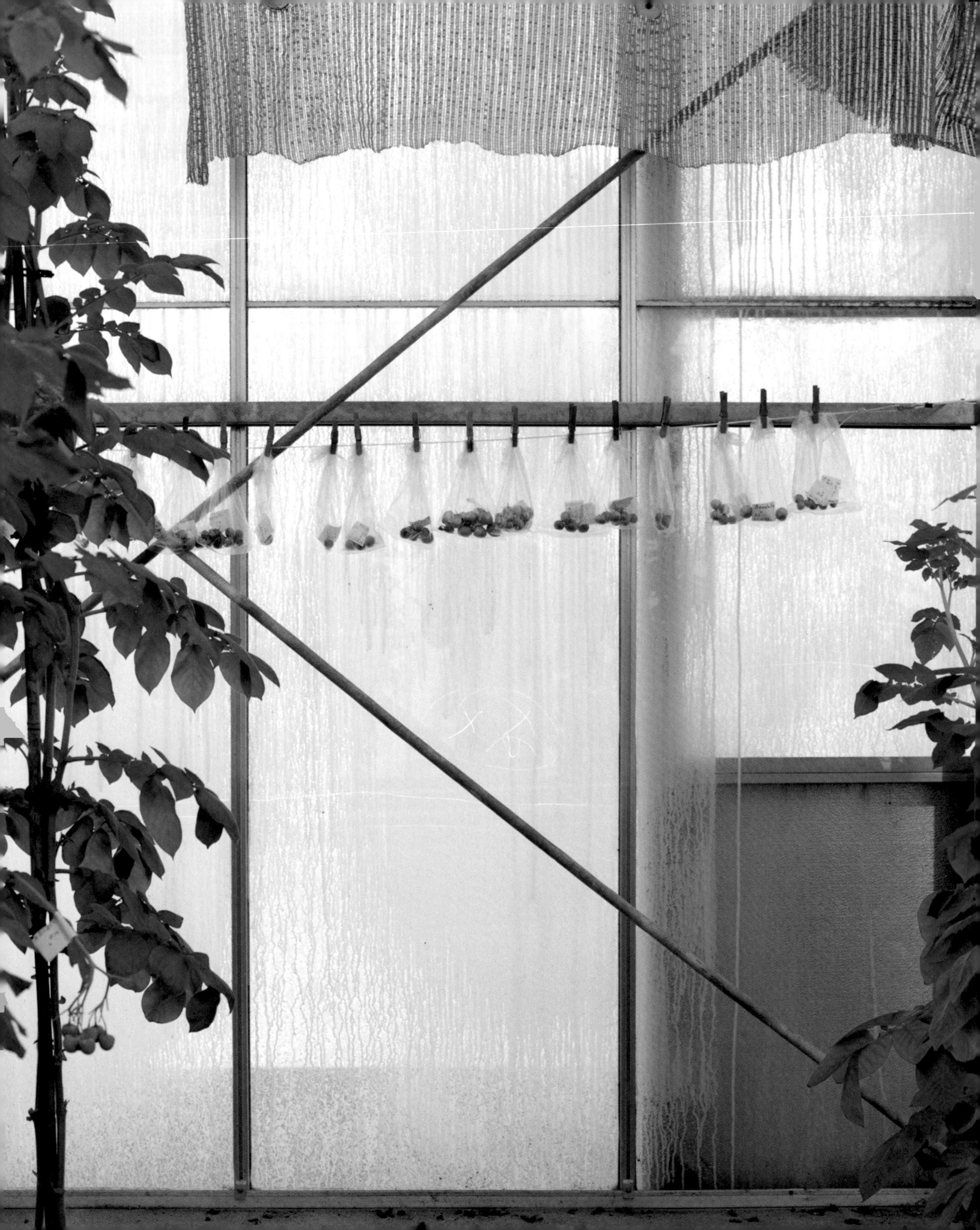

Eiland 7
Tales from Suburbia

Theo Baart

Ideas on Paper
NAi Publishers

Eiland 7
village green
De Muy
De Slufter

I live on an island. Sometimes called Texel, our island – officially known as Eiland 7 – lies between Vlieland and Voorne-Putten. A bridge connects Eiland 7 to the mainland. Situated on this island measuring 200 m in width and 400 m in length are 300 homes, largely made of wood. On Vlieland, Eiland 8, the houses have an exterior of gray and shingles of rust-brown stone. Voorne-Putten has older architecture consisting of durable duplexes, two homes under one roof. And by looking between those, I can see the turrets of castles built on Goeree-Overflakkee, or Eiland 5. Each island has its own urban design and distinct architecture. Islands in the polder: all in all, 120 hectares of new housing developments on parcels of land, divided by canals up to 12 m wide. In the middle, however, those canals are only about a meter deep. My neighbor found that out during our first warm summer here, when he took a refreshing leap into the water and landed on construction refuse. Anyway, in the middle of the polder, where potatoes grew only a few years ago, it's actually possible to live by the water.

Before moving here, I lived in the Bijlmermeer, part of Amsterdam's *Zuidoost* district. The last year and a half was spent in a large apartment that had been spruced up at considerable expense. On the ground floor were apartments with studios, the idea being that artists would give a boost to this depressed neighborhood. What a great idea. But the combination of caring for two growing sons, dealing with upstairs neighbors who threw trash over their balcony onto our terrace and putting up with constant noise and brawls at the front door, eventually got the better of me. I sought safe, calm surroundings and a healthy distance from my neighbors. But also space, since our three-man household was about to expand with the arrival of my new girlfriend and her two daughters. We became a six-person household: two adults, one working at home, and four adolescents with a need for privacy.

So where does one find this kind of space? In the Dutch *nieuwbouwwijk*, the recently built housing development: in its suburban duplexes, upscale townhouses and landed residences. The safe haven for the middle class.

Not only did practical considerations influence our decision to buy a place here, of all places, on Eiland 7. Deviating from the norm, this design by a talented architect was placed in an unusual sort of subdivision. If we had to live in a new development, then this was an attractive option, we thought.

I see our house as a stack of wooden containers. The ground floor is a fairly large container holding the kitchen and the living room. The middle container is huge and extends beyond the others. Here are the two bathrooms (the *boys'* and the *girls'* bathrooms), four bedrooms for four children and a study. On top of this is the smallest container, which has a bedroom/work space and a large deck.

Following our instincts, we sign a 'purchase and building contract' in January 2004. And we accept an offer from a mortgage bank: welcome to the world of mortgage holders. On June 18 of that year, at the project developer's request, the builder starts on the construction of the house. Within two days, it's standing there – well, at least the outside walls are. These are unloaded from a flatbed truck and set against a steel frame. On December 15, 2004 we move into the new house from two different addresses. During one week this house is occupied by four children and two adults. During the other it's nearly empty. That's when the children are with their other parents, and the mortgage holders have the place to themselves.

Eiland 7 is part of the neighborhood 'Floriande,' in Hoofddorp. I know Hoofddorp. After 28 years in Amsterdam, I'm back in the village where I grew up. The village still has its original name, but everything else there has changed. Now I live about 5 km from my parents' house. Between our new home and it lies a sea of dwellings, a whole range of new neighborhoods from various decades. Hoofddorp happens to be an outdoor museum of Dutch postwar housing.

Even while I was living in Amsterdam, Hoofddorp continued to fascinate me. After my departure for art school in Amsterdam, the boundless dynamics of demolition and construction, of filling the polder with office parks and residential areas, were reasons for me to grab the camera. For 20 years I followed the process of change with the astonished eyes of an involved outsider. At the end of the 1990s, I grouped those photographs in the book *Bouwlust, the urbanization of a polder*.

Now that I'm back, I notice the advantages of life in a new neighborhood: the giant parking garage beneath the giant supermarket, being able to walk in a recreational area next to our neighborhood and the fast public transportation to the center of Amsterdam. Although it may lack identity, the place does offer comfort and convenience: that soon became evident enough.

I've seen and photographed many new residential areas, usually while passing through them. Now, being implicated as it were, I'm participating as the buyer of a house which constitutes part of the transformation process taking place in the Netherlands. The western part of the country is turning into one big new neighborhood, dotted with infrastructure, shopping centers, golf courses and recreational zones. And I am a consumer of this utilitarian landscape.

In the first ten days following the move, I'm overwhelmed by the sense of calm. For the first time in over a year, I've had an undisrupted night of sleep. Leaving my car unlocked gives me a childlike thrill. Shall we put a string through the letterbox, I fantasize recklessly, so we can open the front door without the key?

During that initial phase, there is also the adventurous feeling of being a pioneer. For awhile, we don't exist: the navigation system can't find our new address. Anyone visiting for the first time has to be steered here by phone. 'Watch out for the bus channel. Don't try going through it.' A friend misses the warning sign, but the specially designed pavement doesn't miss his crankcase. I believe his greasy tire tracks still run through our street.

November 2007: we've now been living on Eiland 7 for three years. As I look out the window from my work space, I see houses right up to the horizon. What does the island look like now? Narrow streets, small gardens, parking places: an enormously intensive occupation of space. The 'residential park' is situated along the northern side: 88 wooden owner-occupied homes and 30 rental homes, all with exterior walls of brick and gold-colored aluminum sheeting. Situated in the middle of the island is the *brink*, or village green. A *brink* is traditionally a community pasture surrounded by farms and houses. This one consists of a basketball court, two areas with playground equipment for young children, and 300 trees. On the north side of it are 50 brick homes, in rows, and an apartment building. On the south side is a long row of 34 duplexes and an apartment building for renters. And presiding over this green, as it were, is an apartment building in dark-brown brick, bearing a large '7' on its side.

This place has two speeds. During the day, things are quiet here. Each home requires two working people to pay off its mortgage; so between 6:30 a.m. and 8 a.m., you see a stream of cars gliding over the island's access bridges. A bit later the bustle begins on huge parking lots near the schools: double parking and traffic buildup. After that, the second family car leaves the neighborhood, on its way to work. And then comes the hush: dead silence.

Over the past three years, residents of this island have hardly been idle. Now the homes are furnished, the gardens thriving. An unbelievable variety of mini chalets, log cabins and tall sheds have been built in the yards and on parking places. It doesn't seem as though every inhabitant shares the designer's ideas on the use of private and public space. Many of the fences and shrubs put in by the project developer were replaced with wooden partitions during the first months. Some parking spaces that are to be landscaped by the residents themselves look as though they've been flooded. They're littered with remnants of fencing, piled high with dirt. Washed up like a dead whale on one parking space is an enormous inflatable rubber dinghy.

This picture hardly corresponds to the one sketched in sales brochures some time ago: a living environment where the car had been banished from view. Added levels, extensions, storage areas – anything goes now. Could this have been the original intention? Worried residents, disappointed by what they regard as the degradation of the island, write letters to the municipality. They ask for an enforcement and implementation of conditions stated in the purchase contract. The municipality responds by saying that 'viewpoints have been exchanged' with the project developer and that 'agreements have been made with respect to the potential for enforcement.'

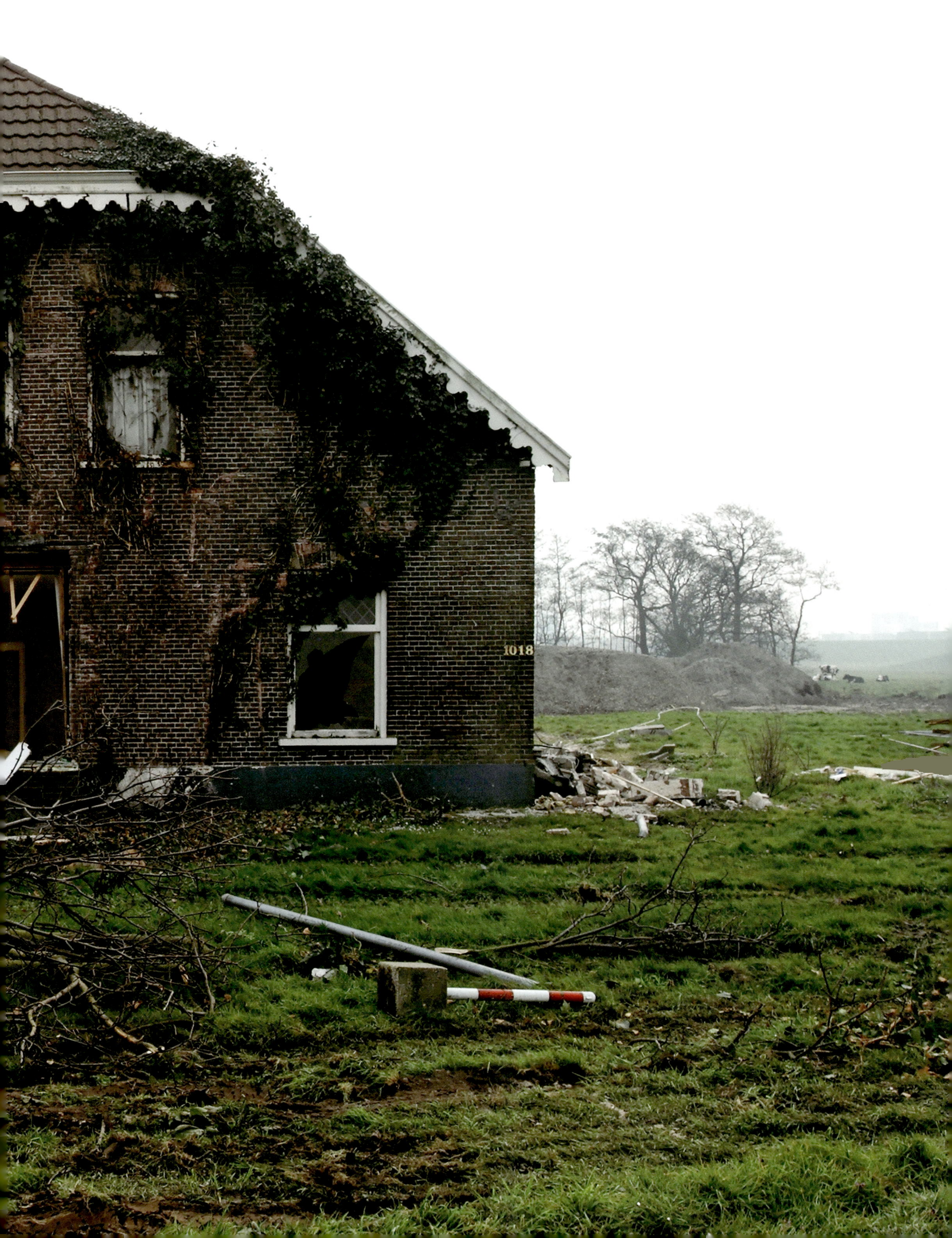

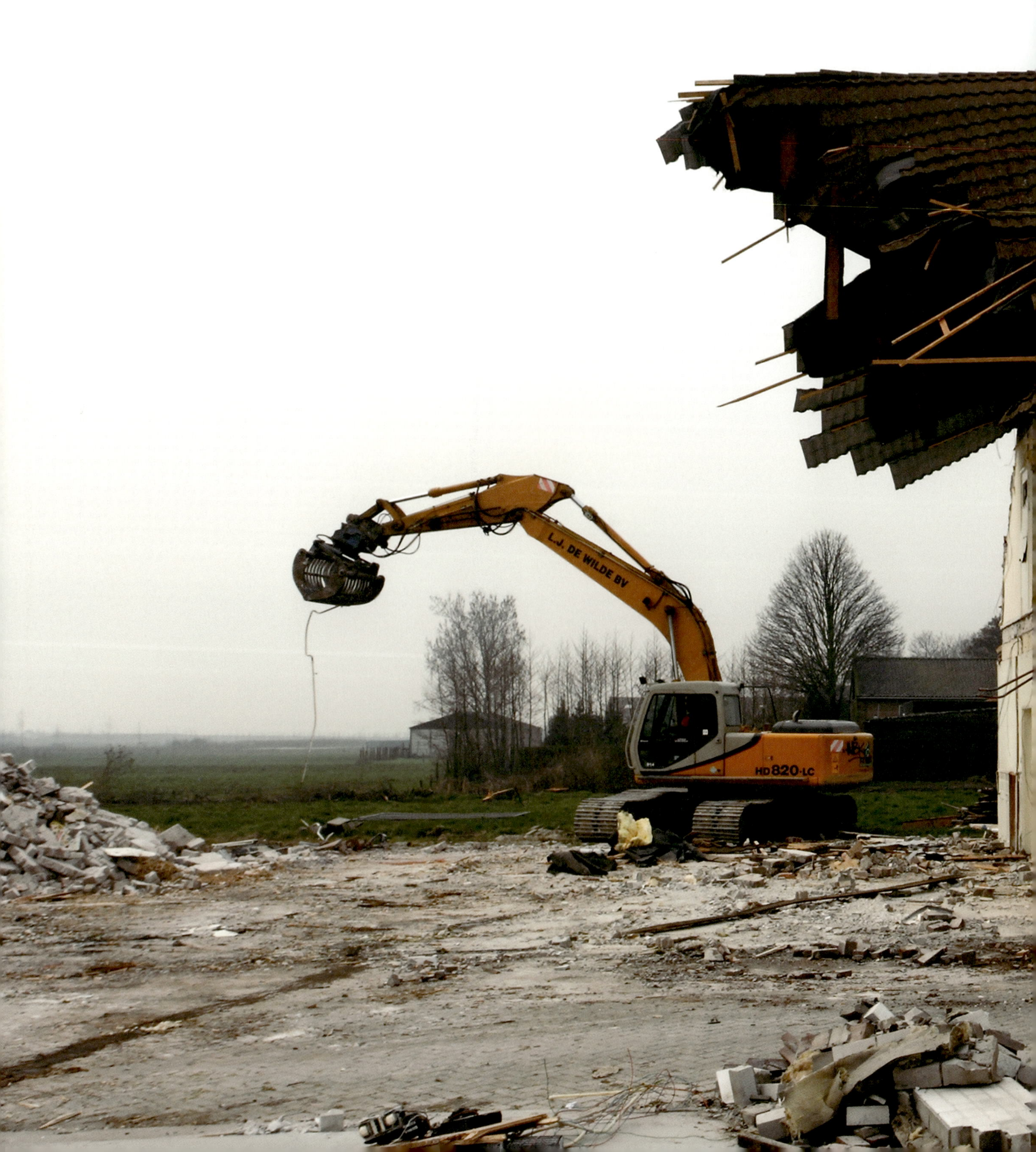

L.J. DE WILDE BV
HD 820-LC

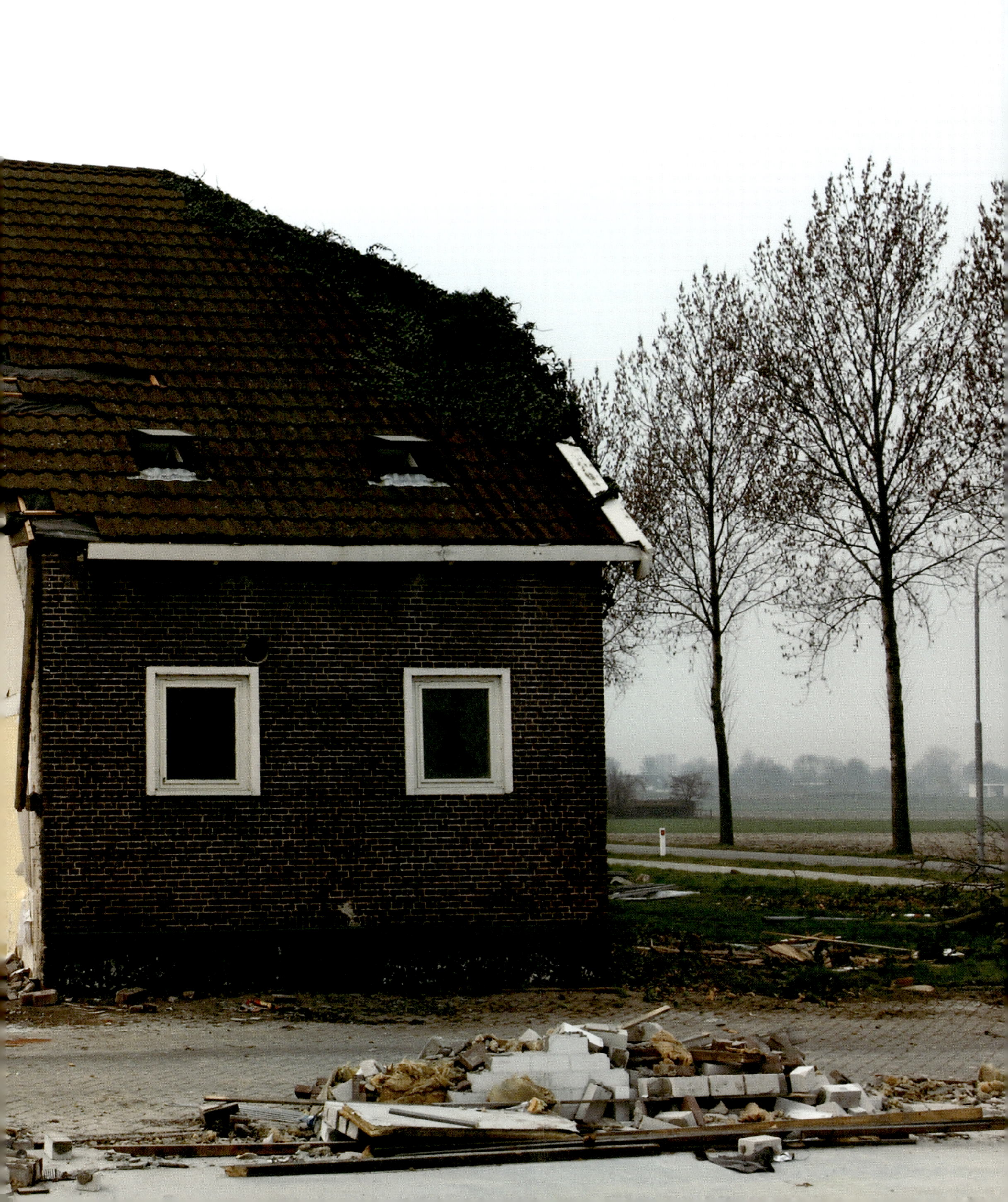

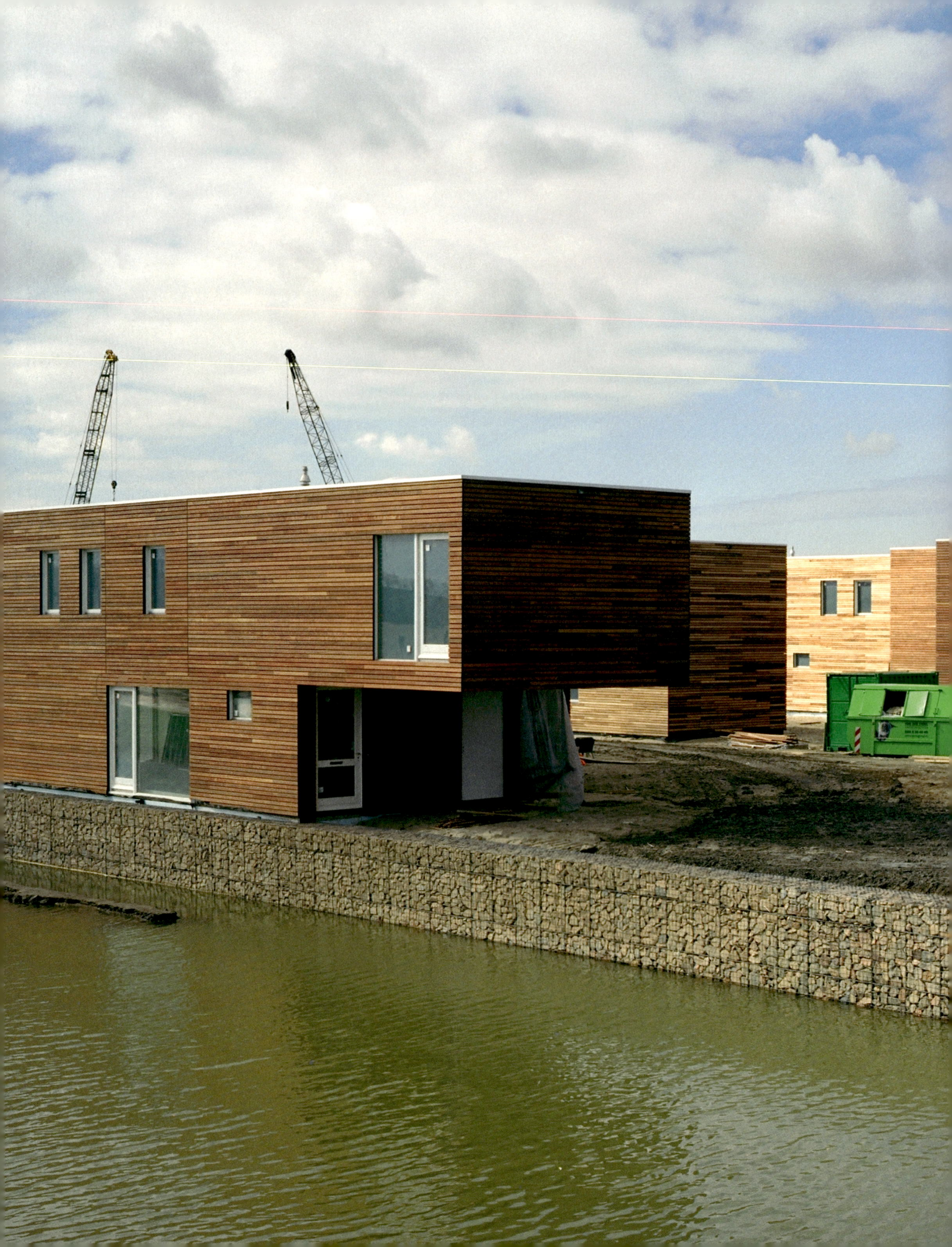

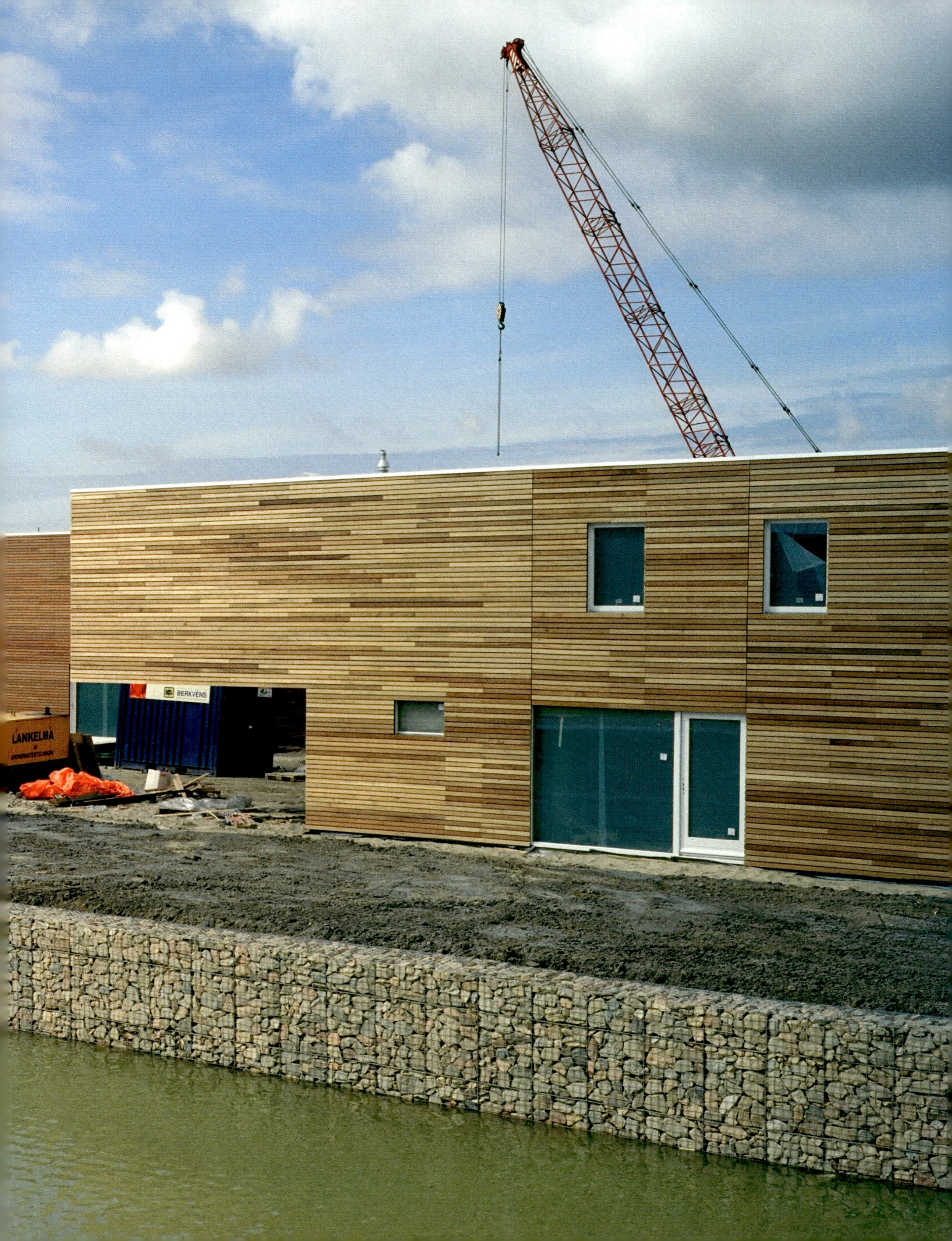

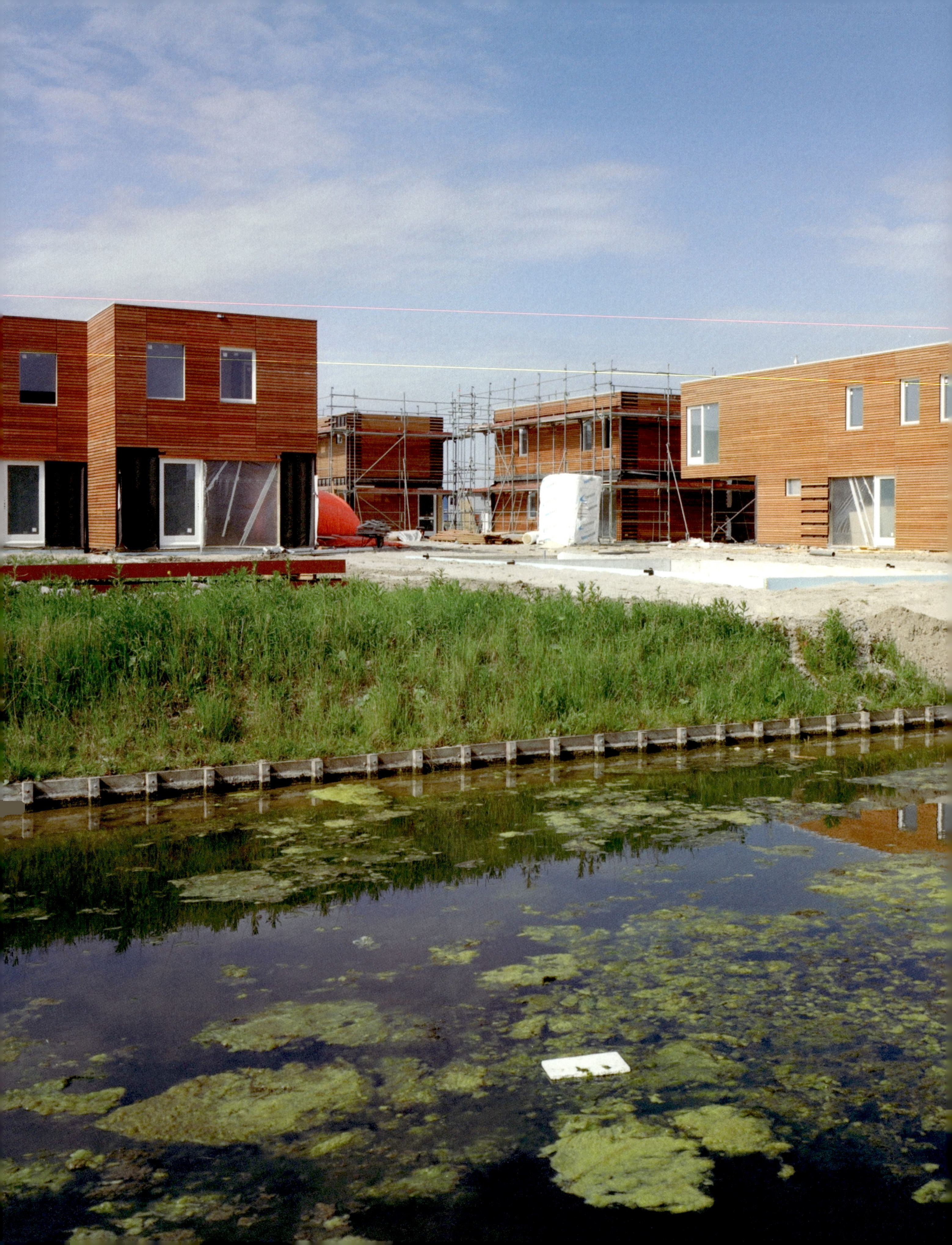

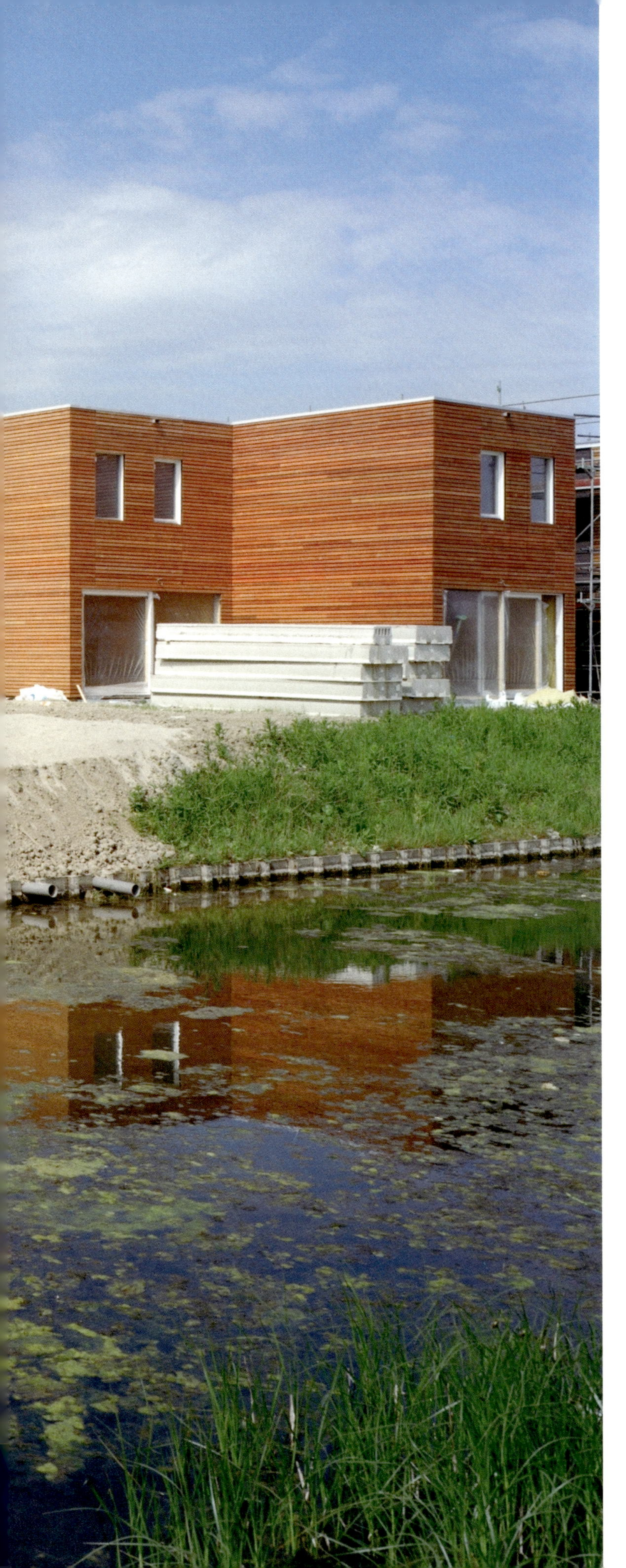

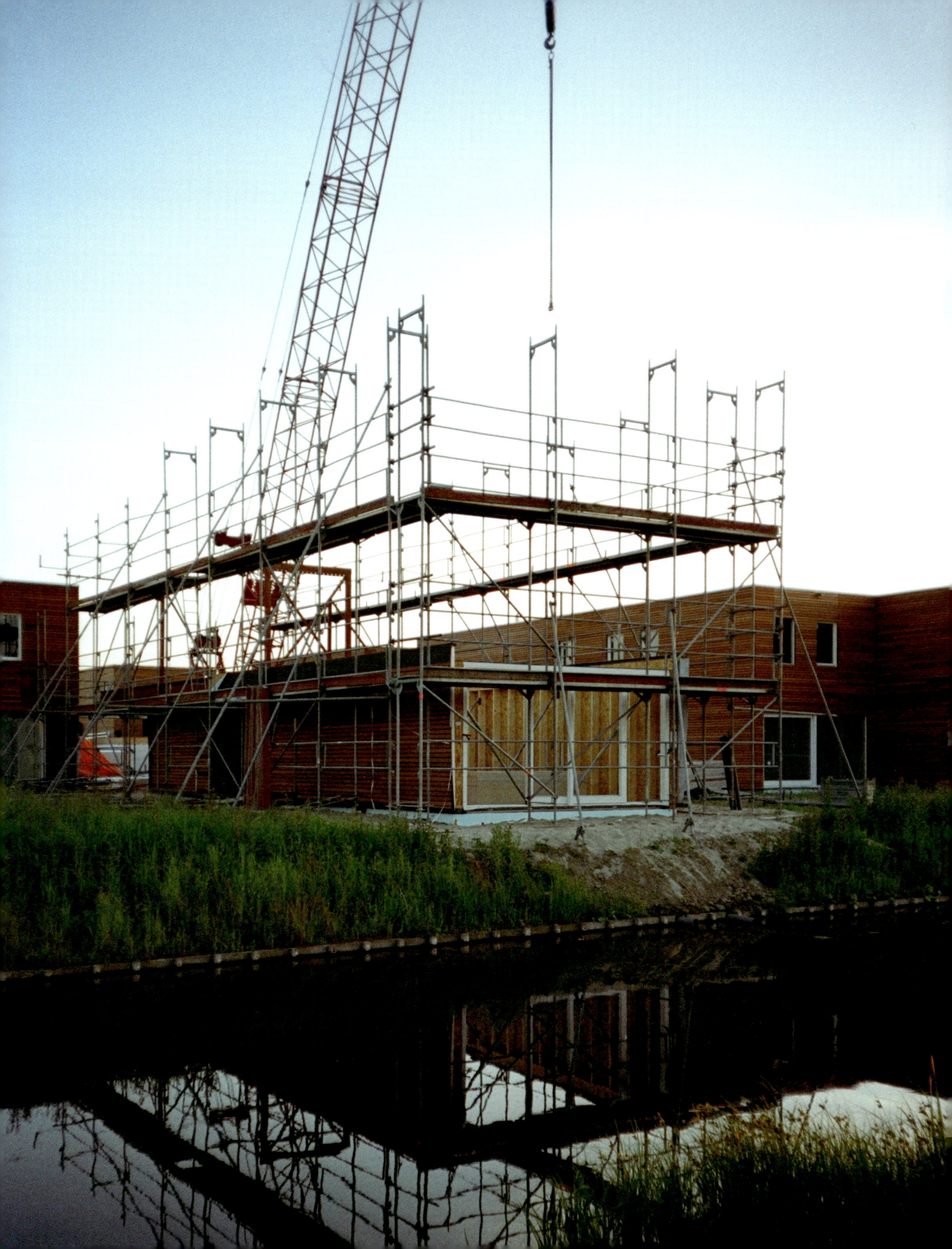

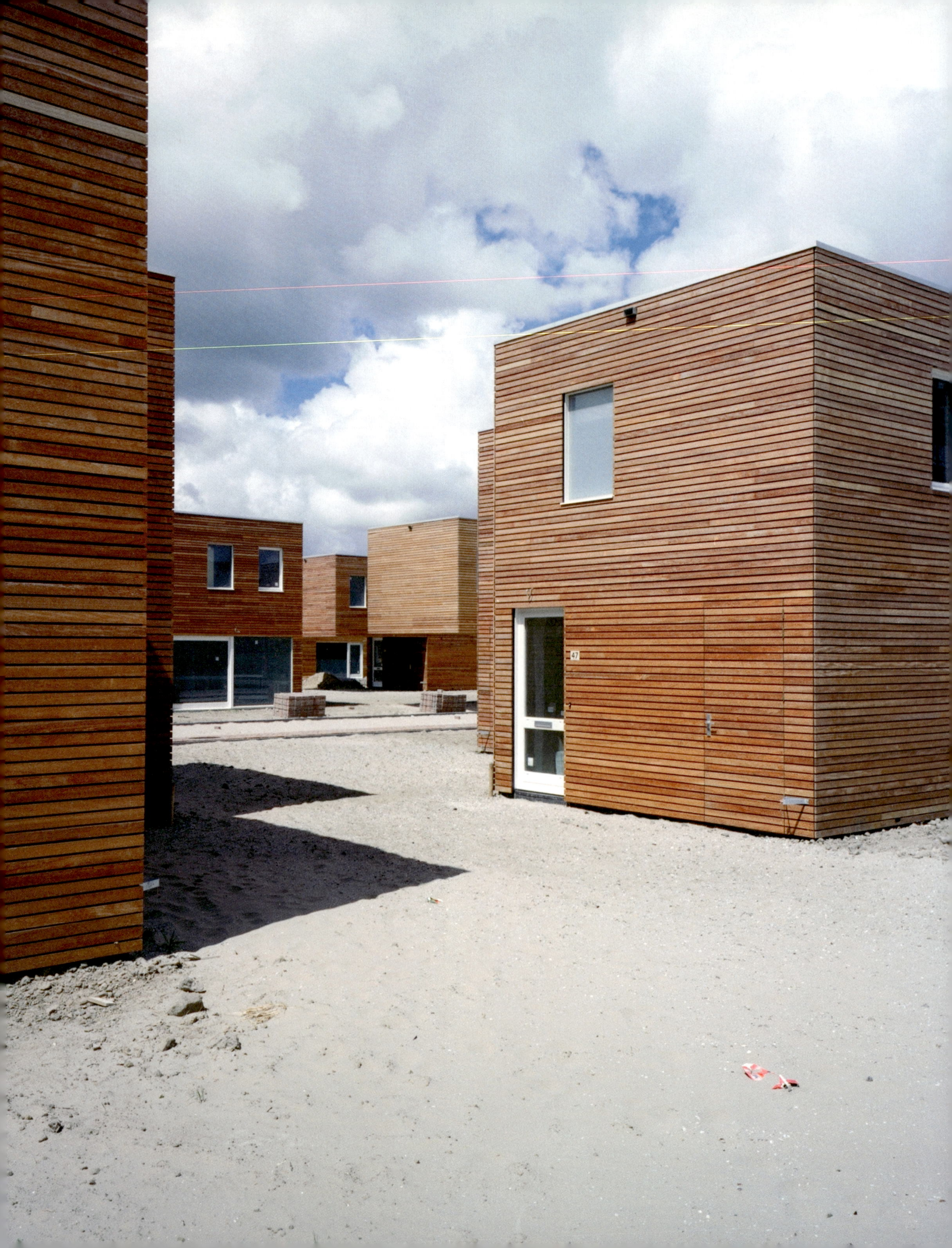

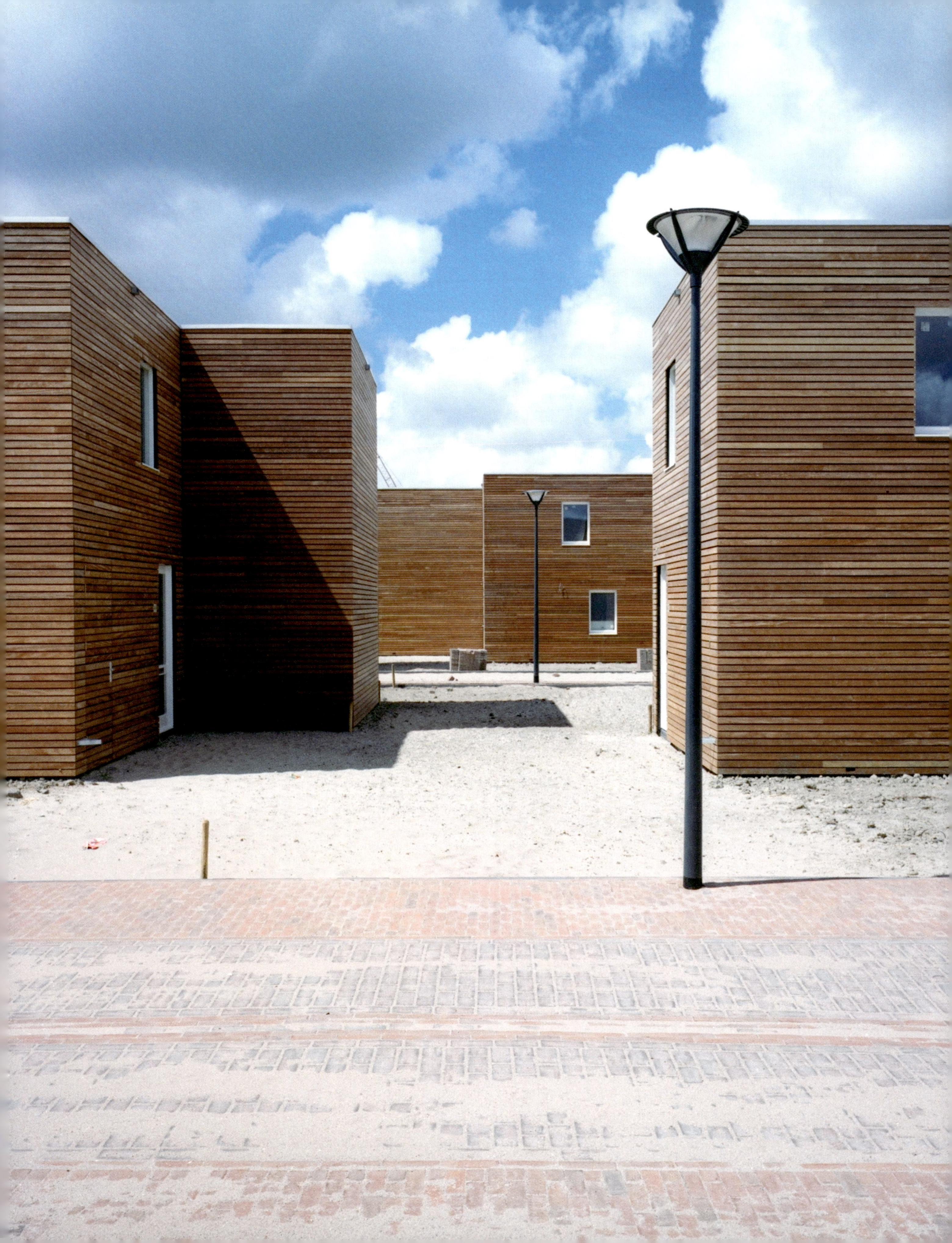

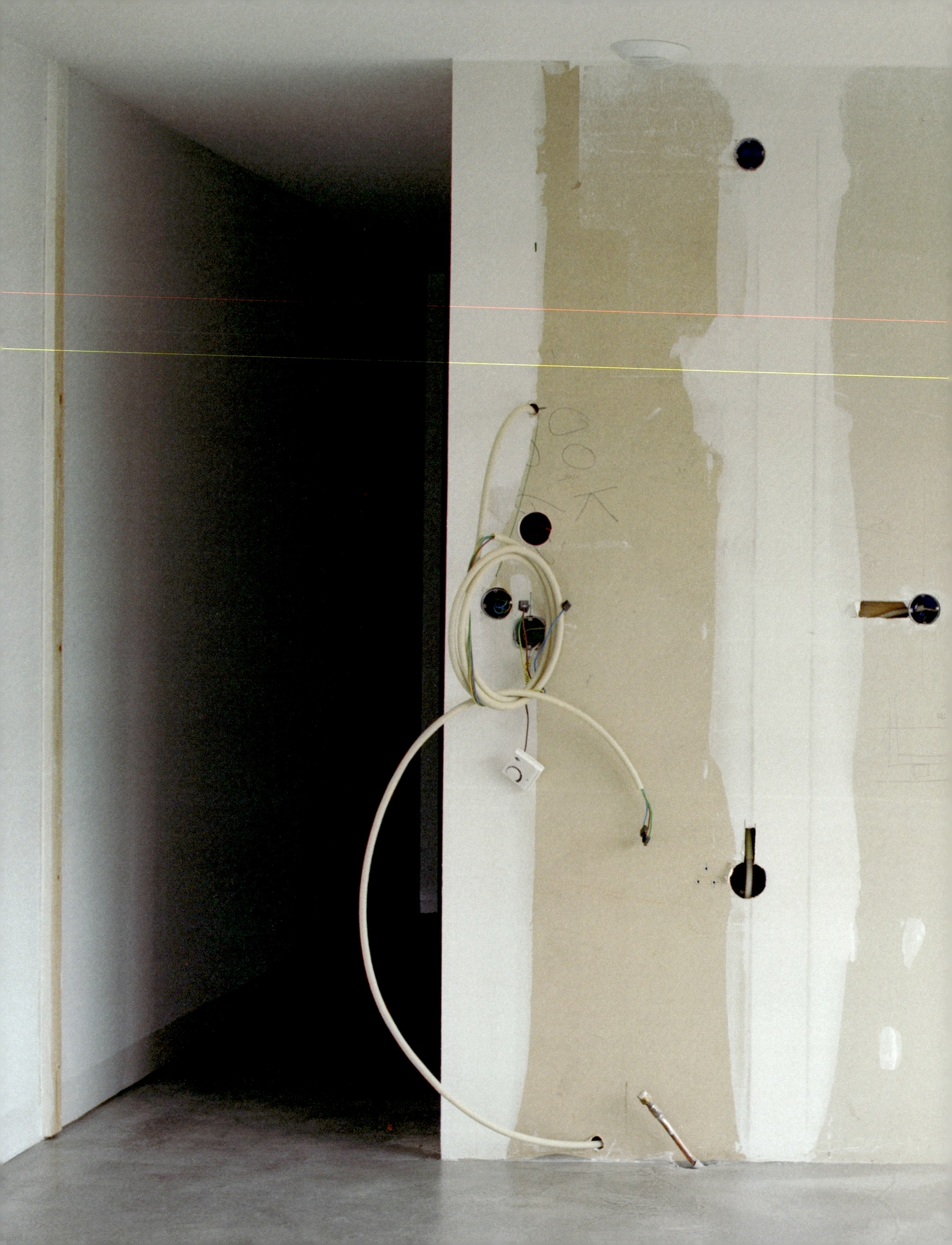

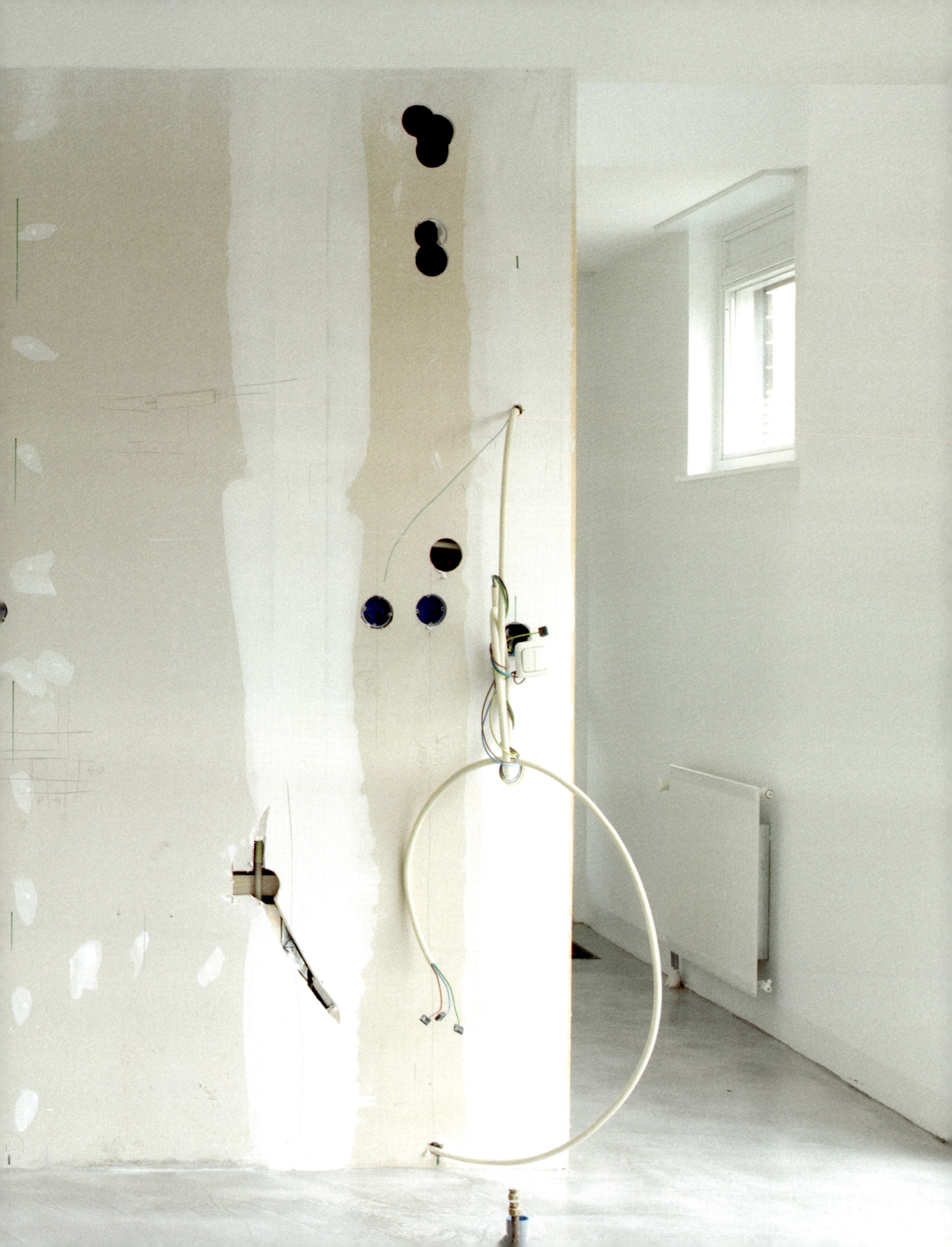

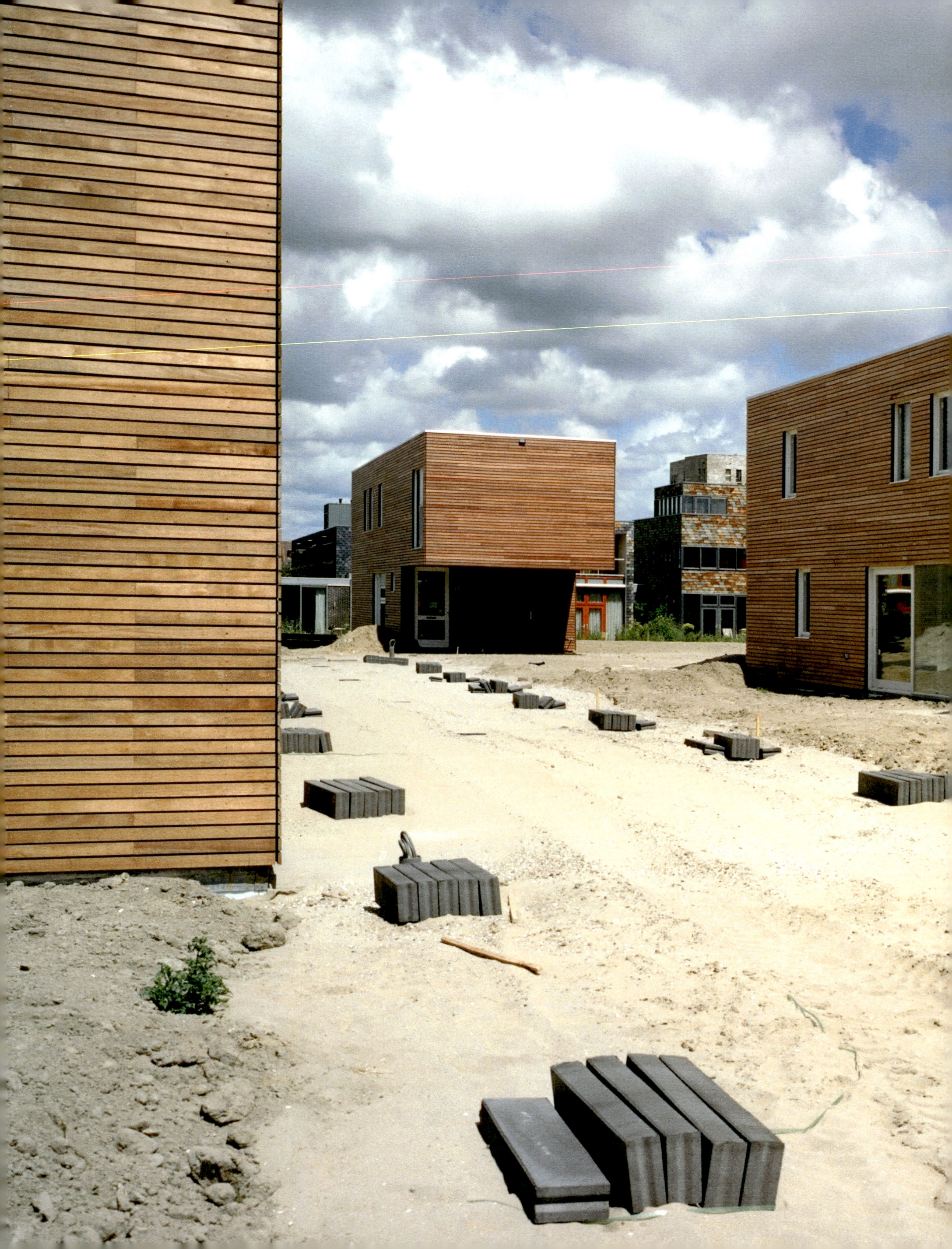

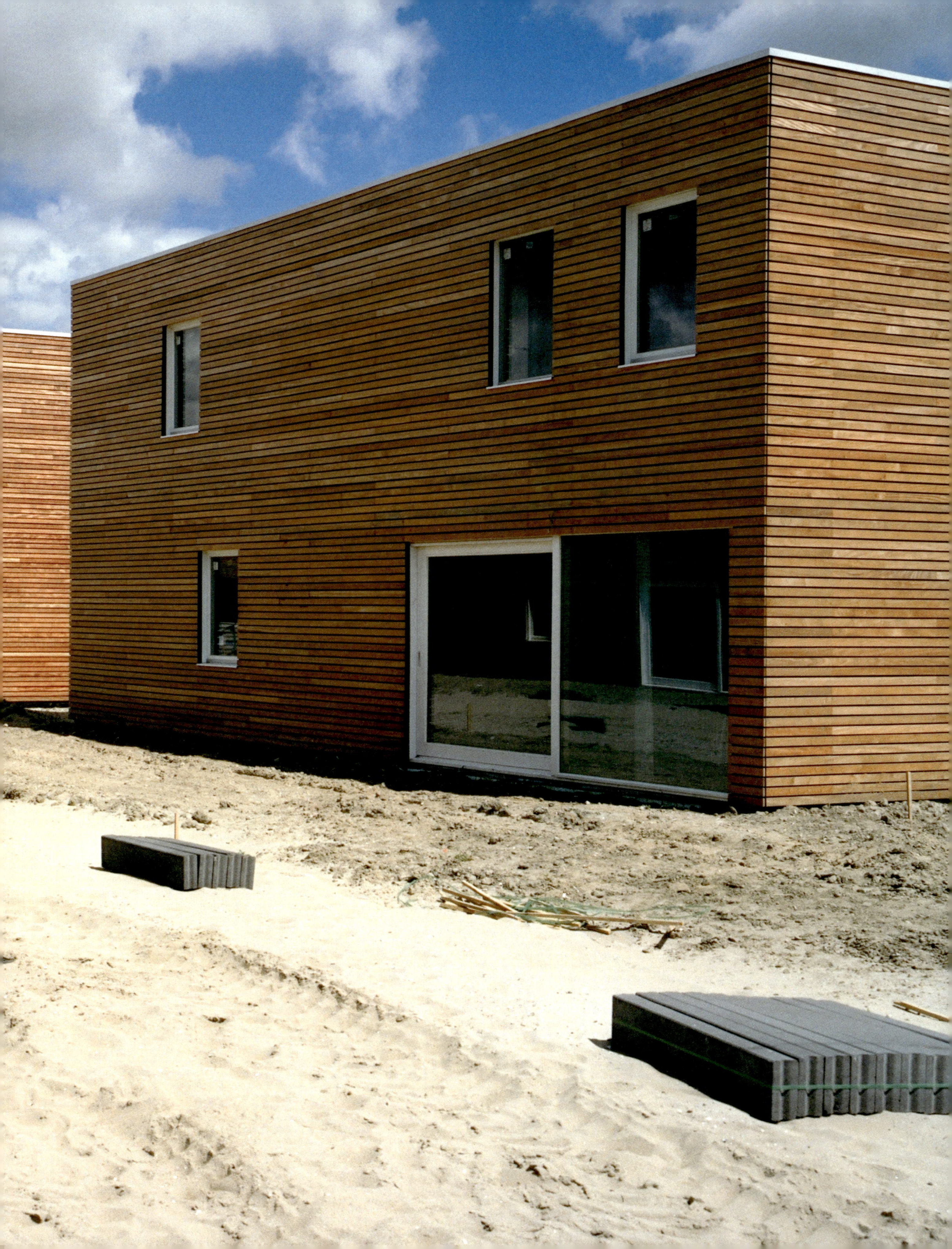

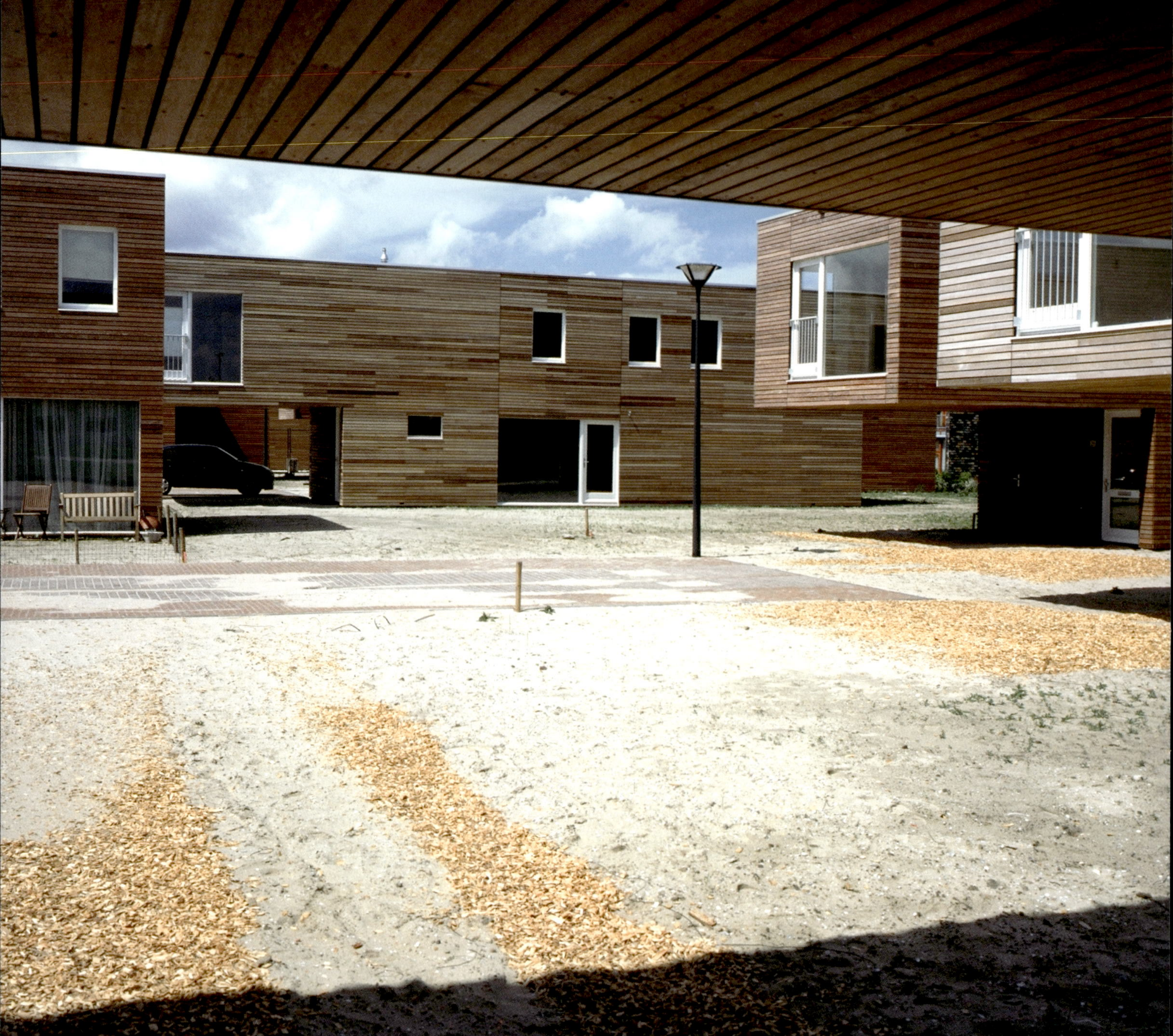

I want to understand why we build and live like this in the Netherlands.

How do such popular residential areas come about, I wonder. What happens, in fact, when someone in an office places a red dot next to an area zoned for agricultural purposes? Who gets the short end of the stick? Who are the players, and who bears the consequences at the end of the process? What do home buyers actually pay for, and how much do they get out of it? Why do all of the new housing developments look so much alike? Who comes up with the idea that it might be good to do it all differently for once? And why? And if the ambition to break the routine gets translated into a deviant plan, why is that ambition only partly realized? What is the designer's position? Is the outcome of such a complicated process as this inevitably the lowest common denominator?

Leaving my observation post on the roof, I set about to reconstruct the developmental history of this island by speaking with the farmers who sold land, with the buyer of that land, the project developer, and with the sales advisor, the realtor, the urban planner, the architect and the financial controller. What were their ideas, and how did they eventually take shape? How do they look back on the making of a new neighborhood? Is there a recipe for this?

I pay visits to my fellow inhabitants on this island. What were their considerations on buying a home in this particular place? Did the pronounced character of the architecture play a role? How did they define their territory? When will it be time to go?

This book paints a residential landscape, but it can also be seen as a financial landscape. Money and land play an important role here. Land changes hands, and houses change hands. And then everything changes, inside and out, once the loan comes through.

Money makes the world go 'round, even in Hoofddorp.

Eiland 7, De Muy
Gita (40)
Richard (39)
Angeline (10)
Lindy (7)

Gita:

We just happened to see this project being advertised in the newspaper. Actually we had no intention of moving at all, but in the end we did. Richard wanted to get his hands on another garden at some point. This had to be bigger, and the house had to be worth moving for, too. After we signed the purchase contract, it took a year-and-a-half to complete. During that time, we were busy thinking about how to furnish it. The house struck me as being quite straightforward and modern. I tend to prefer more rural homes, but the use of wood does make it warm. Looking at the floor plans, we had to figure out if everything would fit. Though we wanted to take our old furniture with us, we ended up seeing all kinds of fun stuff and did buy a lot of new things.

We went to one of those places where you can pick out a kitchen. It had to be kind of rural-looking – cozy, not slick. With shoeboxes, we made a little replica of the house; that's basically the shape of it. Then we placed the neighbor's house next to it, on the same scale, to see whether their extra level would be visible from the living room.

Together, the kids and I picked out the colors for their rooms. Angeline really wanted a room with dolphins. It had to be a kind of 'underwater room,' so that pretty much meant blue. And yellow floor covering, to make it seem like sand. Lindy was still going through the 'princess' stage. She was given all sorts of pastels: pale pink and lilac. We chose a pale green for our bedroom. That didn't turn out to be such a good idea. Pretty boring. But we dealt with that by painting one wall red. I had made a folder with all kinds of color samples, pictures of furniture and kitchens, to see what looked good together. We had a planning book for the post-completion activities. Everything was scheduled: the laying of floor covering, the spray-painting of walls and the installation of the kitchen.

We had 12 days to make the move. It did seem tight, but we managed. Only the bathroom turned out to be a problem, since the guy who was supposed to install it failed to show up. Everything else went fine. We brought along the curtains from the old house, and those really need to be replaced now.

2

It starts with land.

Anyone who owns land in the Netherlands can build on it, as long as the land is zoned for housing. Project developers need to have 'land locations' in order to build anything. In the Netherlands the project developer is the builder's client. The builder builds.

In 1993 our Minister of Spatial Planning published the 'Fourth National Environmental Policy Plan,' which soon became known by its Dutch abbreviation *Vinex*. This plan designated the areas in which 250,000 homes had to be built by 2005. For the municipality of Haarlemmermeer, that would amount to 13,000 homes distributed among three locations. The largest construction area to be designated lay within a rectangle of 3 x 1 km (300 hectares) to the west of Hoofddorp, along the Spieringweg.

Well before the publication of this plan, land speculators drove by many a farm to make an offer for the land. Everyone could see what was coming to this polder: so close to the large cities of Amsterdam, Haarlem and Leiden – and right next to Schiphol. Now it was only a matter of waiting for the change in the land's zoning. And who is allowed to change the agricultural zoning status of a tract of land? That would be the municipality, by way of its zoning plan, with or without the pressure of a higher government. In the Netherlands, construction can be seen as an interesting *pas de deux* carried out by the government and the market sector.

The Haarlemmermeerpolder has the shape of a potato. After the land had been pumped dry in 1851, the polder was divided into segments of 3 x 2 km. Fifteen subdivisions, each 200 m wide and 1000 m long, were situated along a farm road. The farm buildings were placed on the shorter, 200 m side. Everything had to have a use in this polder. Here and there, a tree was planted alongside the road. This gave the landscape a certain scraggy look, which might even be called beautiful; the opinions on this have tended to vary. I always found it wonderful, until the polder started filling up with office buildings, highways, residential areas and the ever-expanding airport Schiphol. That's when the landscape became fascinating in my view.

During the 1970s the municipality of Haarlemmermeer had a visionary mayor. He wanted new housing projects to be free of project developers and land speculators. So the municipality itself went about the task of acquiring land. Buying land is a game: the trick is to get into the game as quickly as possible and not to let anyone know what's going on. For a municipality this is no simple matter. Participation in this game is difficult to reconcile with the taking of public responsibility required of a government.

From 1970 onward, the municipal official Geert Deddens purchased land for the municipality Haarlemmermeer. Agrarian land. He's been retired for some time now. In municipal department 'number 4,' this man dealt, as it were, with land issues. Later the notion 'land' became so big that an entire municipal enterprise was set up. By the end of the 1990s, 20 people were working there.

When Deddens started out to purchase it, land wasn't expensive. He was buying at 'agricultural prices,' the value that arable land has for farmers. Even the financing costs weren't all that bad. Twenty hectares of land would sell for 250,000 euros: that's 1.25 euro per m². After its purchase the land would be cultivated by a farmer employed by the municipality, and proceeds from the crops would generally cover about half the interest charges. 'It was all pretty feasible. Refusals to sell were rare,' says Deddens. 'Farmers love it when you come along to buy them out. Selling the place is the only moment when they can make a good profit from the business.'

Half of the farmers in the Haarlemmermeer were tenants. So business had to be done not only with the owner of the land, but also with the tenant. There was an accepted formula for lease compensation: nine times the annual income. 'We offered a tenant 1.12 euros per m², 11,200 per hectare, without having to look at the bookkeeping,' says Deddens. 'Everyone accepted that offer.'

During the early 1990s, the land market became tight. Schiphol Airport was buying up a great deal of land. At that time, the Ministry of Agriculture, Nature and Fisheries was buying land in order to have 'green zones.' And project developers were eager to be in the right positions for inevitable construction projects. 'For years we deliberately bragged about various plans,' says the former land buyer for the municipality. A smoke screen was created. The municipality wanted to buy up as much land as possible and knew, all along, precisely where it would eventually expand. The price was no longer an issue, since that had already risen from 12 to 13.50 euros per m² (2,700,000 euros per 20 hectares) in 1993. Quantity was the issue. 'We used this tactic, because we wanted to have as much land for the municipality as possible. We knew, of course, who owned the land, but not who had granted an option on his land or who had signed a contract. Our purchases, too, were usually carried out by way of various front men. It was quite a game,' says Deddens, looking back.

Those involved in the market, especially the project developers who wanted to start building, attempted to find out precisely where the municipality intended to expand. They purchased land at locations where they suspected plans for municipal expansion. These parties always paid more for land than the municipality did. They paid farmers the anticipated value, the value that the land would have after the municipality converted its agrarian zoning to a residential one – that being a much higher price.

Before it became known that a *Vinex* location would be designated along the Spieringweg, the municipality had already purchased two farms in the area intended for its expansion. And the purchase of a third farm (60 hectares) was still being negotiated. If the municipality could also purchase a fourth, the potato-breeding business owned by the Könst brothers, it would own two-thirds of the land for the *Vinex* location on the Spieringweg. The remaining land was bought by project developers. As such, the municipality had a strong negotiating position with respect to the project developers. Due to the large quantity of land being contributed by the municipality, it was able to influence the building program substantially.

Geert Deddens and I drive over to Hoofdvaart. This is where the Könst brothers continued their business after leaving the farm on the Spieringweg. Until 2002 they farmed the tract of land on which Eiland 7 has been built. We park alongside Peter and Vincent Könst's new farm on the south side of Hoofddorp. Well, if you can call it a farm: a large warehouse with an office in front, not the usual farmhouse. This building could be anything. The sign at the entrance says *Könst Research bv.*

Unannounced, we walk in. They're having a coffee break, and we're invited to pull up a chair.

'"The expropriation procedure has begun," is what Deddens said when he came to us in 1993. And I replied, "I'd do the same if I were you,"' says Vincent Könst (38), who owns *Könst Research* with his brother Peter (42). Geert Deddens can laugh about it now, but says there was no getting around it at the time. Situated right in the middle of the project, their land was vital to it.

Interest in their land was nothing new for the Könst brothers. Talk about the possible expansion of Hoofddorp already began during the 1970s. The Könst parcel along the Spieringweg would be part of it. Now and then, an interested buyer would drive down the lane with a great offer to trade it for a farm three times its size. But Könst had no interest in more land. They bred seed potatoes, and that doesn't require much land.

'Selling wouldn't do a thing for us. Quite the opposite, in fact: it would only put us at a disadvantage. We were rooted to this land. That's why we were the last to sell farmland on the Spieringweg,' explains Vincent Könst.

Jan Könst (1912), father of Vincent and Peter, took over the family business in 1932 and started breeding seed potatoes on 100 m² of land. Breeding means introducing improvements in crops. A crop thereby yields more in terms of weight, but also in terms of quality and resistance to disease. 'The plant breeder helps nature make the product more attractive. Knowledge, insight, the right kind of soil and stamina are needed for this. Periods ranging from 10 to 15 years are normal for introducing changes in a crop,' Peter Könst tells us.

Father Könst carefully documented the development of his crops in small notebooks. His first big success was the seed potato 'Meerlander': a potato for the Dutch market. He acquired the rights to breed it. The breeding rights for improved crops are issued, under license, to a commercial establishment. The proceeds from licensing, royalties, make up the profit earned by the breeding business. In the description of the breeding rights, the 'Meerlander'

Het nieuwe huis

15 september wordt ons nieuwe huis opgeleverd. Het staat in de Floriande.
Froriande is een lange rij met eilanden. Ons huis staat op eiland zes. Mijn moeder
vind dat het luciferhuisjes zijn omdat ze bekleed zijn met hout. Onze buurman
heeft er een heel lelijk schuurtje aangebouwd. Fien heeft er een foto van
gemaakt. Ons huis heeft als enige nog een verdieping erop. Hopelijk kunnen we
snel verhuizen, want daar heb ik hele erge zin in.

Cato   7-9-2004

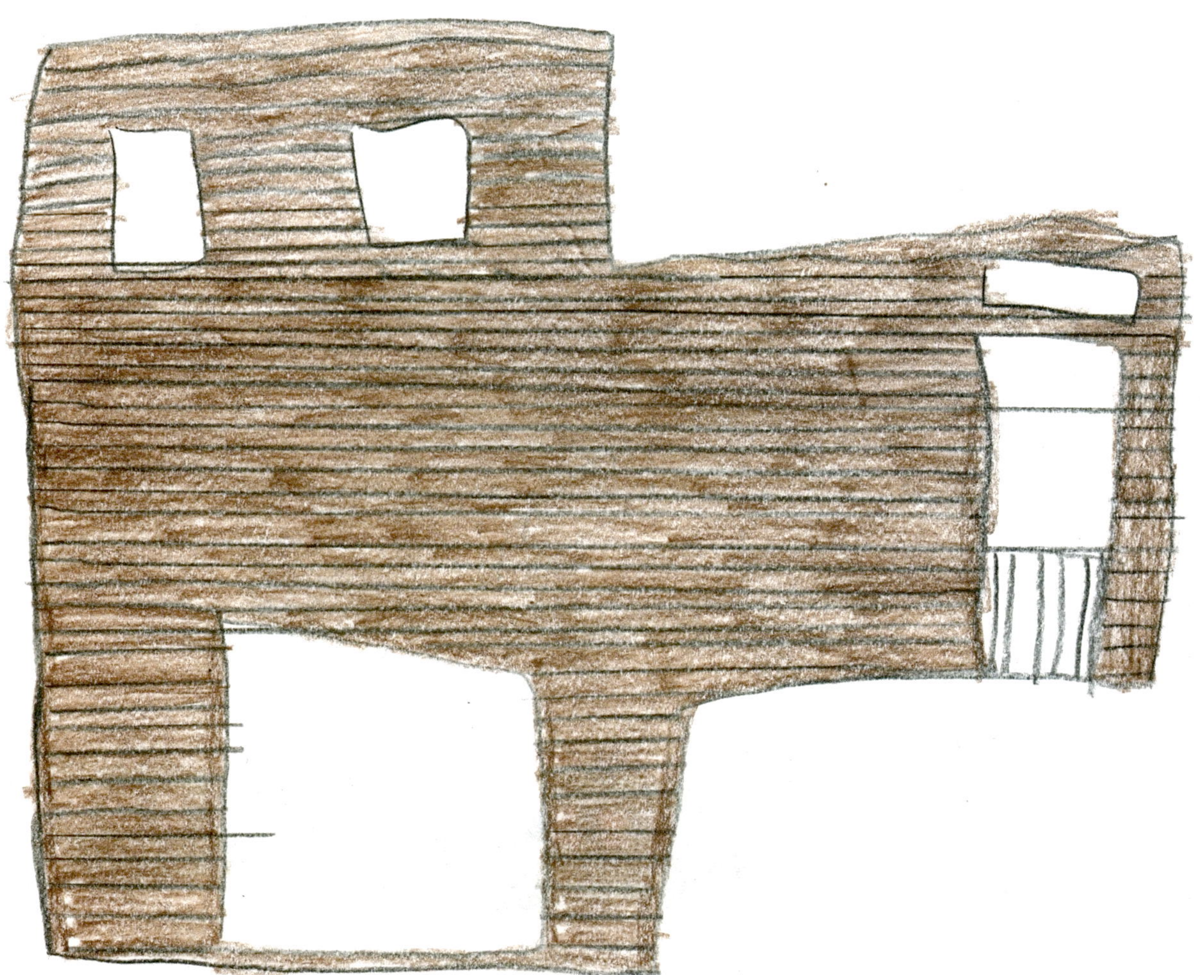

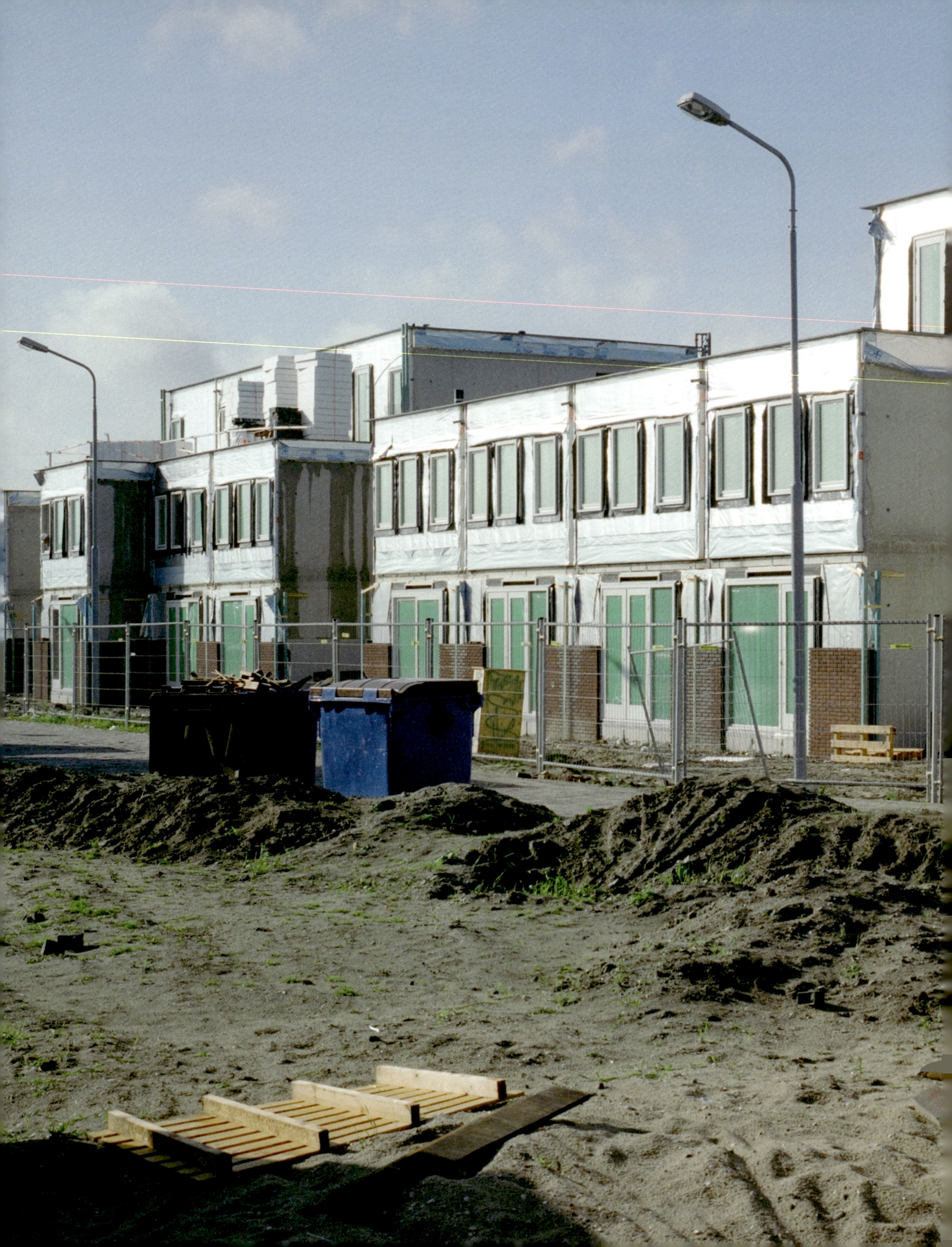

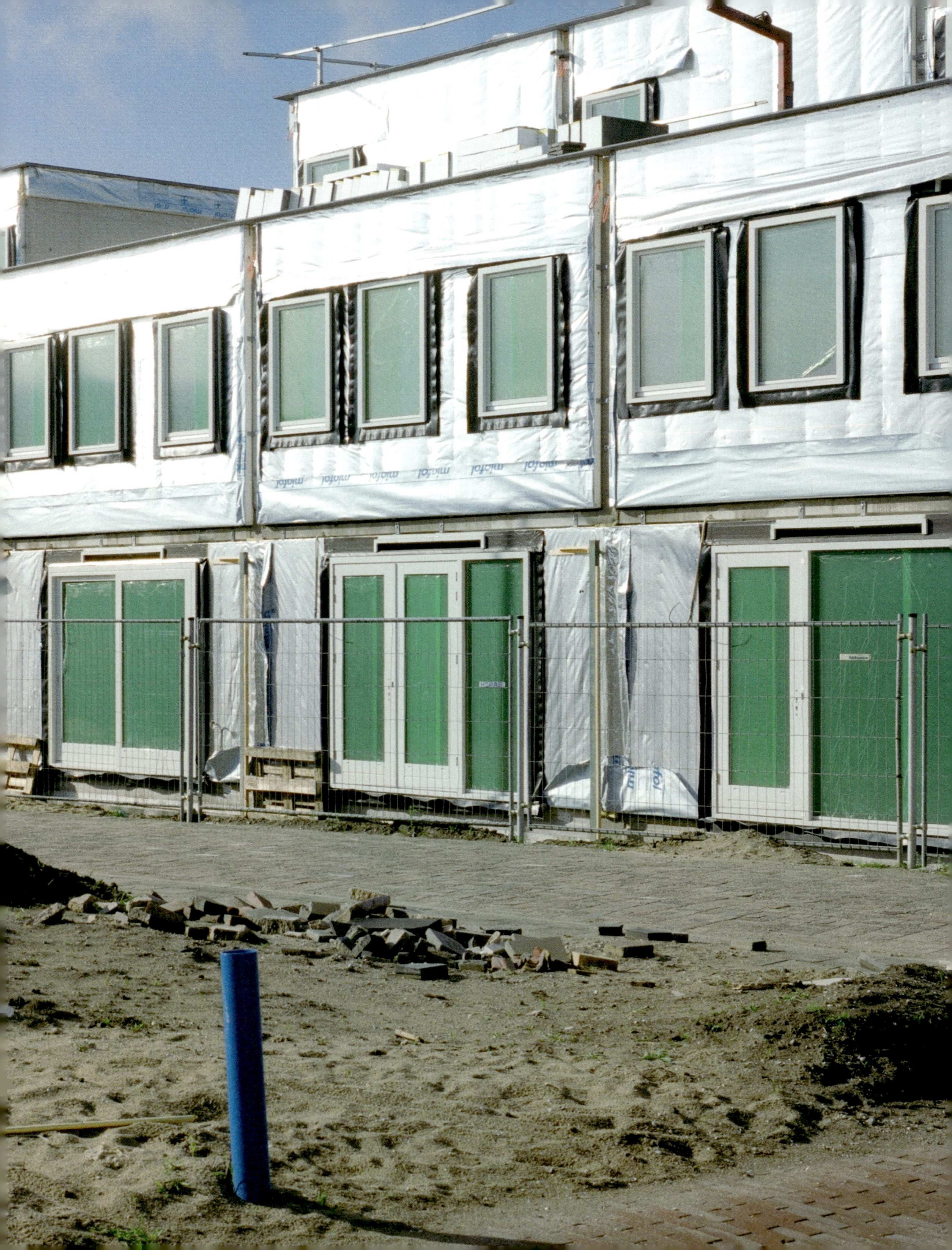

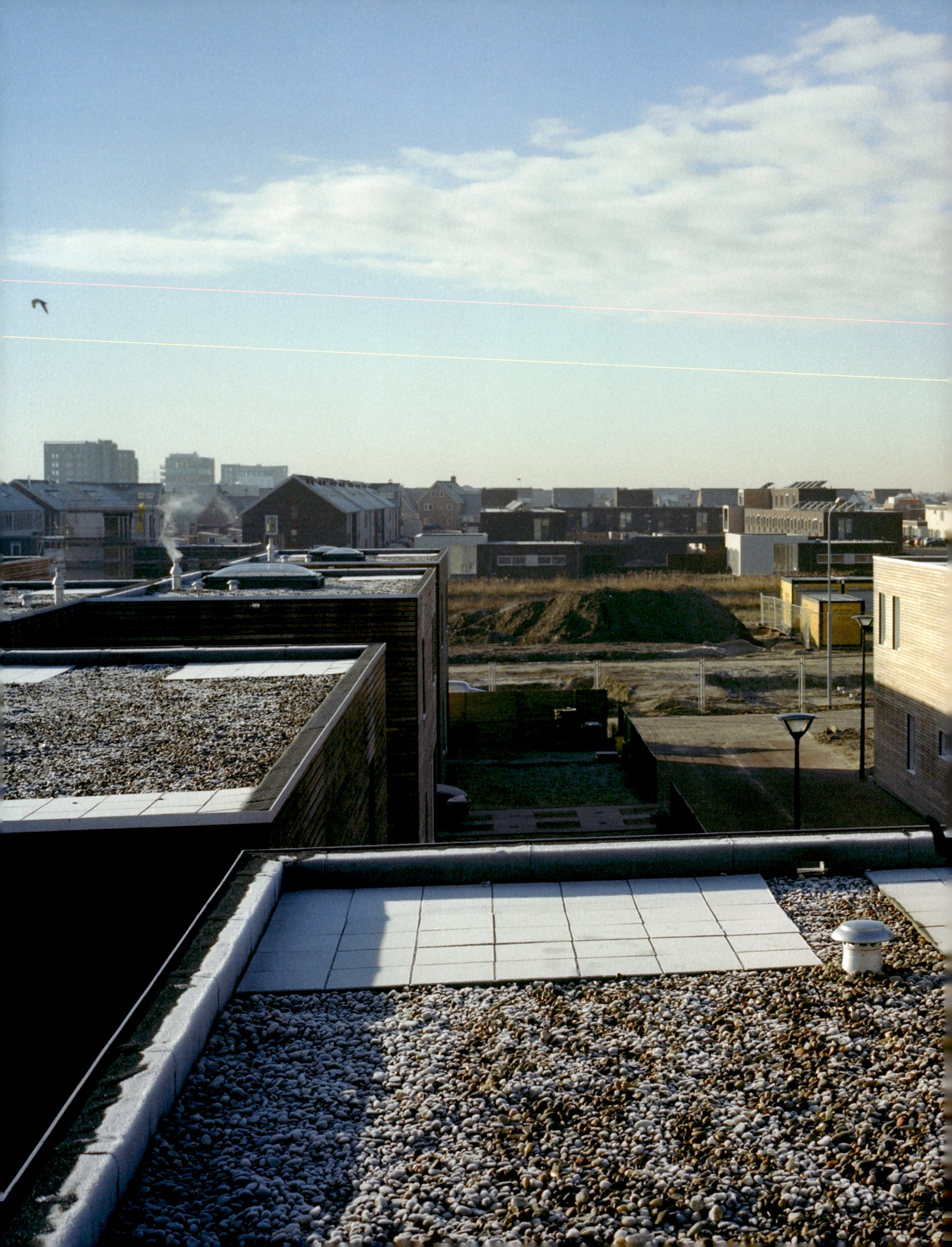

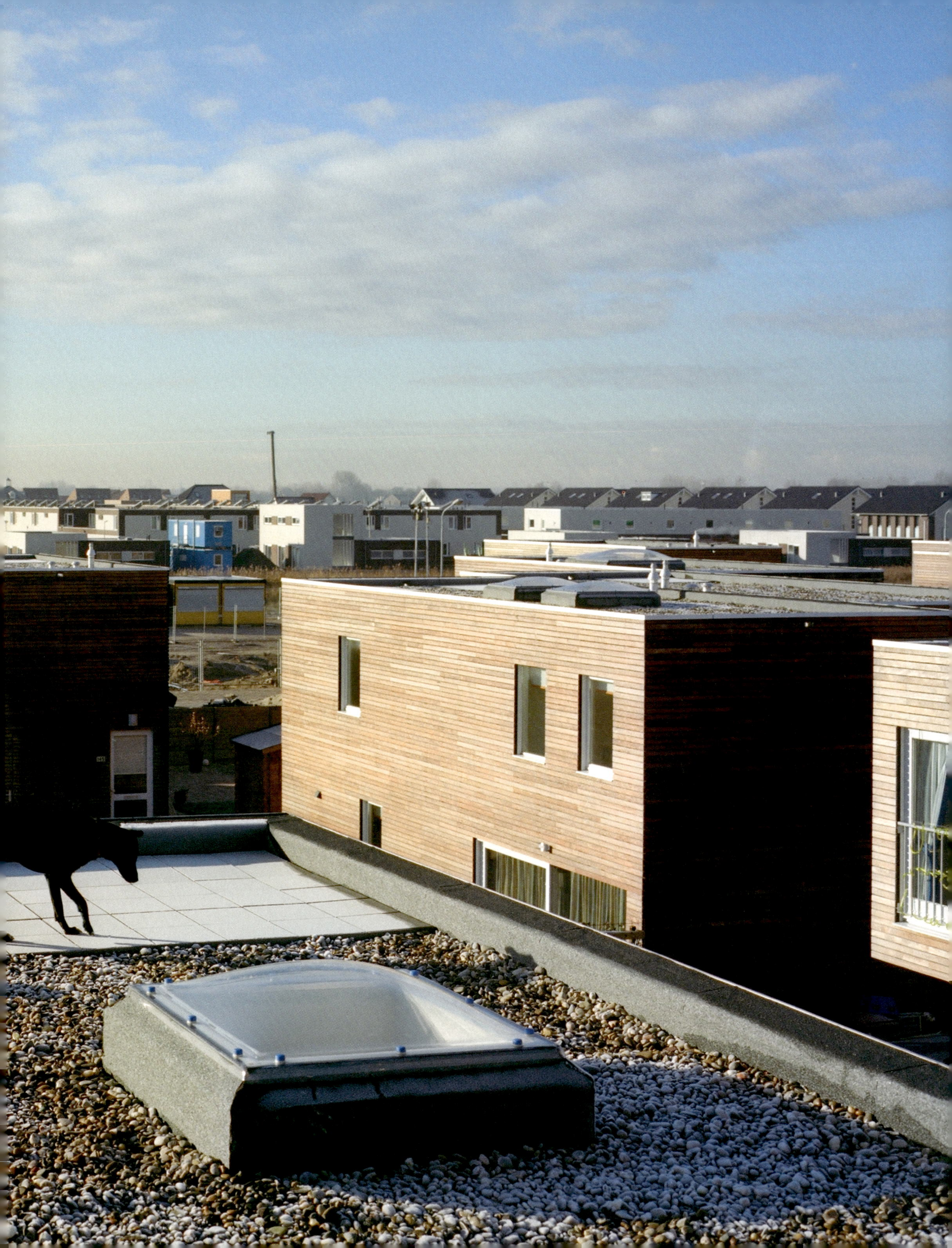

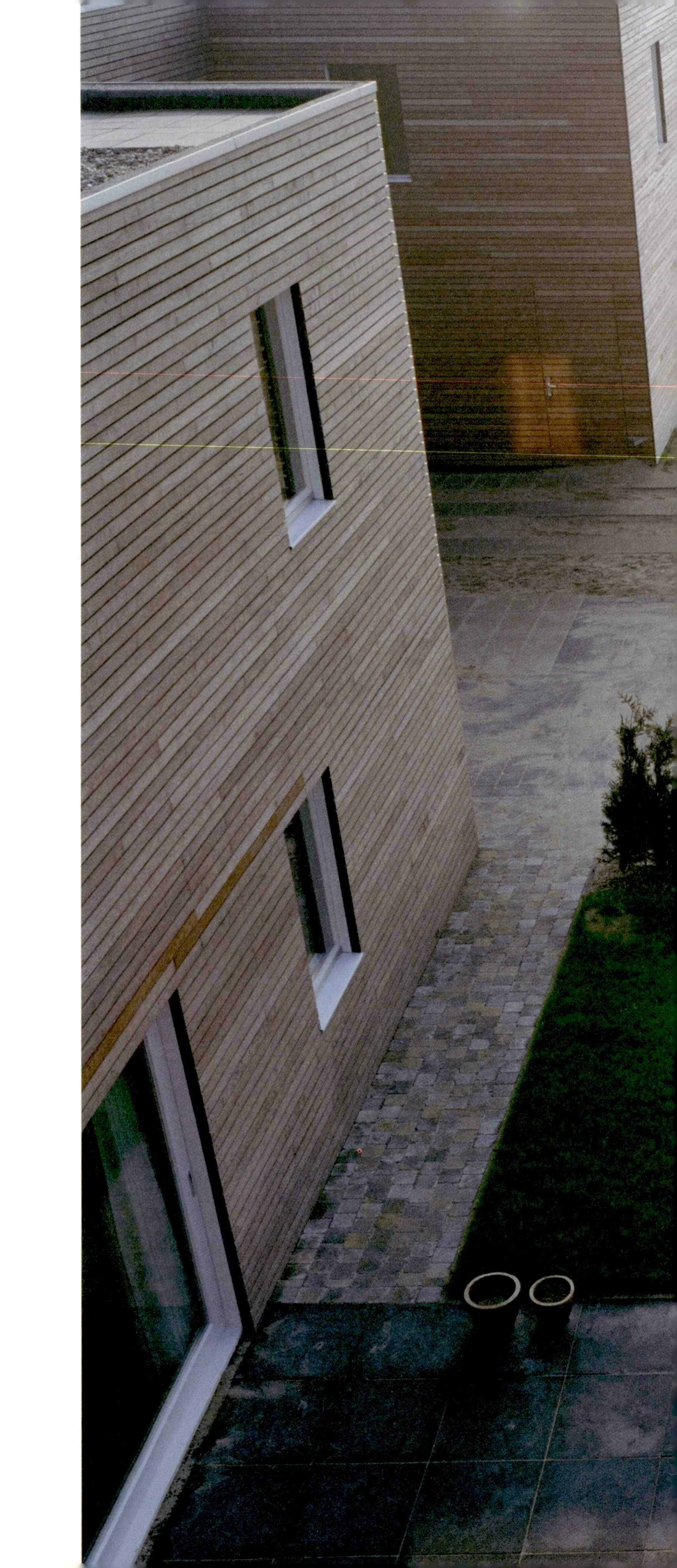

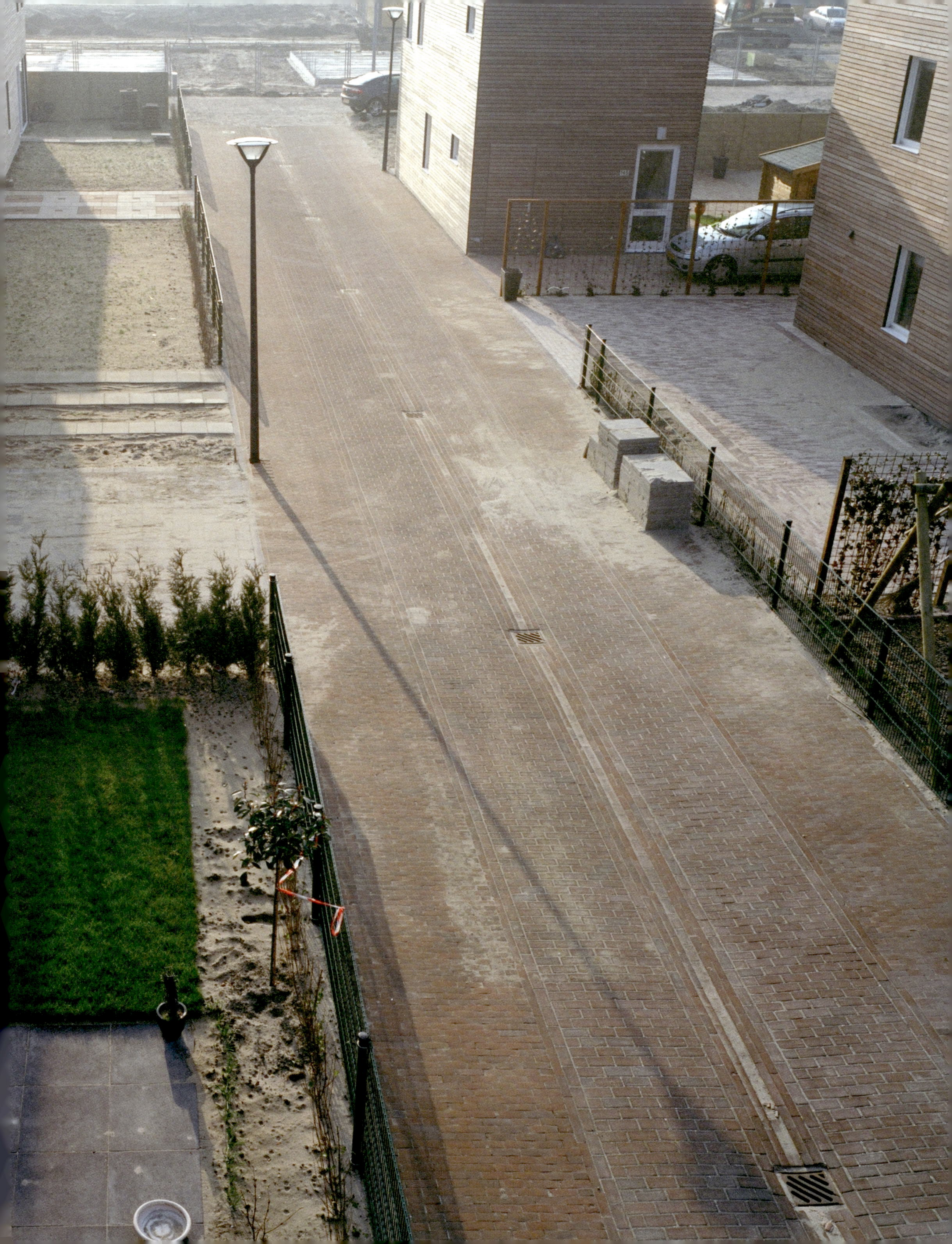

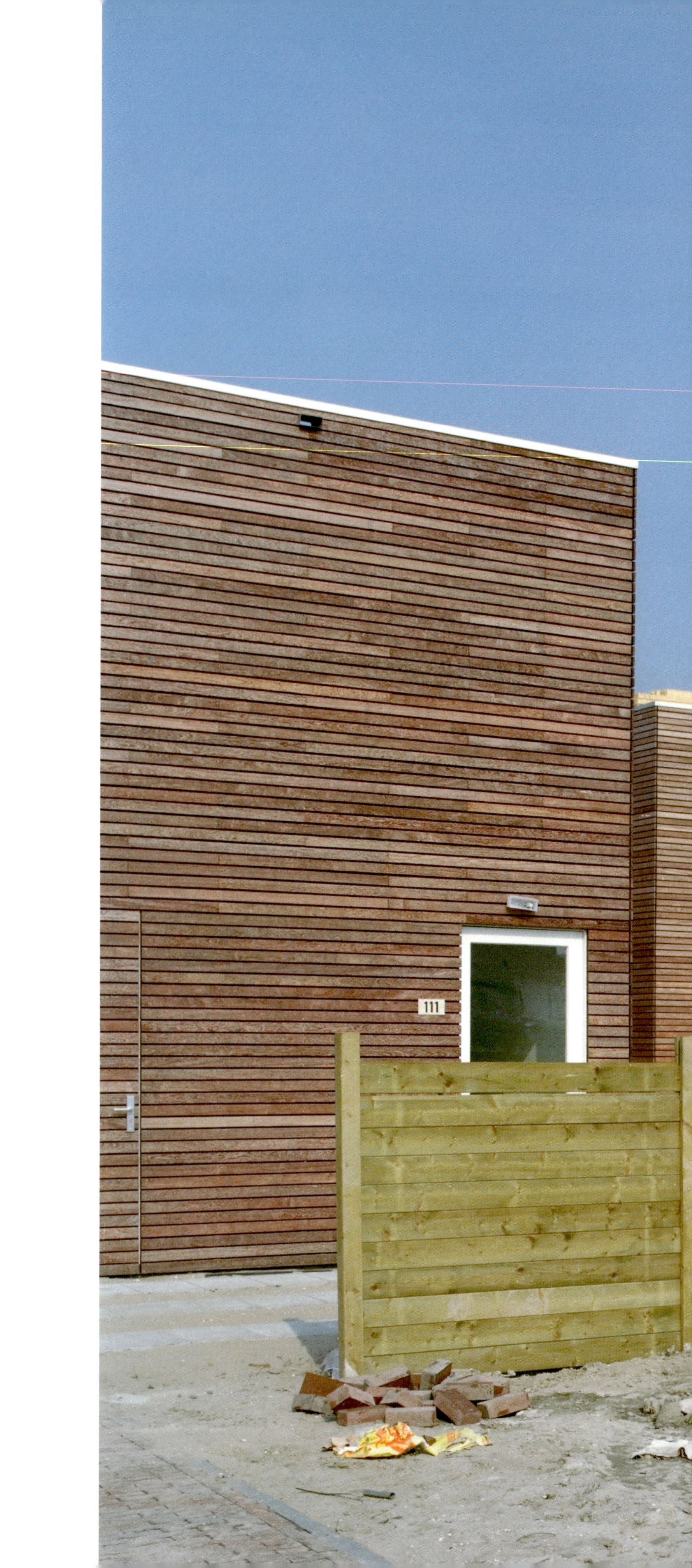

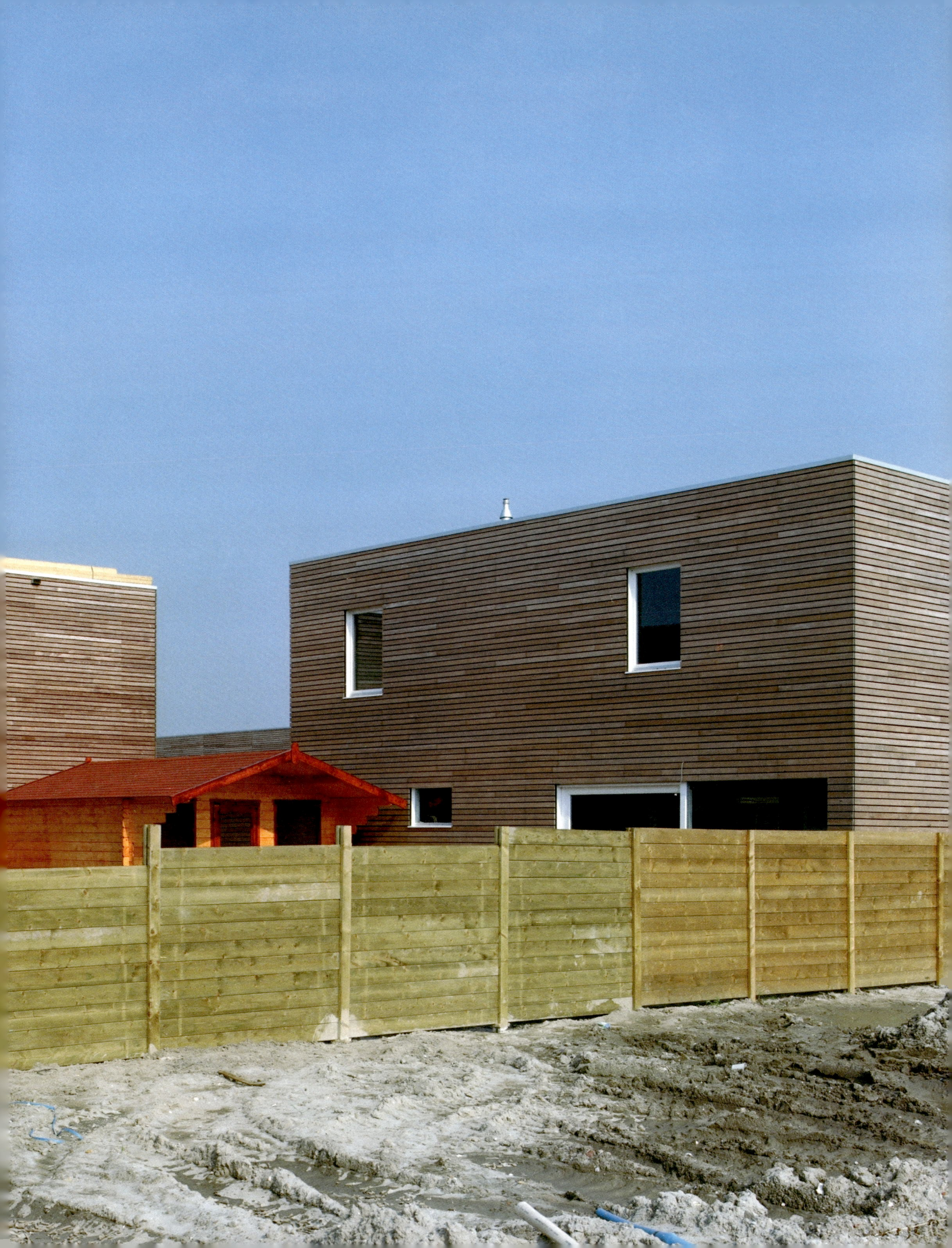

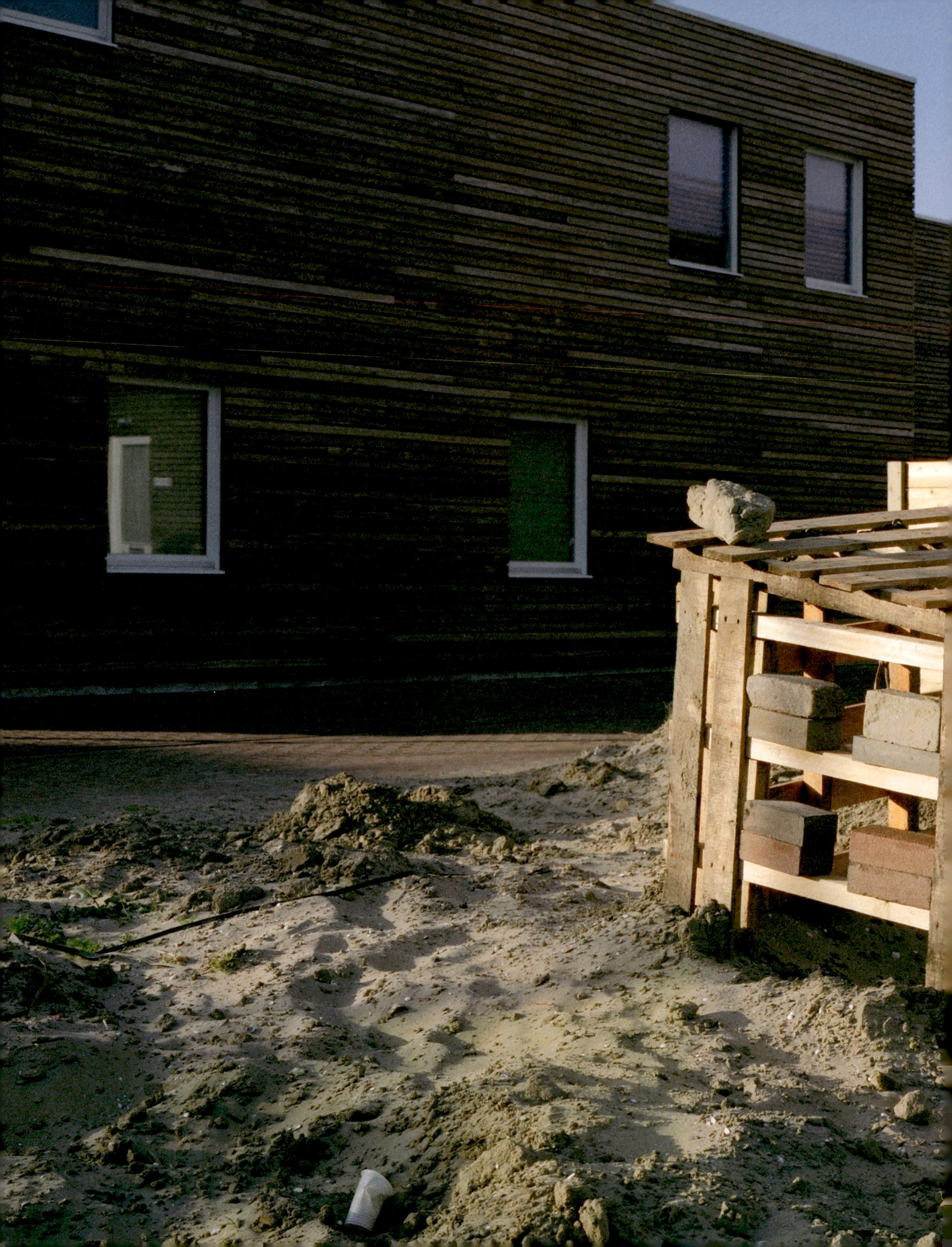

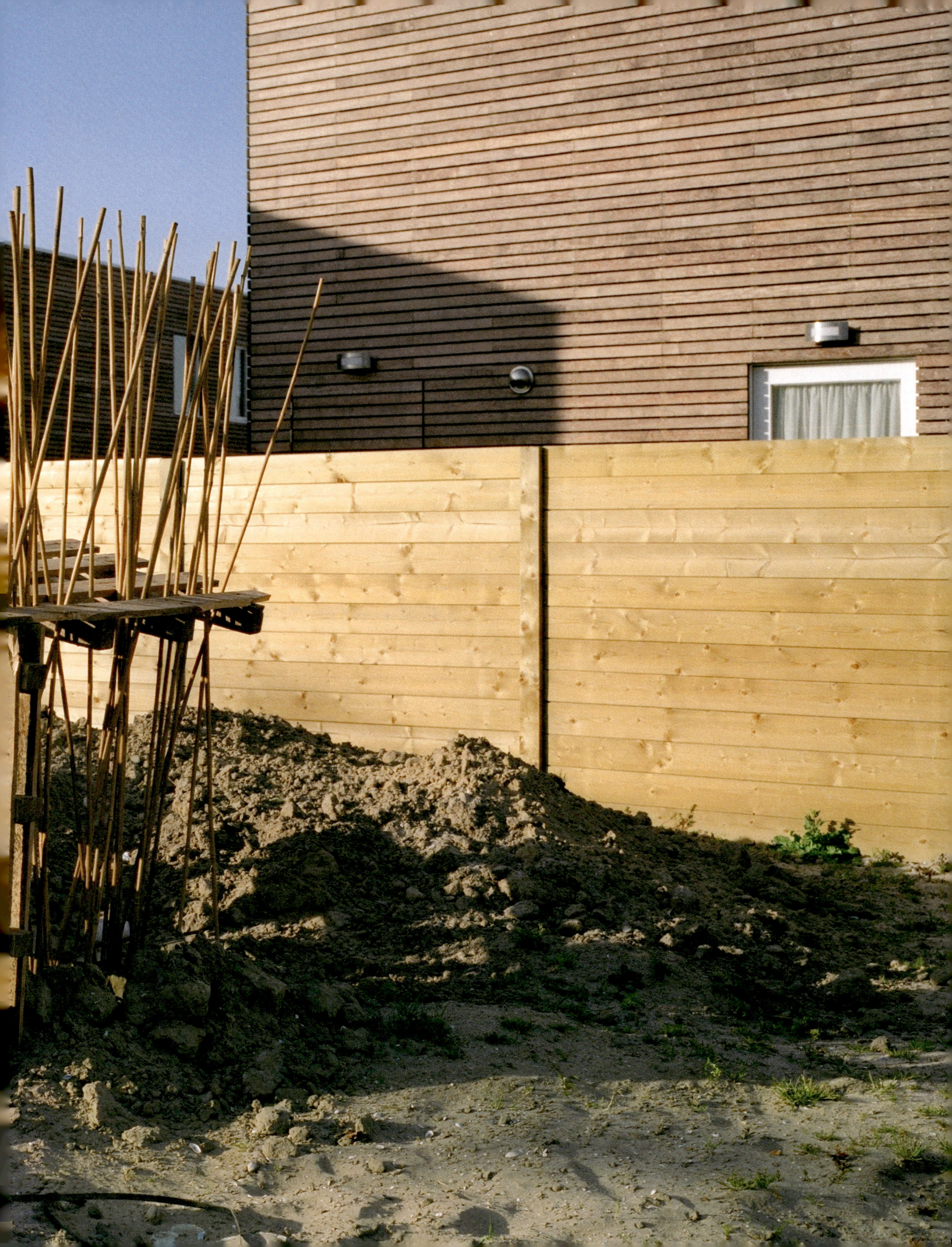

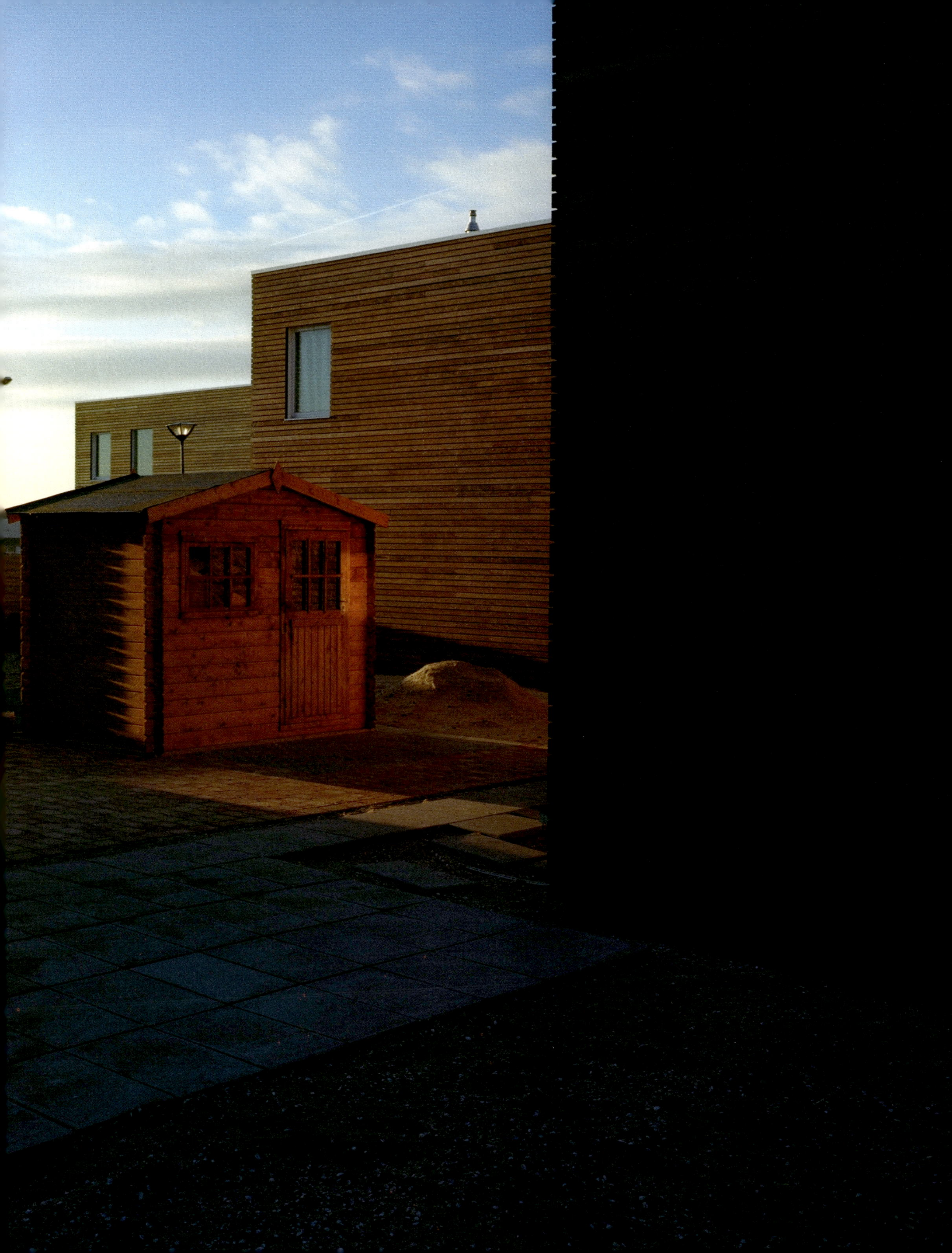

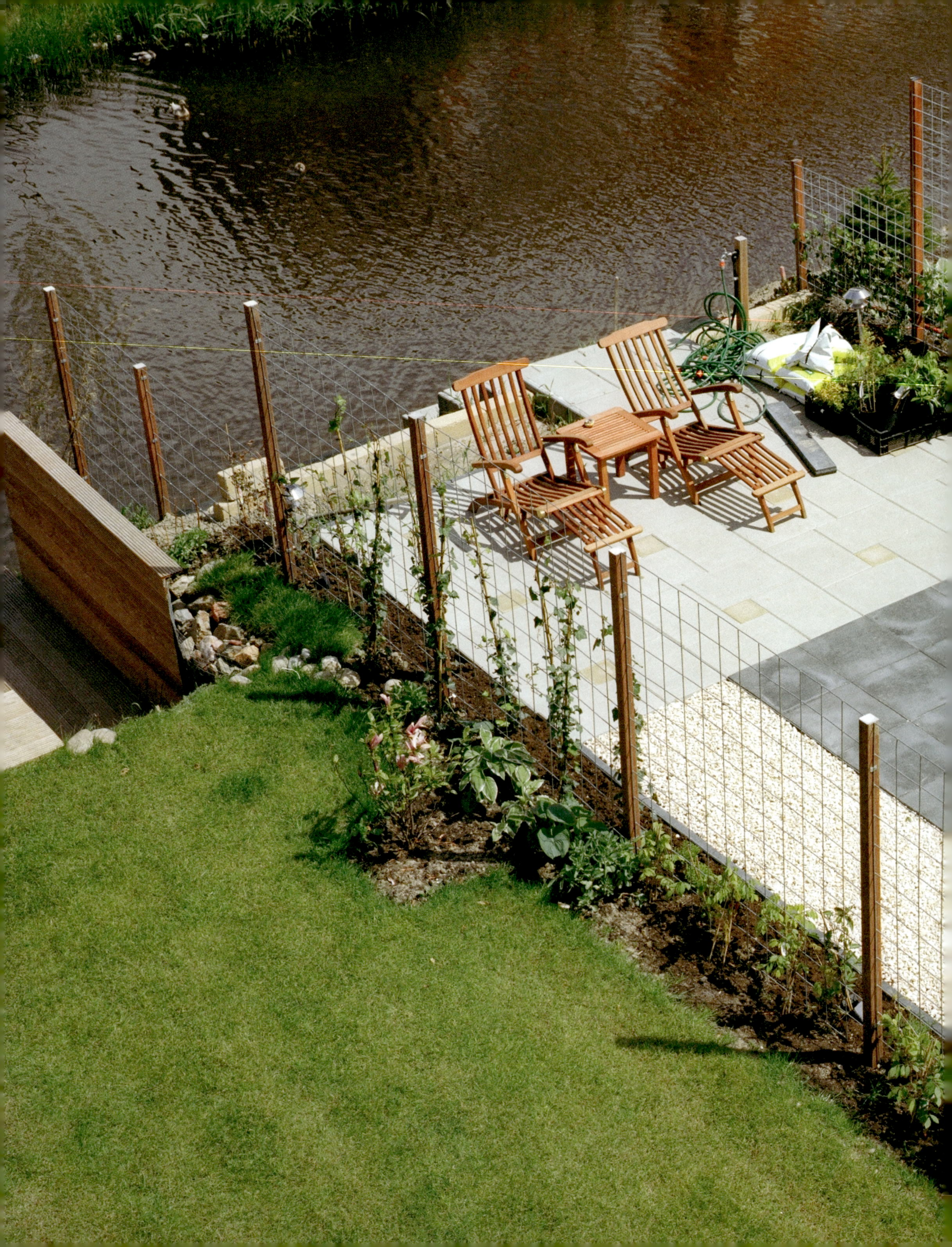

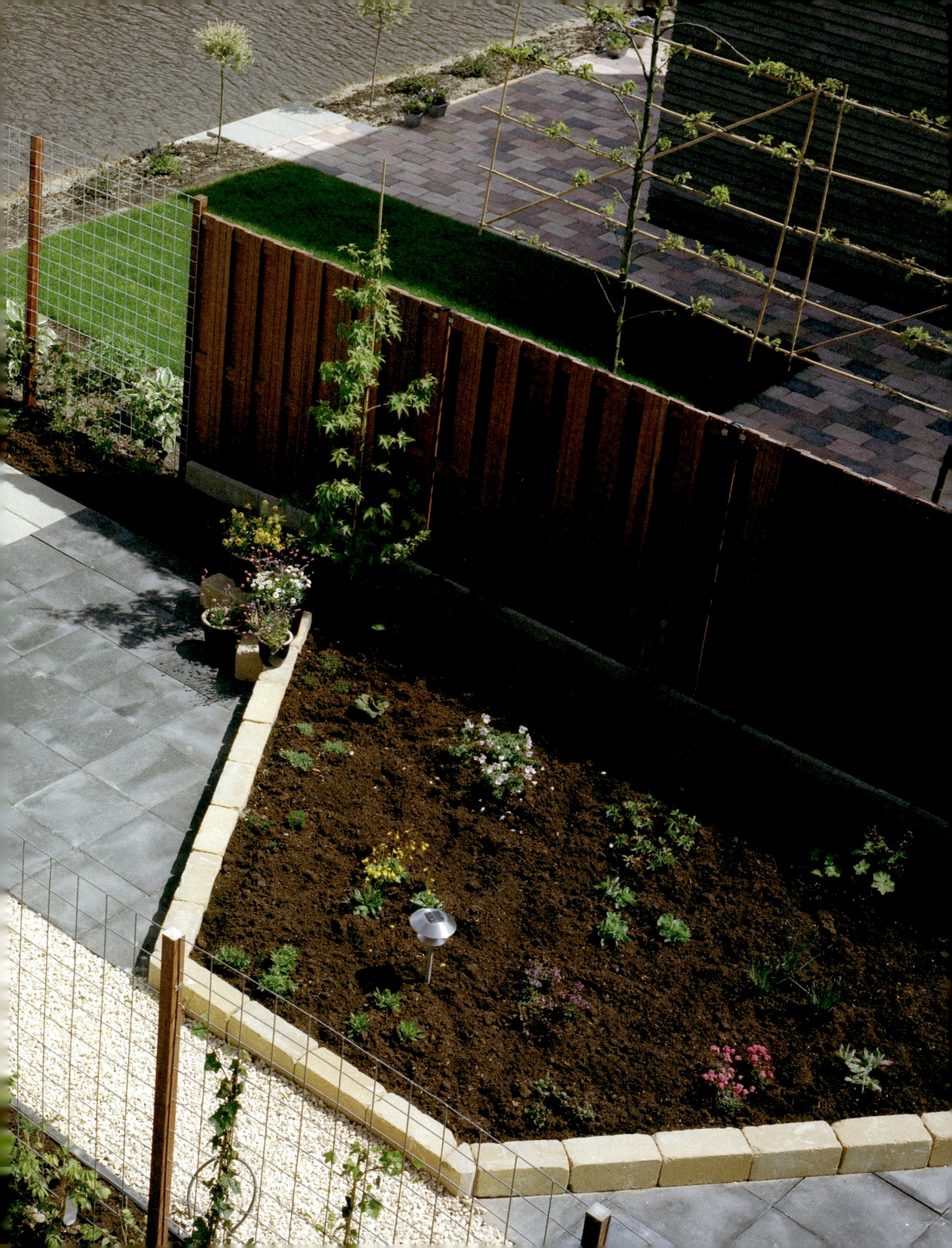

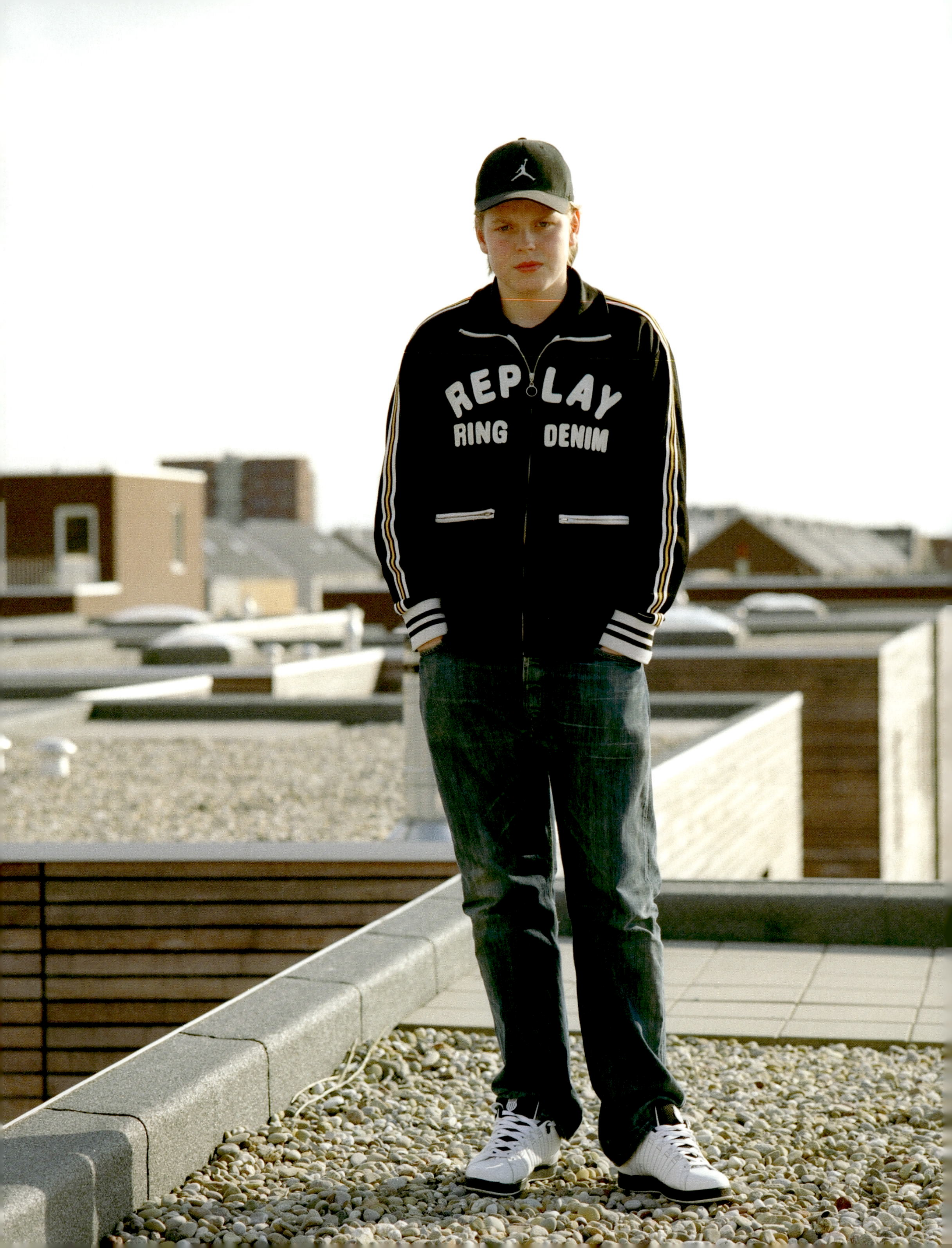

is referred to as being 'fairly crumbly, sometimes having the tendency to become mushy; the color on the plate is slightly grayish.' This is compensated by the fact that 'the taste and smell are quite good under favorable circumstances.' Then, in 1943, the 'Meerster' makes its debut. This potato plant has 'abundant, sturdy foliage.' Other successful new seed-potato breeds follow: Arka, Rubinia, Concorde, Ausonia, Wilja, Fianna, Cosmos, Cornado, Marfona and Kondor.

In 1993, when Geert Deddens wants to buy the land from the Könst brothers, the business is in a strong position. Almost a quarter of the breeds shipped by the largest seed-potato exporter in the Netherlands have been developed by Könst. And more seed potatoes are exported from the Netherlands than from any other country in the world.

The brothers always accepted invitations to discuss the possible sale of their land. But they invariably took a business-like approach to this. 'We did want to talk; but being business men, *time is money*, so we charged them for our time. That made things clear right away,' Peter Könst says now. The brothers kept a folder with newspaper clippings on all the announced plans for construction and attended meetings of the town council. They knew that, because of their farming business's special character, the run-of-the-mill buy-out formula would not apply to them. They could expect an entirely different compensation, well beyond that given to the 'ordinary farmer.' Once the project developers realized this, they pulled out: this high-priced business would just have to be bought by the municipality. Peter and Vincent weren't surprised, therefore, when municipal official Geert Deddens came forward with an offer.

The Könst brothers had clear-cut demands. They wanted to continue their business in the Haarlemmermeerpolder; they wanted to be able to cultivate two different tracts of land over a long period; and they wanted appropriate compensation for relocating the business. And that's exactly how it went. Independent experts drew up a report describing the business's special character, its value and the conditions for relocating it. The municipality acknowledged the conclusions of this report.

Having bargained that all compensation, for the buildings of the business for instance, would be reflected in the price of the land, the Könst brothers were in a fiscally advantageous position. Ultimately, the municipality awarded them five times the amount paid to other bought-out farmers per m². Furthermore, they were able to continue farming on the Spieringweg for another seven years. In 1995, Vincent and Peter Könst started construction at their new location, 10 km to the southeast. This enabled them to make comparisons in the behavior of their seed potatoes, grown on two different parcels of land. But as a result of that, the project developers were forced to work from the north and from the south, toward the center of the planned residential area. The construction of new housing on Eiland 7, the new name for Könst's tract of land, would thereby have to wait: the land was not available.

Eiland 7 spends many years as a potato island among the new neighborhoods that are gradually sprouting. During the final year of their buy-out agreement, Vincent Könst sows 100-m-high letters of winter radish in the grass for his girlfriend, who flies down from Sweden every so often. The words I LOVE YOU can be read from the sky.

Eiland 7, De Slufter
Kees (58) retired maintenance
    technician
Marian (46) human resources
    manager
Milou (18) student
Romana (15) student

Kees:

I used to pass the construction sign for Floriande as I drove by Hoofddorp. That's when I'd think: wouldn't be caught dead in this place. Until we saw an ad for 13 'waterside bungalows' to be built on Eiland 6, freestanding houses by the water for an attractive price. We were living in a smaller home in Haarlem, but had no urgent need to look for anything else. Simply out of curiosity, we went to have a look. My wife said, 'You won't get me here for all the tea in China.' She was rooted in Haarlem; Hoofddorp was unfamiliar to us. When construction on the houses began, my wife did get enthusiastic. We signed up for a waterside bungalow, but missed out on the draw. What a letdown. So by that time, clearly, the die was cast. We were ready to leave Haarlem.

The project developer's sales advisor told us that another wonderful project would be starting on Eiland 7. An information evening was held in Febuary 2004; only about 20 people attended. Later we saw two of them again, once the project was finished.

At the meeting, two types of homes were presented by two architects. We were most attracted to the design by SeARCH. That's what we said that evening, and we picked out this lot where we now live.

We thought it was all arranged, but suddenly there was a phone call from the sales advisor. Not enough demand for the design by SeARCH. What now? The type that would indeed get built wasn't our choice. 'Either we do it, or we don't; but then it'll be the last chance we have at this type of home,' we reasoned. A place like this would cost at least another 200,000 to 250,000 more in Haarlem. And in Hoofddorp they're not building any more of these for the time being.

But the house did cost 400,000. We took a long time to make up our minds. What you mainly opt for is a large house, with a large garden by the water. Value for money, but without knowing what Hoofddorp would have to offer. We moved in the day before Christmas, 2006. Now Hoofddorp doesn't seem all that bad, and we think it's been a good decision. A great house with a wonderful garden, despite the fact that it was our third choice.

3

Preliminary sketches for the *Vinex* location along the Spieringweg took shape in 1995. After a competition was held among residents in the area, the location was given a name: Floriande.

Fred Kaaij, city architect for the municipality of Haarlemmermeer, supervises all construction projects carried out here. He has asked Rien de Ruiter, of Klunder Architects in Rotterdam, whether he'd have any interest in a position as coordinating architect.

On the evening prior to his interview for the job, Rien de Ruiter traced part of the Haarlemmermeer map and came up with a general layout for the area to be developed. 'The whole structure was already conceived while the land was being reclaimed; it was already there. Nothing else needed to be done. Okay, the ditches were a bit narrow. My proposal was: work from the existing structure and make the ditches around the parcels wider. Then you'll have islands.' With this sketch De Ruiter gets the job. For the next three years, all sorts of urban planners think up alternatives, but this proves to be the best plan.

The gist of De Ruiter's sketch is carried out: this polder landscape's underlying structure serves as the basis for the design. And that results in 12 islands, each measuring 400 x 200 m. Running straight through the development will be a secondary road and, to the west of it, a greenbelt. A 100-m strip along a drainage canal on the eastern side, next to power pylons, will be zoned for schools and other facilities. Here, too, lies the road providing access to the islands.

Fred Kaaij: 'Rien de Ruiter drew a display card with a different color for each island, twelve different flavors.' Next to the bridge came an apartment tower. There had to be a wide range of options. 'When you walk down the boulevard, you're walking past a bookcase; you can take that book, or any other book,' says De Ruiter.

The commission involved the following: 300 homes per island. According to the *Vinex* norm, that meant 35 per hectare. For the various developers, this was a pleasant concept. 'Each developer was given his own island. That eliminated the potential for complaints about who would pay for the lighting or the paving stones in the alleyways. Cultural history and organization converged here,' Kaaij explains.

Keep the structure austere, and seek to achieve this in the urban-developmental and architectonic innovation: that was De Ruiter's motto.

And it led to great diversity among the islands. Eiland 2 has 'conservative architecture' (as Fred Kaaij puts it), and on Eiland 3 a variety of very wide homes were built. Eiland 5 was 'regulation-free,' which meant that the buyers could build their houses as they saw fit.

On Eiland 7 an experiment would be undertaken. Municipal architect Kaaij believes that a relatively young city facing an enormous construction task should have guts and not be afraid to experiment. AM Wonen, the project developer of a few islands, including Eiland 7, proposes Bjarne Mastenbroek, from SeARCH, as the urban planner and architect. Rik Bolderheij, civil servant and later director of the *Vinex* program office, is present at Bjarne Mastenbroek's presentation. 'At that time there was an alderman very interested in quality – a bit less concerned with costs and revenue. Mastenbroek held a strong presentation that made a good impression on the alderman.' It was a simple proposal: two large strips of homes and, in the middle, a large area with 300 trees. Clearly different from the other islands.

'When I was asked to do the job, they said: we want an out-of-the-ordinary *Vinex* neighborhood. That appealed to me. I'm critical of the *Vinex* program. What you often see is that developers have no interest in what happens to the project after its completion,' says Mastenbroek.

The developer had made a report. These were to be unusual homes; the '*Vinex* look' had to go. All of the houses were given an extra room, so that inhabitants could work at home. 'It seems worthwhile to me, but then I'd like to do it really differently, I told the developer,' Mastenbroek recalls. 'These were wealthy times. They could afford to experiment. People wanted a bit more, to experience more with such a neighborhood.'

In the Netherlands, today's new neighborhoods are often being designed to look like old villages. But according to Mastenbroek, that creates only the *image* of a nice village; the social cohesion that characterizes an old village does not automatically come with this. A village is not a village because it looks like one.

Mastenbroek created space and airiness in his original (1999) urban-development plan. Sweeping all the green areas together, he gave the

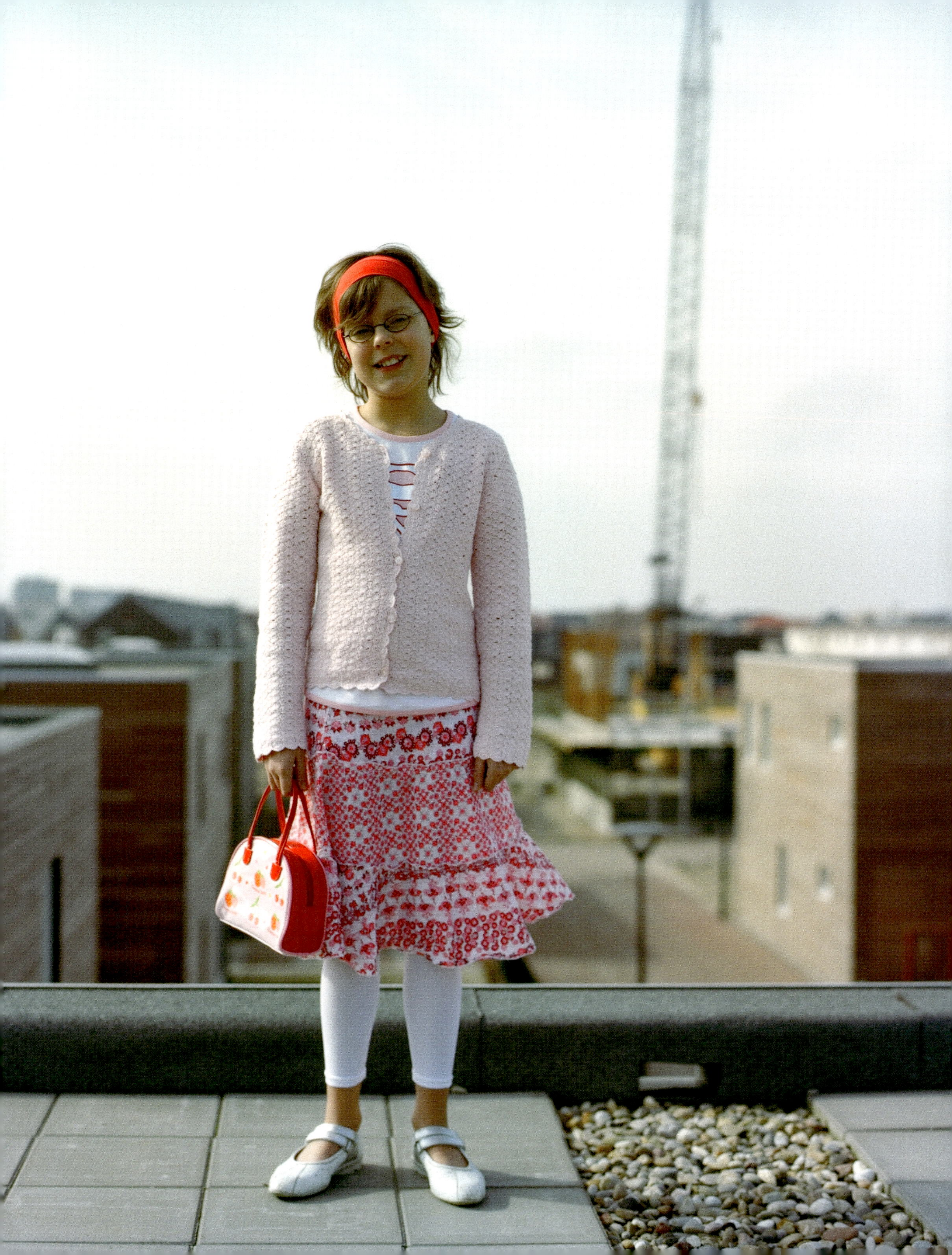

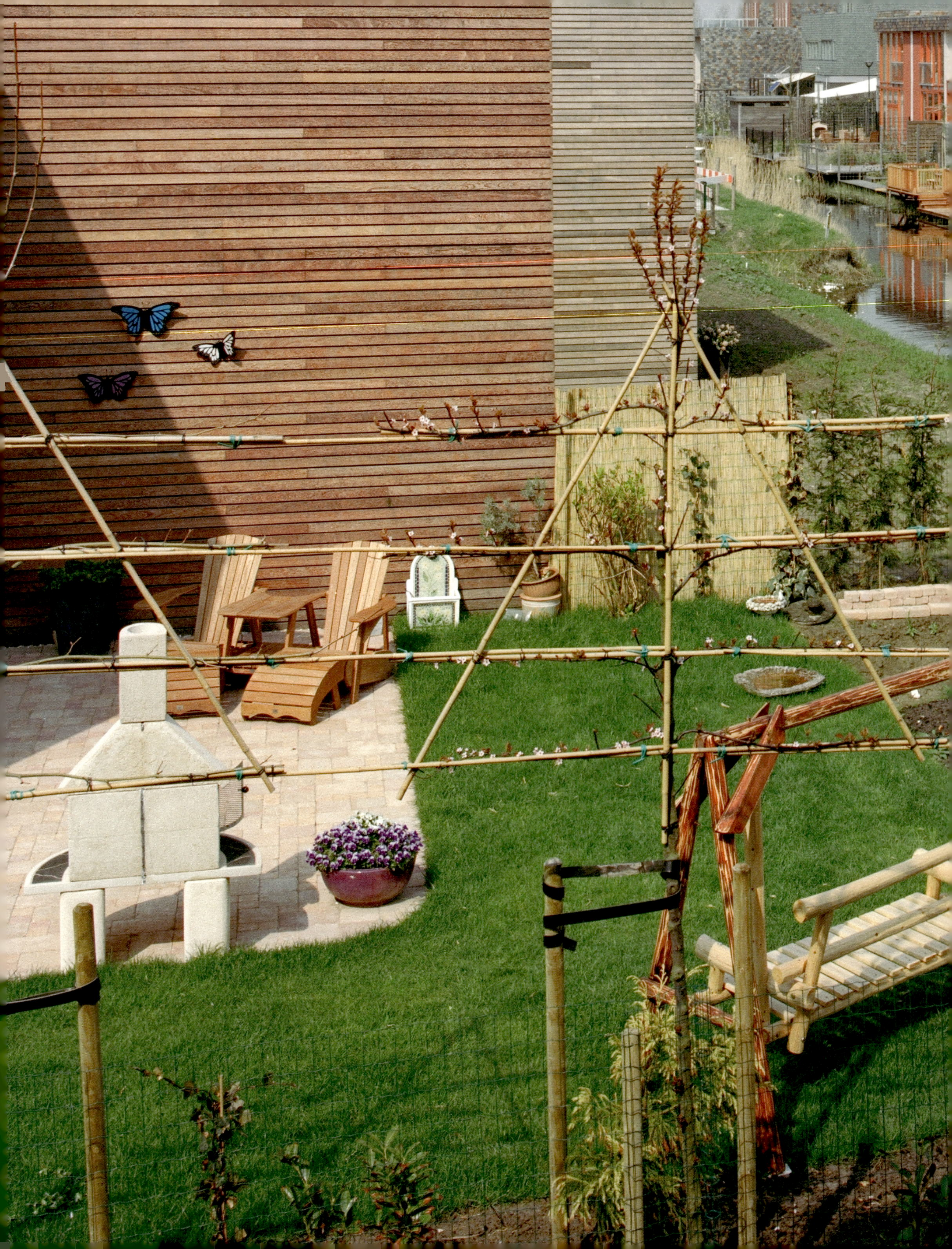

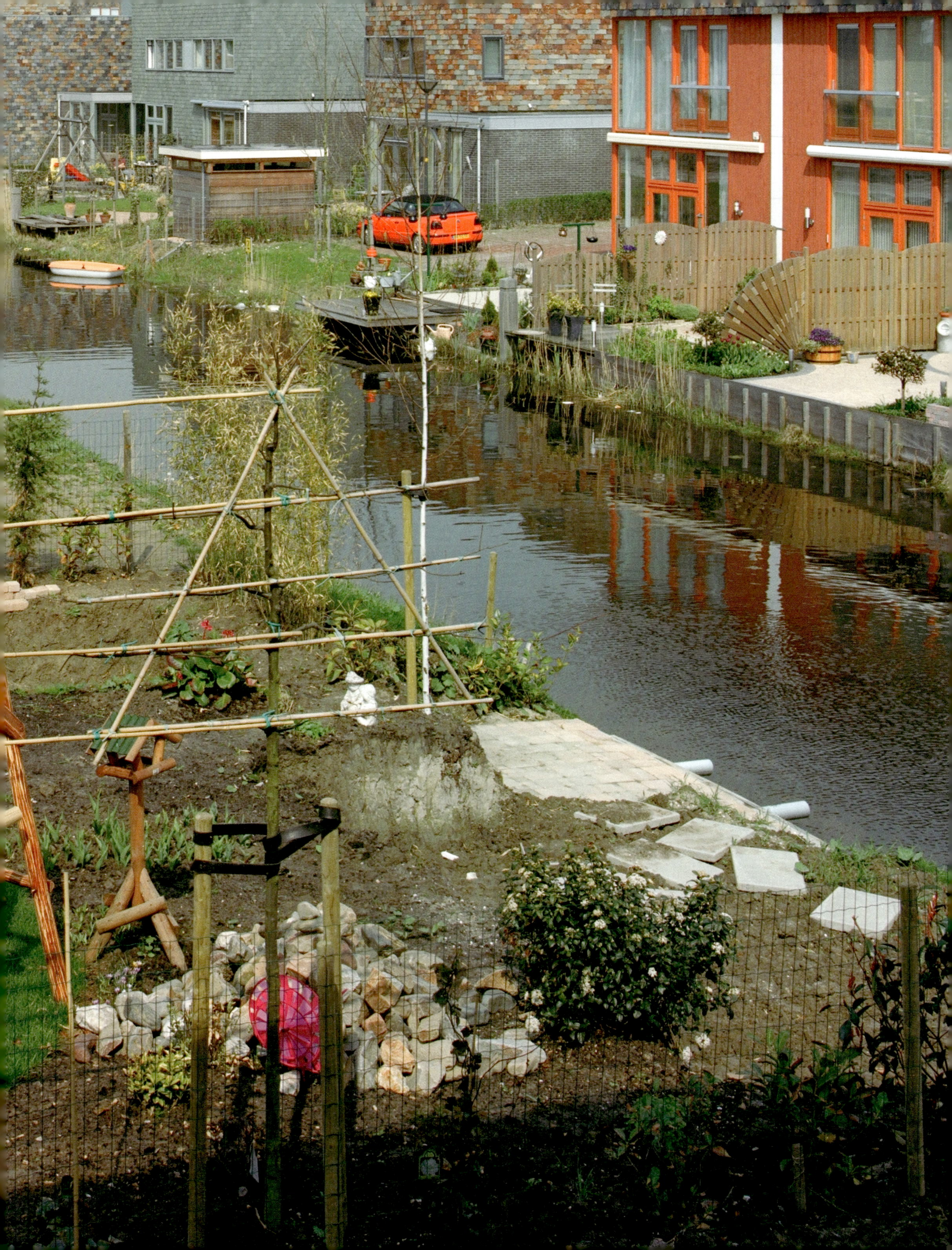

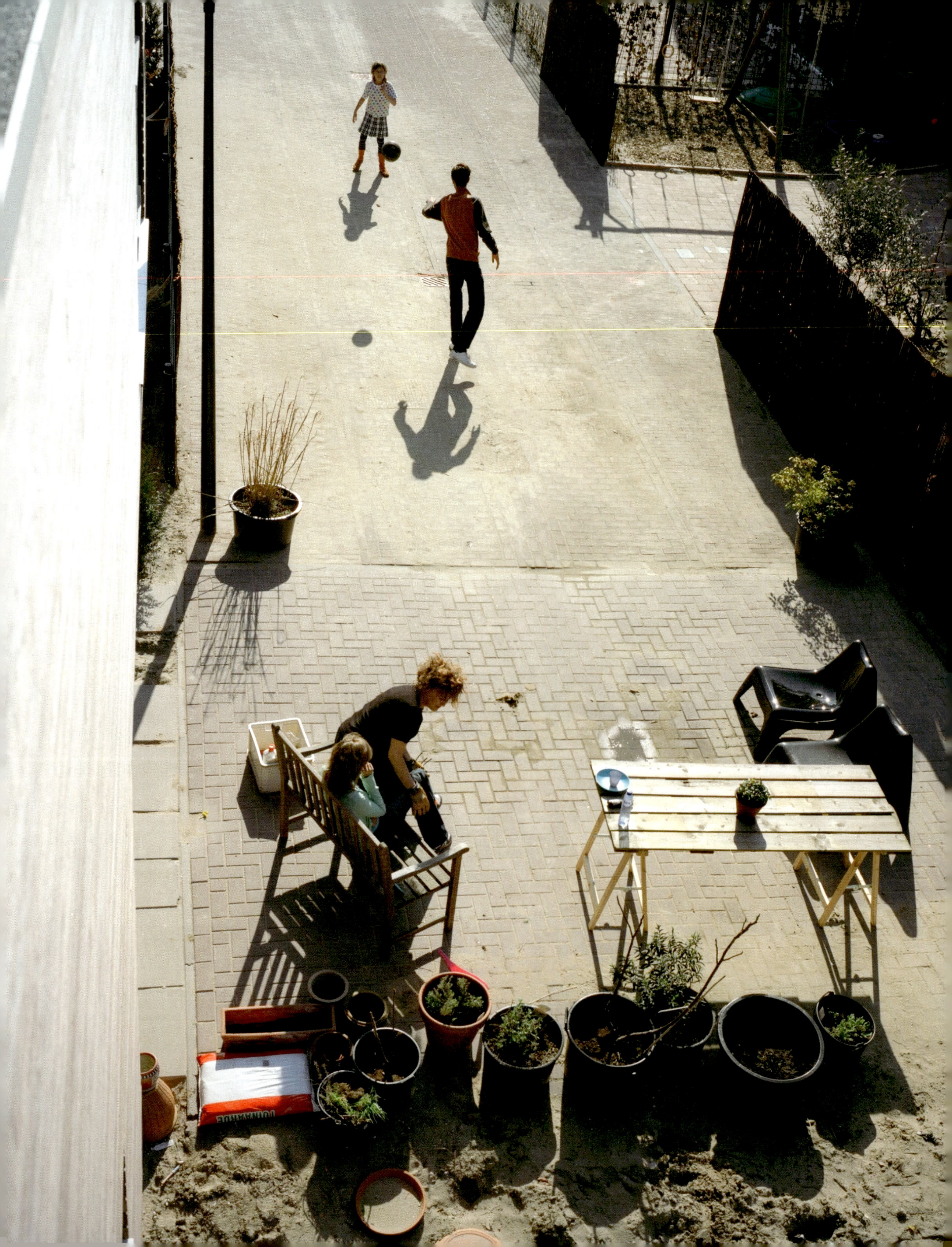

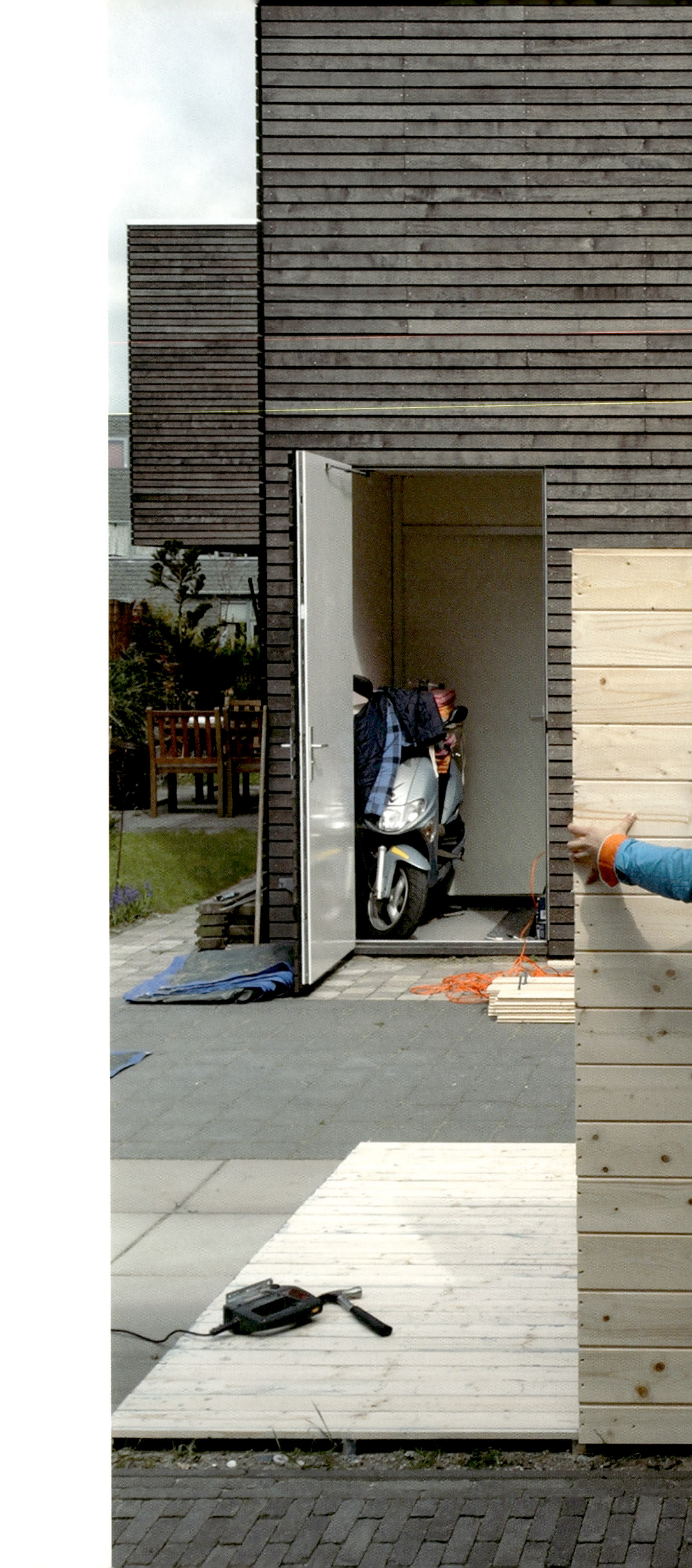

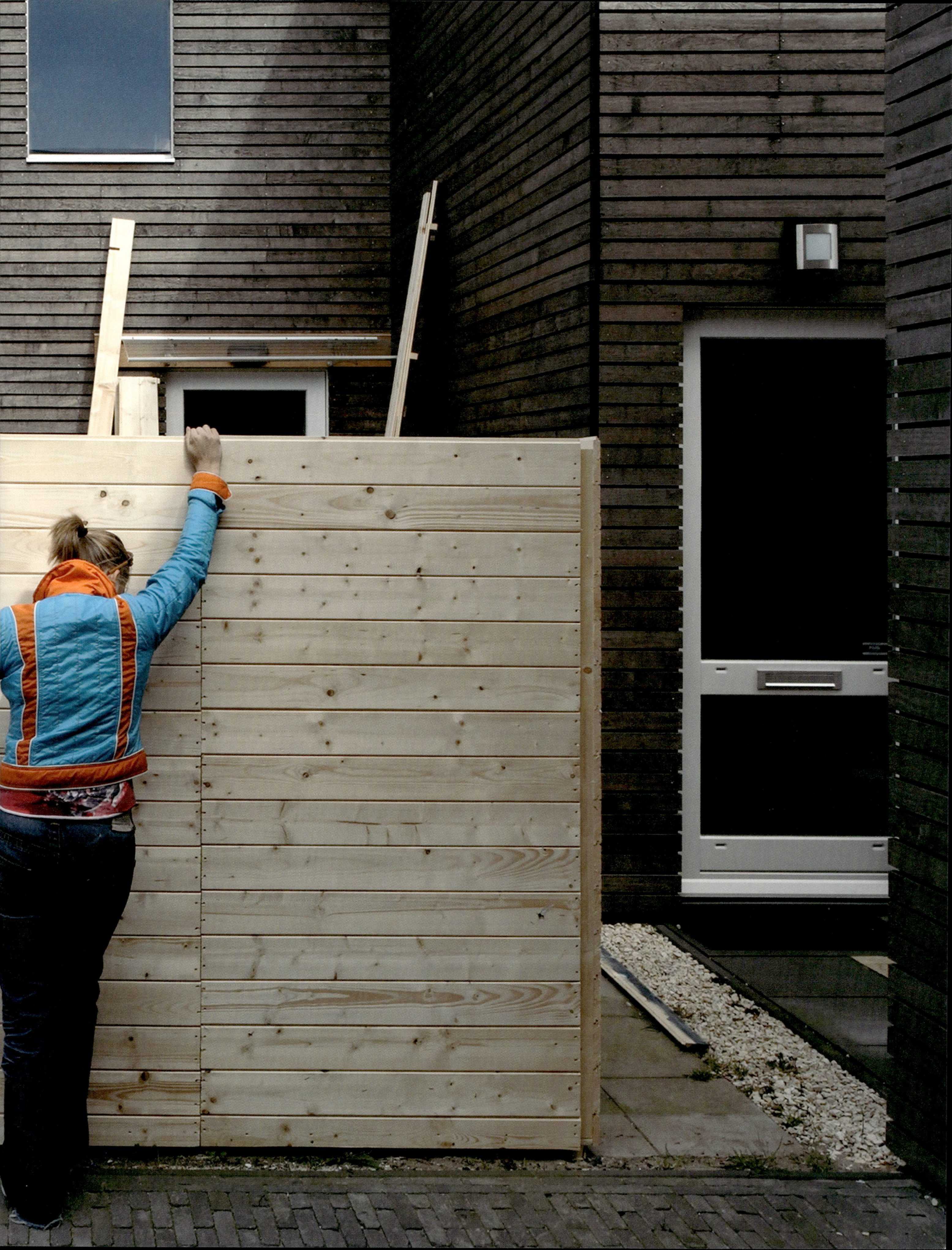

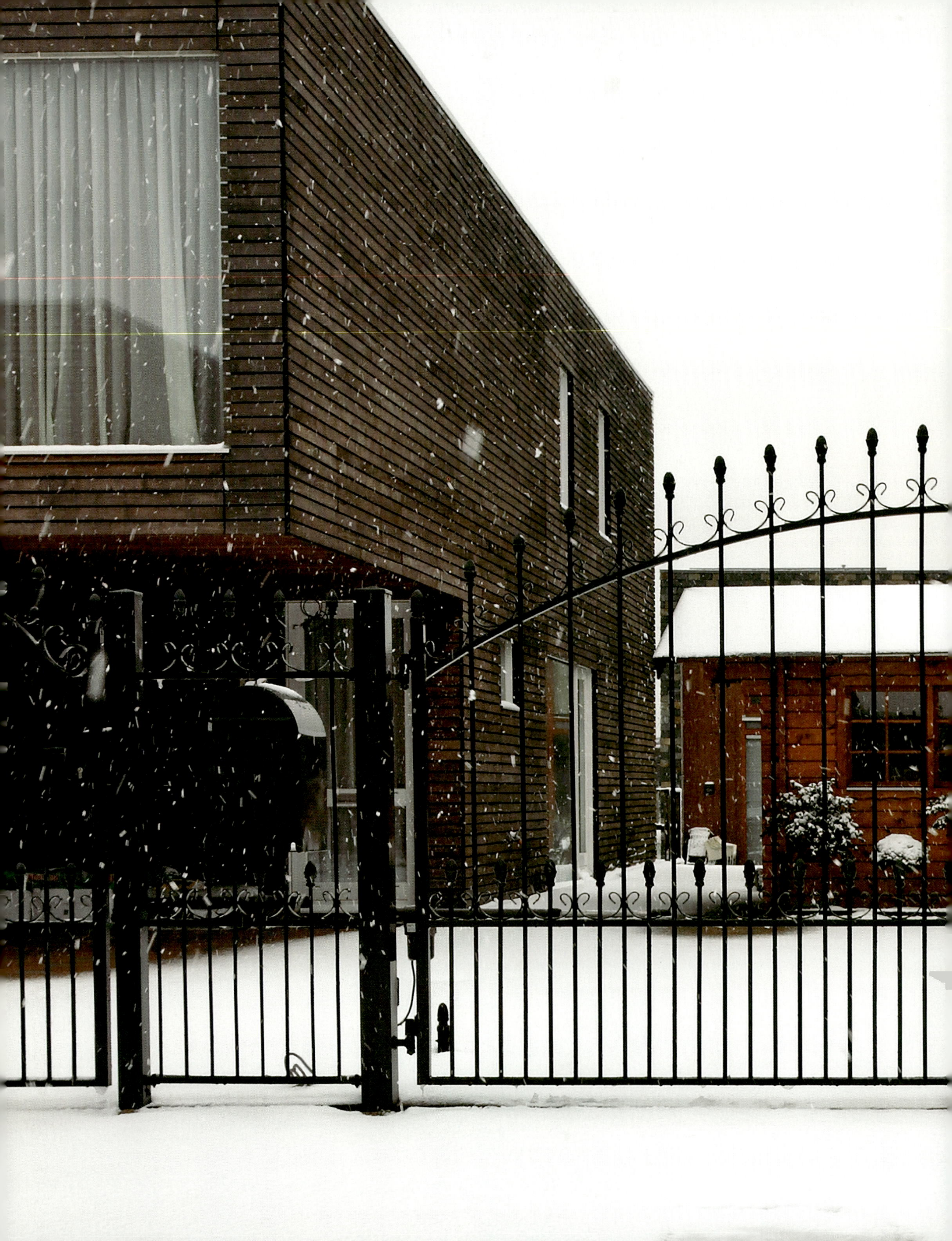

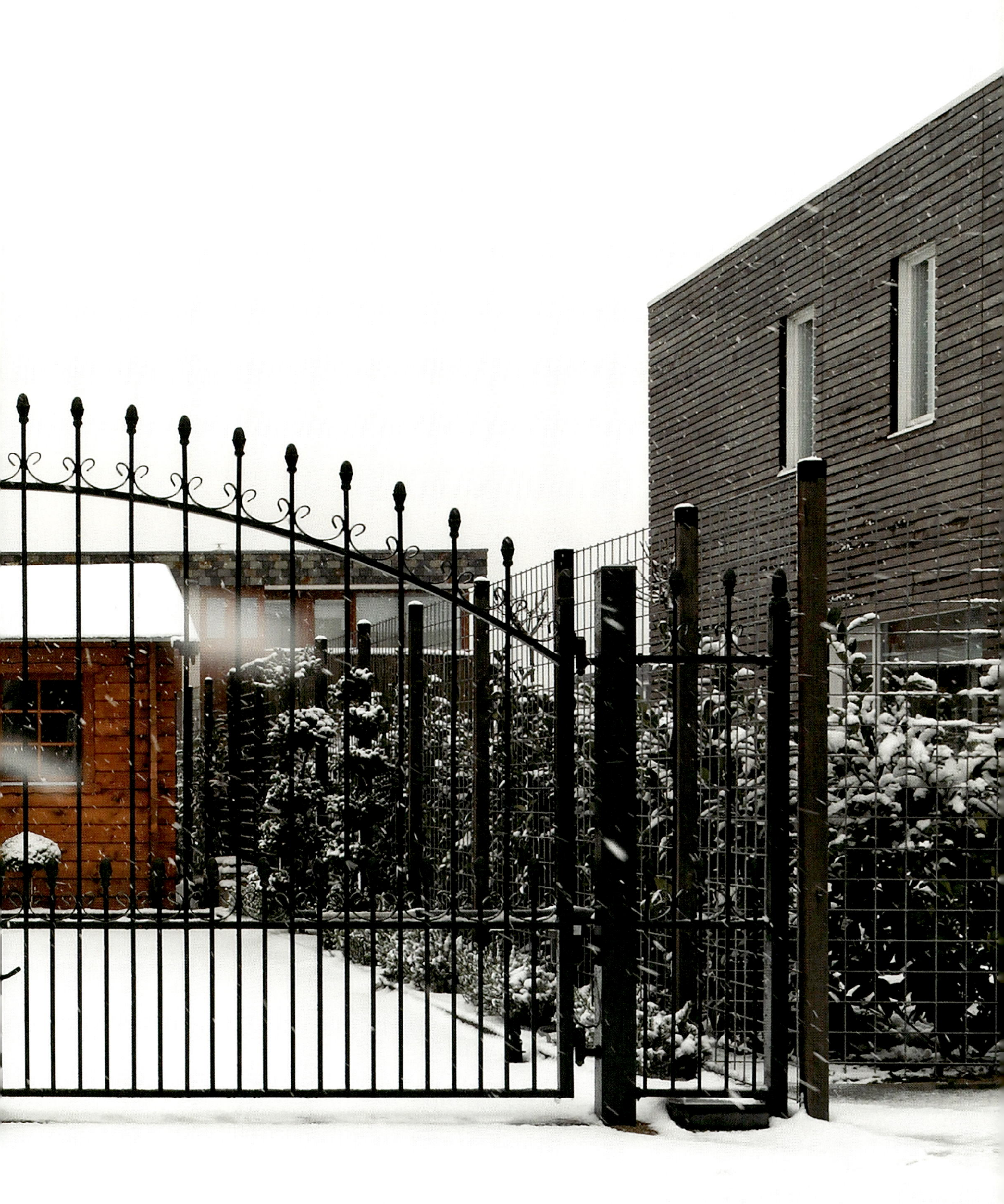

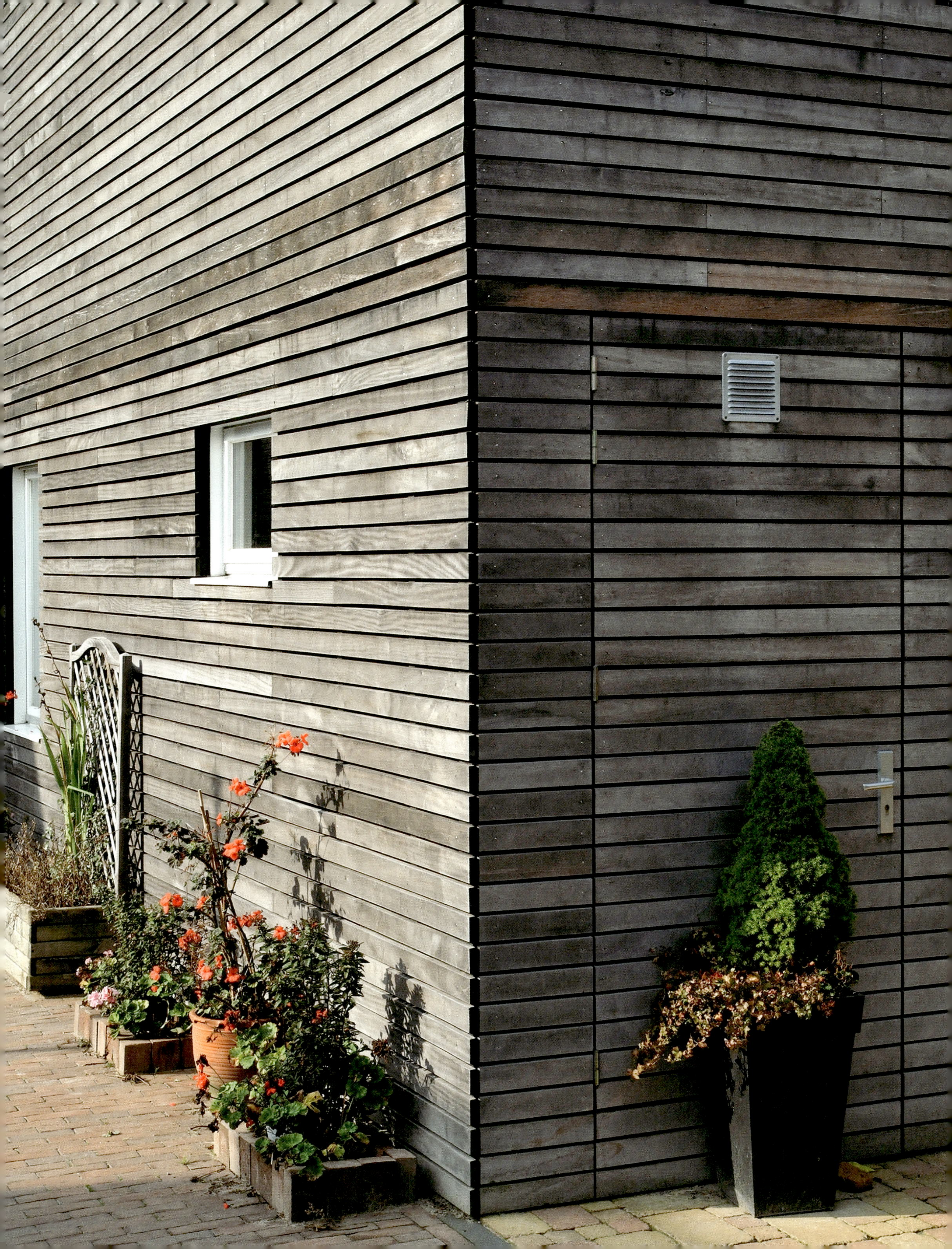

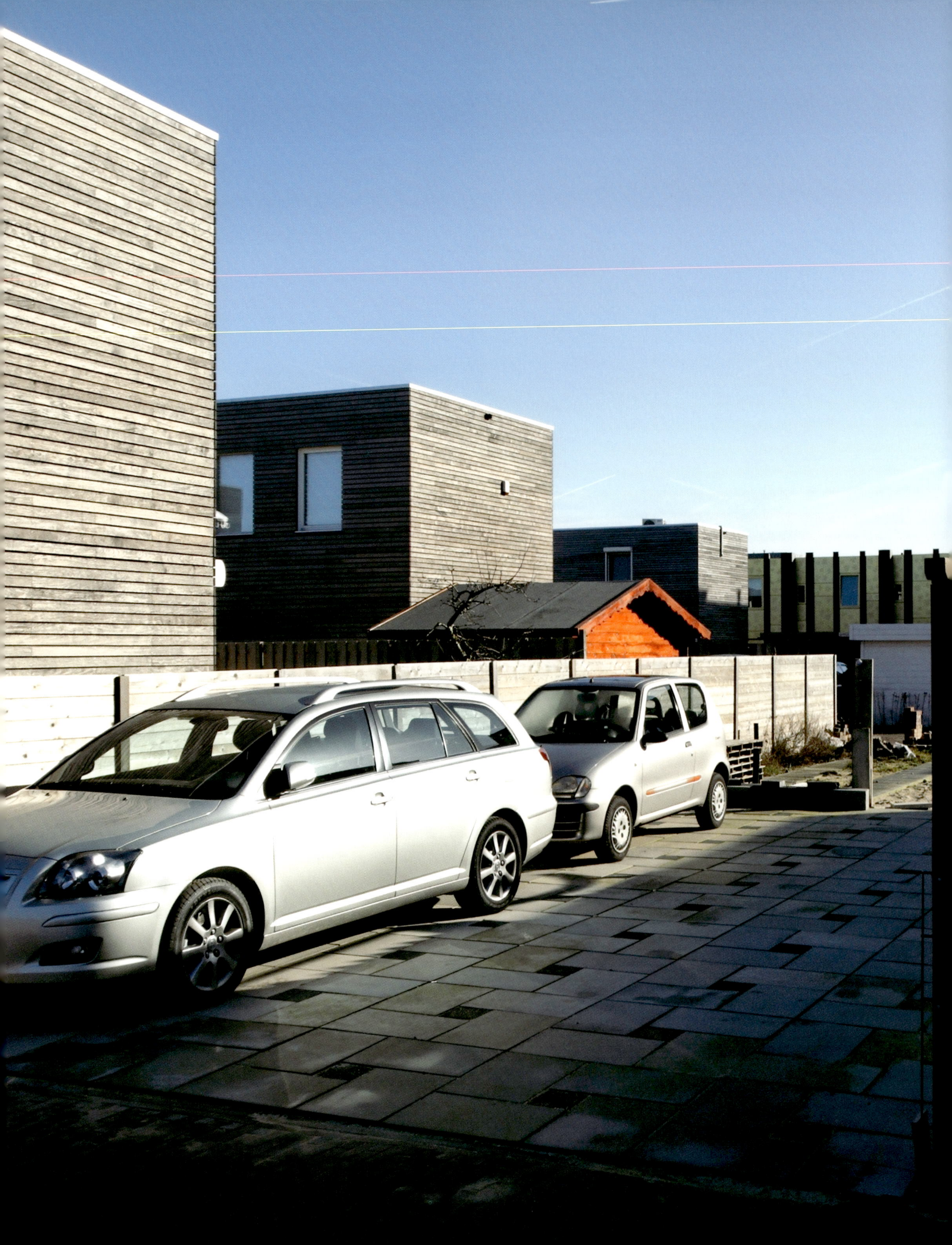

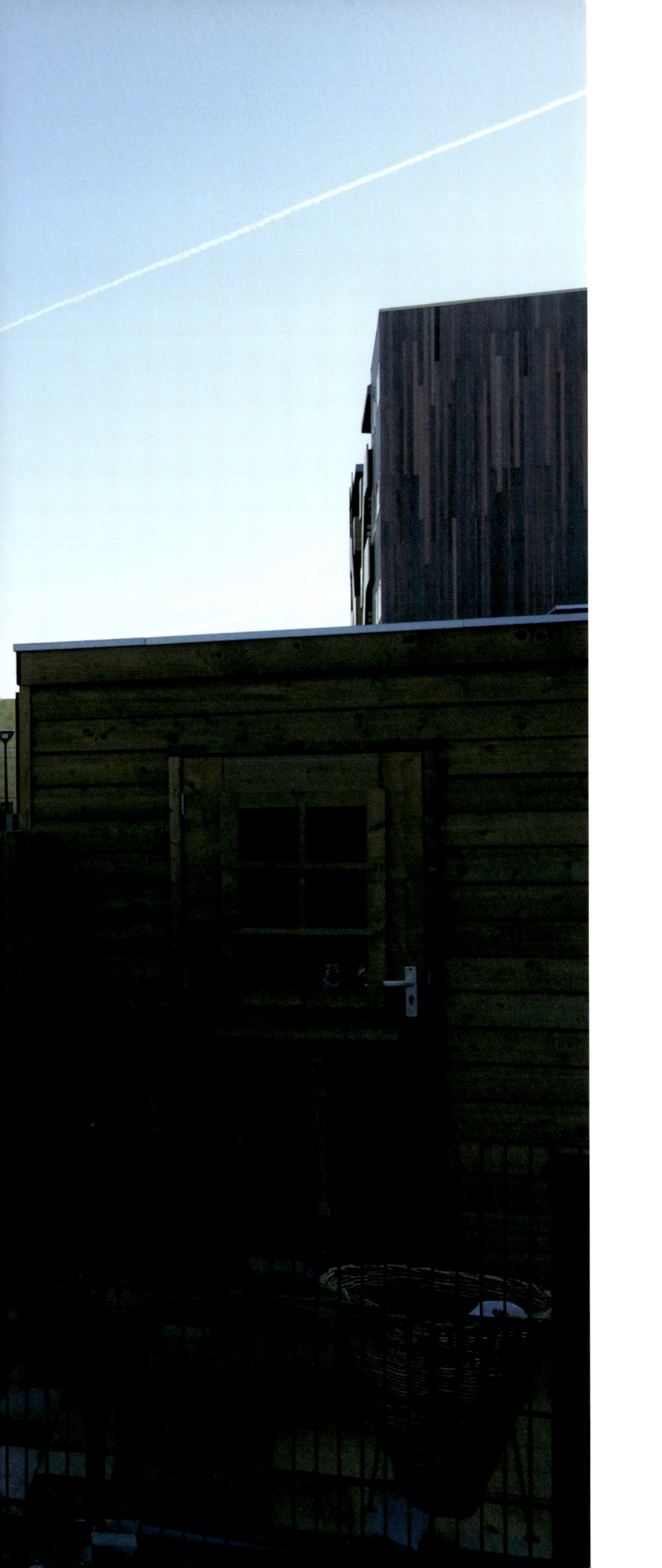

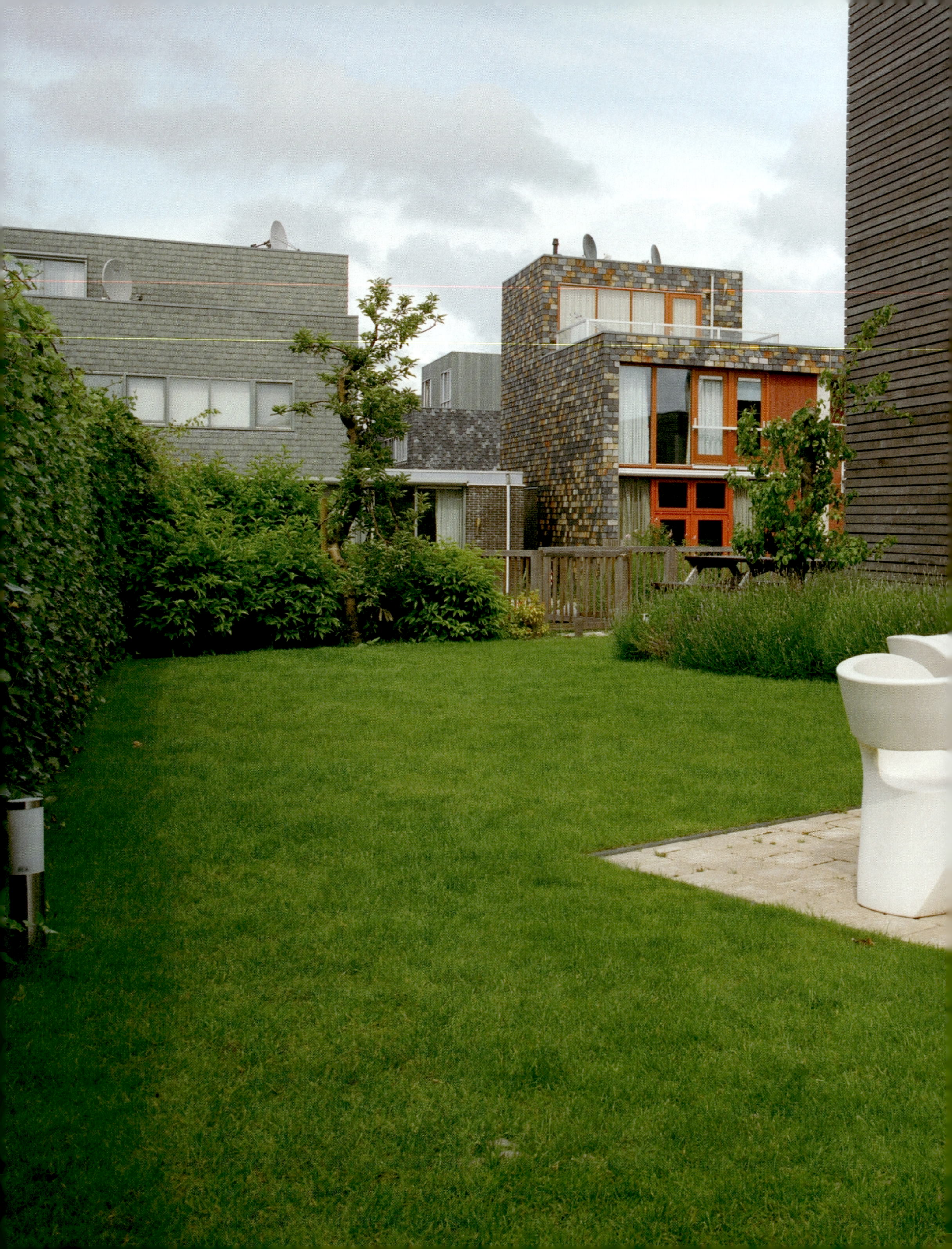

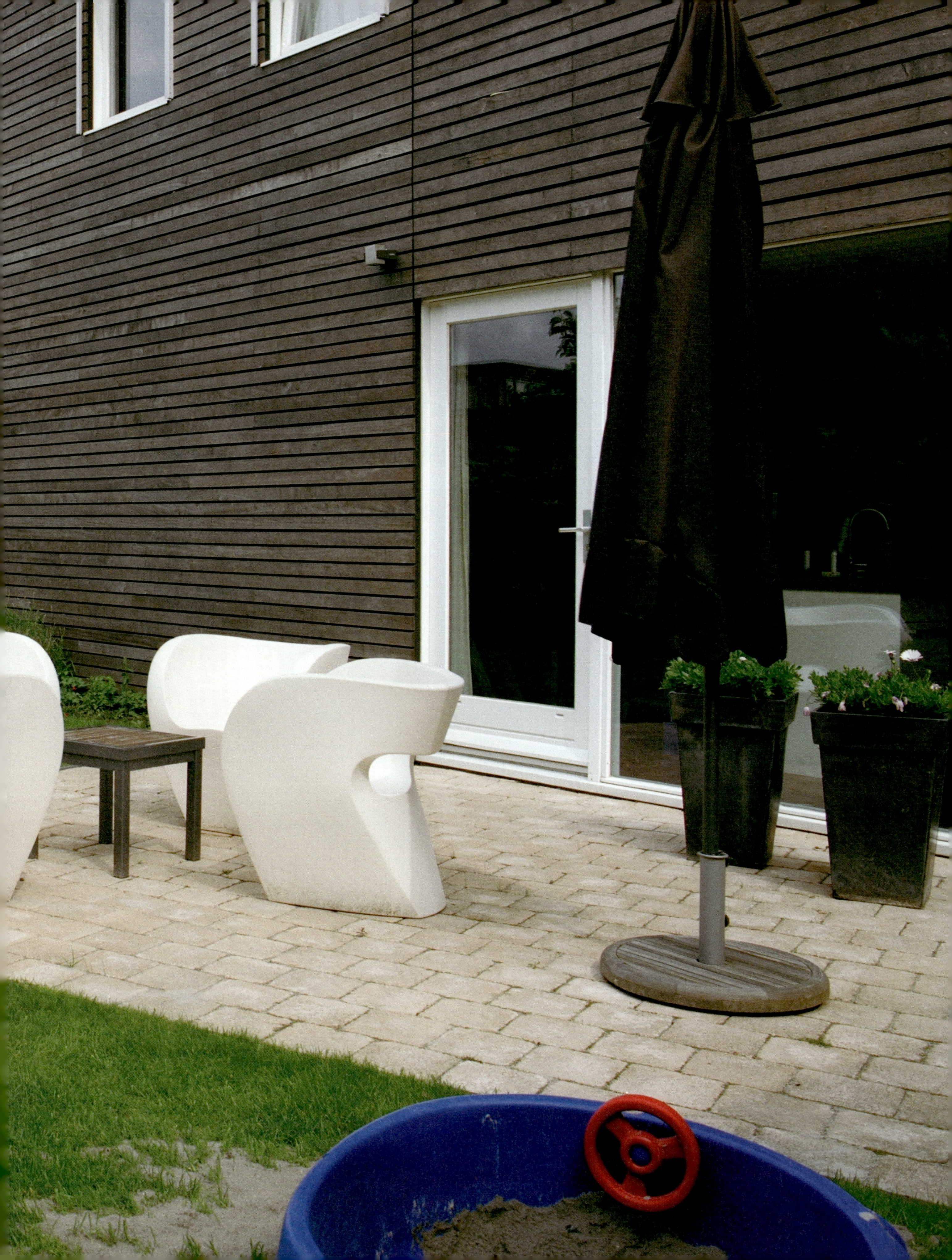

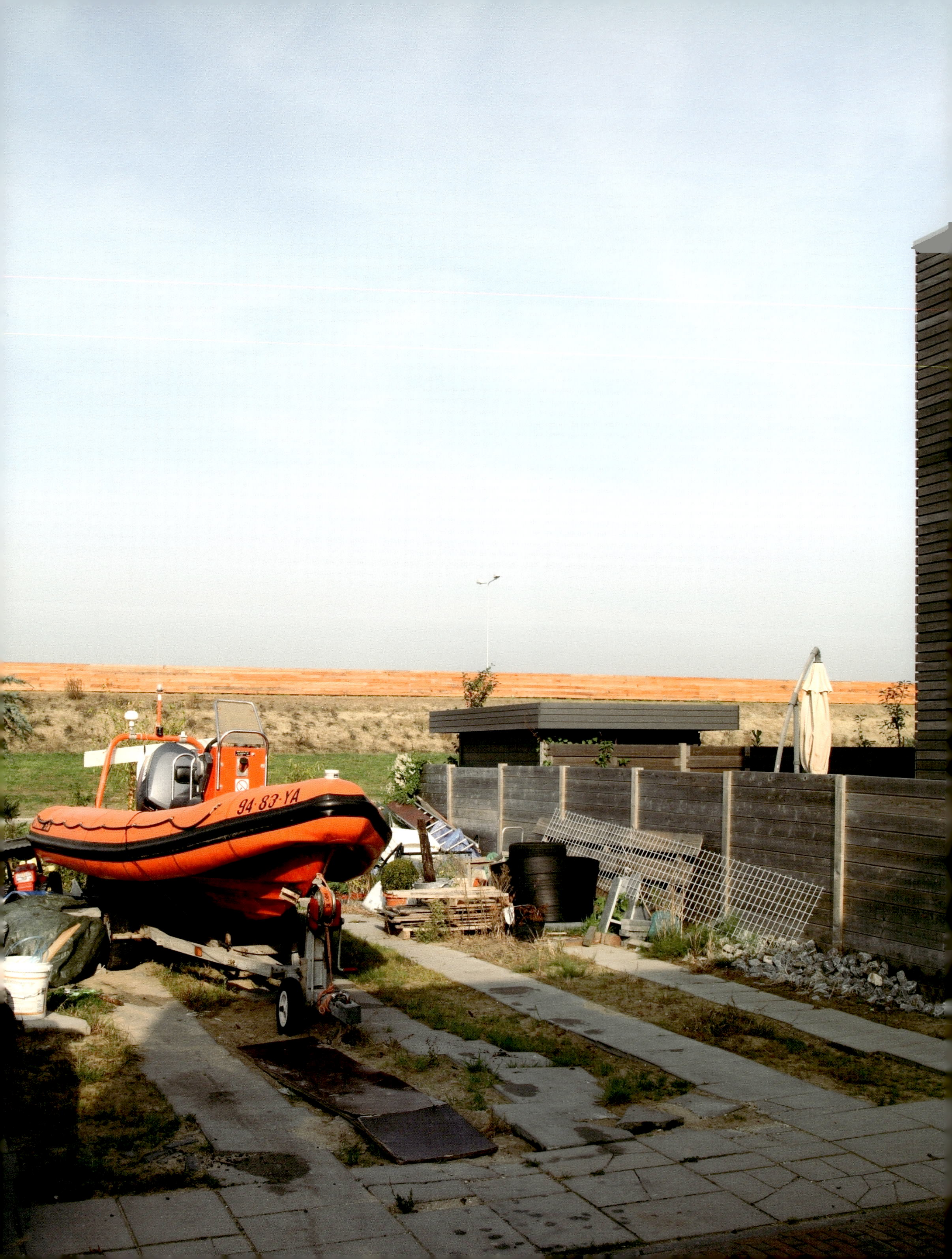

island a central *brink,* or village green. This meant that some streets would become little alleys. The less expensive houses would be freestanding; the more expensive ones would be row houses situated on the village green. 'By dividing the lots cleverly on Eiland 7, you get more ample gardens and a large green with 300 trees,' explains Mastenbroek. 'But what you don't get is that all-too-familiar alignment of the street. Nor are there any grassy public slopes along the water. Everyone wants to live by the water, that we know, so situate the gardens along the water as much as possible. That creates a beautiful environment, which tempts you to stay right at home on your day off. Kids can go out boating. The houses should look as though they're there for you. For living in green surroundings, in a lovely garden.'

The decision to use a timber frame allowed for a more rapid, less costly construction. These houses are lighter, and because of that the foundations are less expensive. This is one method for producing freestanding homes on a limited budget.

Bjarne Mastenbroek's basic idea was the following: to create a beautiful green island and well-designed public space. The consequence of this was that residents would have to keep their belongings inside: indoor storage, parking beneath the upper-level 'overhang.'

Mastenbroek: 'We said: we'll build a home that'll be your carport. Can't be any simpler. When we produced the design, we immediately drew up a zoning map for the island. The rights and wrongs have to be well indicated; otherwise residents will run away with this vulnerable plan. That zoning plan made it clear that putting a storage shed in the garden was out of the question. If people want to expand their houses, then this had to be done upward, with an extra level. And the green partitions dividing the lots had to become the property of the municipality.'

A year later, to Mastenbroek's great surprise, the municipality appeared to have come up with a very general type of zoning plan. No details were specified on the map; only the maximum height of the buildings (9 m) was indicated: two residential levels, plus one on top. 'With a zoning plan like this, you could forget about maintaining any of the intended qualities,' says Mastenbroek. 'A shrewd buyer could get away with just about anything.'

Eiland 7, De Slufter
Nancy (35) has a massage practice at
home
Ramon (36) account manager for an
Internet business

Nancy:

Having seen a striking ad in the newspaper for duplexes on Eiland 7, we were immediately taken with the size of the lot, but also with the 'village green' and the idea of living by the water. The garden faces south, and the front is on the green. That alone makes it unique. Aside from adding to the pleasure of living here, such things also add to and stabilize the value. Probably the value will just go up and up, since these houses have everything going for them.

Eleven years ago, you were really an idiot if you came here to live. I'm still saying I live in Hoofddorp, 'of all places.' But nowadays Hoofddorp is beginning to acquire a certain status in Haarlem. When people see the shopping area in the town center, they're really impressed. Even friends of ours from Haarlem have moved there.

We're interested in architecture and design. The house that Mastenbroek designed for SeARCH was our choice. He had made a beautiful model. It caused some discussion at the meeting for buyers. 'How am I supposed to wash my windows?' Prospective buyers were thinking in very practical terms; there was a room less due to a void. From the window, you could look into your neighbor's house: those kinds of arguments. Only two candidates signed up for the design by SeARCH that evening. When AM Wonen decided not to build that design, we went ahead and bought the other design anyway. Living space, location and price were the crucial factors for us.

The standard version of the house cost 399,000 euros. We were set on having an extra room, so it came to 435,000. Once you add furnishings to that, it easily adds up to 485,000 euros before you move in. We just signed a new the mortgage, ten years at a fixed interest of 4.6 percent. Now we're paying 1800 euros per month for the mortgage. From the start I've said: if we can't afford it anymore, then let's sell it. To me, it's purely an investment; eventually I'd like to end up in Bloemendaal or Haarlem. We bought our first home for 71,000 euros and sold it for 224,000. If you look around here, you sometimes think, 'Boy, they've got money.' We've run out of it right now. But then you talk with the neighbors and ask, 'Aren't you ordering those shutters?' And that's when you hear they're out of money, too. Everyone has just run out of it now, six months after moving in. We're all in the same boat.

4

It all has to do with land and money. A municipality is given the task of building 13,000 homes at three *Vinex* locations within ten years. How does that municipality put a figure on it? How do they manage to pull it off? Do the methods of budgeting determine the quality and appearance of new neighborhoods in the Netherlands? To find out more about this, I visit Hans Zuurbier, financial controller of the three *Vinex* locations supervised by the municipality of Haarlemmermeer.

I ask Zuurbier what a budget for building a new neighborhood looks like – specifically one for these three *Vinex* projects. On a notepad the controller draws a vertical line. This is dense stuff: I brace myself.

To the left of the line are the costs. 'That includes the land bought directly, as well as land that the municipality bought from project developers who acquired it themselves,' says Zuurbier. From the start of the *Vinex* projects, the municipality entered into a collaboration with the project developers. The land was purchased from the project developers for a fixed price of 18 euros per m². Occasionally, that price would be above that which the project developers had originally paid for the land, but usually it was below. To most project developers, this meant taking a loss; but in exchange for that, they were granted a construction permit, a concrete pledge to allow building. The loss taken on the land could later be calculated into the prices of their more expensive houses.

Then there were the costs of preparation, supervision and administration. Those concern the urban-development plans, the hiring of project managers, legal procedures, PR campaigns and the like. In short: the costs of administrative workings and outside personnel. 'When a budget is drawn up, a percentage of the investment cost is used to figure these costs. If you do it the way we did, then it comes to 27 percent,' explains Zuurbier.

We're not there yet, still more costs: the investment itself. The municipality now had control of all the land and started to make the areas ready for construction. That means installing sewer systems, making access roads for the building equipment. When the houses are built, the area must be made 'ready for occupancy': roads and green areas are introduced, streetlamps set up. This basically involves 'furnishing' the public space.

And then there are interest costs. These start with the purchase of the land. Despite the rise in land prices, interest costs are relatively low for the municipality. It had bought the agrarian land at a fairly low price and received income from the cultivation of that land. Interest costs mainly consist of various expenses that are financed in advance, such as the infrastructure needed to make the new neighborhoods accessible. 'Residents want to reach the highway quickly by car. The municipality pays for this, but the project developers have an interest in this, too,' Zuurbier says. 'It's an important consideration for prospective buyers.'

To the right of the line is the income.

The municipality has received subsidies from the government (75 million euros) over a period of ten years. After the land has been made ready for construction by the municipality, the developer starts building. Ultimately, the municipality sells the land directly to the buyers. For the use of the land, the municipality charges the project developer a certain amount of interest agreed upon beforehand.

The price of the land has been determined from the start as follows: the land price is a percentage of the all-inclusive price of the home, into which legal fees have been figured beforehand.

And then it gets complicated. Different percentages are used for the land price: the higher the selling price of the house (the all-inclusive price, to be exact), the higher the percentage that determines the land price. With an expensive house, a great deal more is paid for the land per m² than with an inexpensive house. 'When the land is made available to the project developer, you get an idea as to the selling prices of various houses, but anything can happen in the meantime. It's important for the municipality to establish exactly how those houses will look,' explains financial controller Zuurbier. And especially what they'll cost. 'Optional work' is not reflected in the selling price; this is charged to the buyer separately. And so, for that 'optional work,' no percentage of the profit on the land goes to the municipality. That leads to discussions between the project developer and the municipality.

Zuurbier: 'If bathrooms, extra levels, storage areas and kitchens are offered as 'optional work,' then we could end up with a deficit.' That's why the municipality doesn't get its money for the land until the home buyer arrives at the notary's office, since that's when the ultimate selling price becomes clear.

Zuurbier acknowledges the existence of a natural tension between municipalities and project developers. 'To put it in black-and-white terms, the municipalities want quality, nice homes in nice neighborhoods, and project developers want profit.'

But not only have the project developers earned money on the realization of *Vinex* projects. In retrospect, the municipality of Haarlemmermeer has done rather well financially. It has set up the three *Vinex* locations, with 13,000 homes, for about 600 million euros and the large-scale infrastructure for 200 million euros. On the first rough calculation of the budget, the 'initial land development,' the municipality was in danger of lacking funds; but at the end of the line, money is left over. With this project, the municipality has made roughly 3,000 euros on each home.

Building in an open area is relatively inexpensive. It partly explains the appeal that open areas near cities have to project developers. And it can be a source of income for the municipality. The town council of Haarlemmermeer decided, for instance, to reserve part of the land proceeds for a large sports complex which will cost 45 million euros.

When we arrive at the notary's office in Hoofddorp on July 22, 2004, we see in the settlement that, for 118,319 euros (including sales tax), we've purchased a piece of land measuring 252 m². That's about 469 euros per m². The distribution of private and public property is equal on Eiland 7: for every m² of private property, there is a m² of public space. Consequently, the buyers are purchasing not only their own land for that amount of money, but also – collectively – land needed for the community.

The amount can be broken down as follows: 19 percent, 75 euros, has gone back to the national government in the form of sales tax. The land on this island was purchased by the municipality itself, not from the project developer. Eiland 7 was purchased from the Könst brothers by the municipality for a higher-than-average price: at 29 euros per m², times two (for 'collective' land) equals 58 euros. The investments (making the area ready for construction and for occupancy) are represented in 100 euros. Contribution to the infrastructure costs come to 60 euros. For preparation, supervision and administration, 35 euros; and for other costs (extra investments in schools) 3 euros. Interest costs amount to 50 euros; the municipality's 'profit' is 12 euros; and the last item, the adjustment for inexpensive and social housing, is 76 euros.

At *Vinex* locations, 30 percent of the housing is 'low income' or inexpensive. The item 'adjustment' is intended as a financial contribution toward deficits in this category. The profit from two expensive homes is needed to cover the deficit with low-income or inexpensive housing.

    Not only does the *Vinex* standard (35 homes per hectare) determine the general appearance of *Vinex* neighborhoods. Could there be a relationship between the budgeting methods and the ultimate look of a new neighborhood? Hans Zuurbier: 'Every municipality in the Netherlands budgets in the same way, and that leads to the risk of uniformity in urban-planning solutions. The challenge for a municipality is to rise above that. There has to be courage to make extra investments in public space. The consumer looks at the price of one home and compares it to the price of a comparable home at different location. That price needs to be competitive.' The financial leeway to deviate from this is thereby limited. It's another reason why *Vinex* neighborhoods look so much alike, believes Zuurbier.

Despite this lack of latitude, the project developer, the municipality and the architect undertake an experiment on Eiland 7 in the autumn of 1999: there has to be a different way to do things.

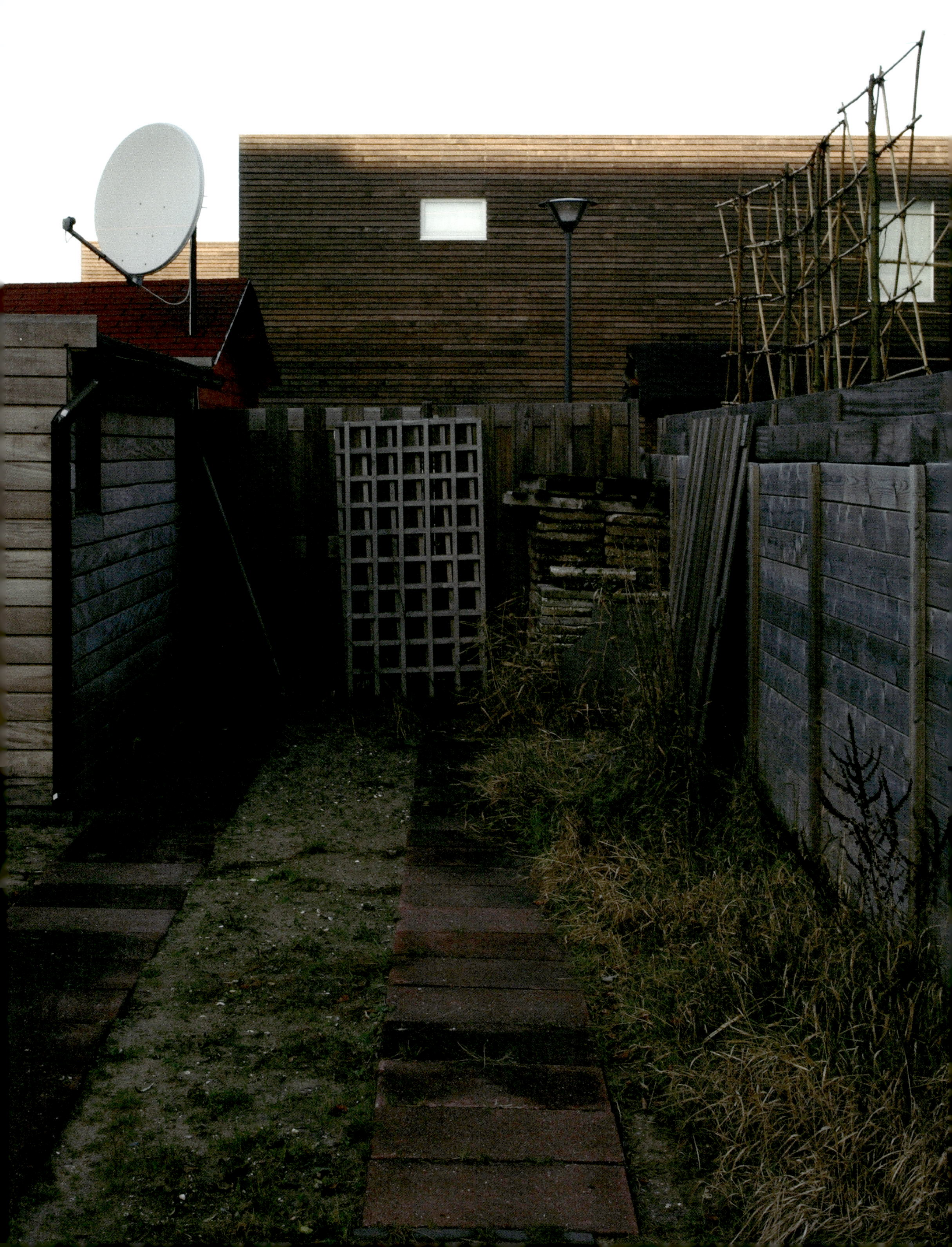

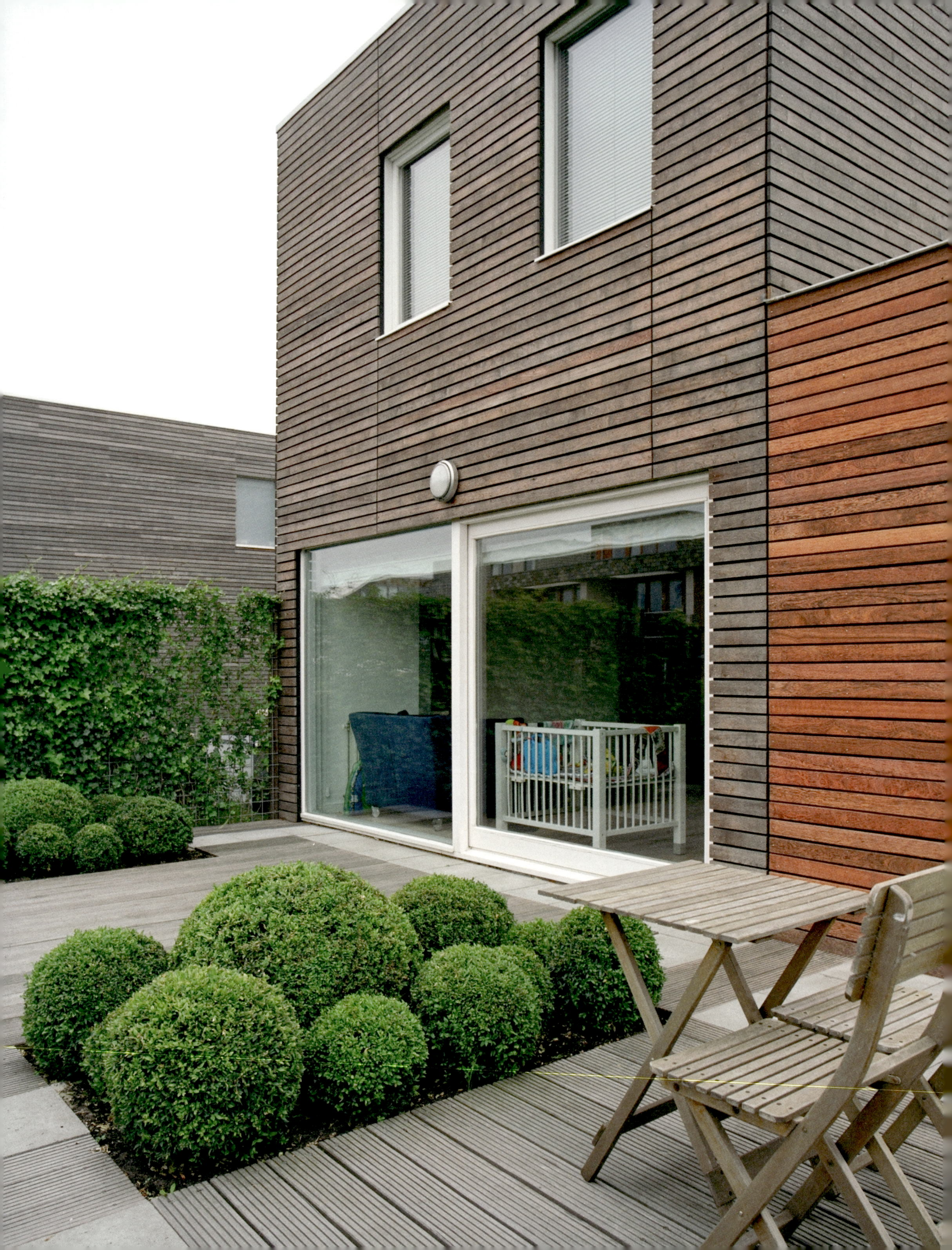

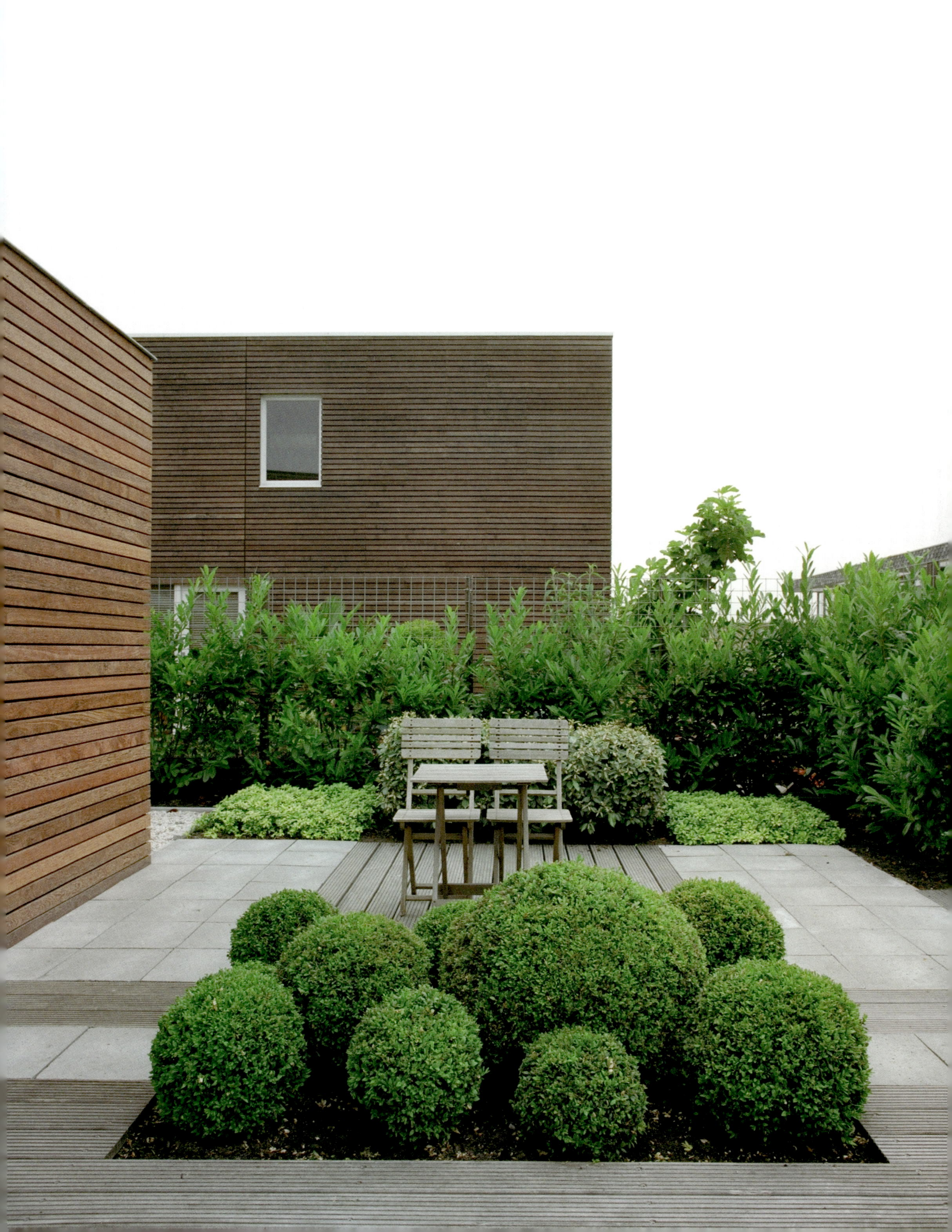

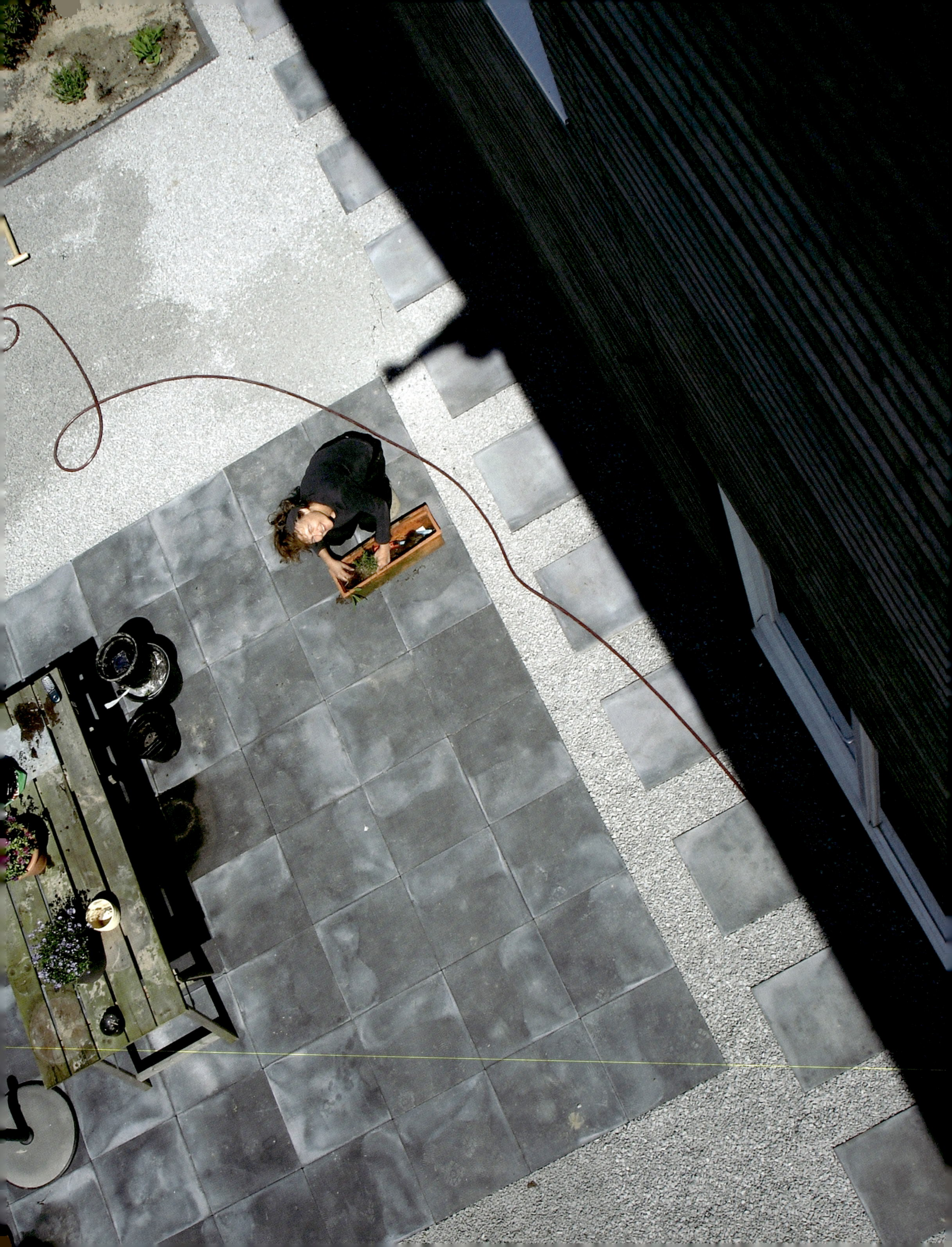

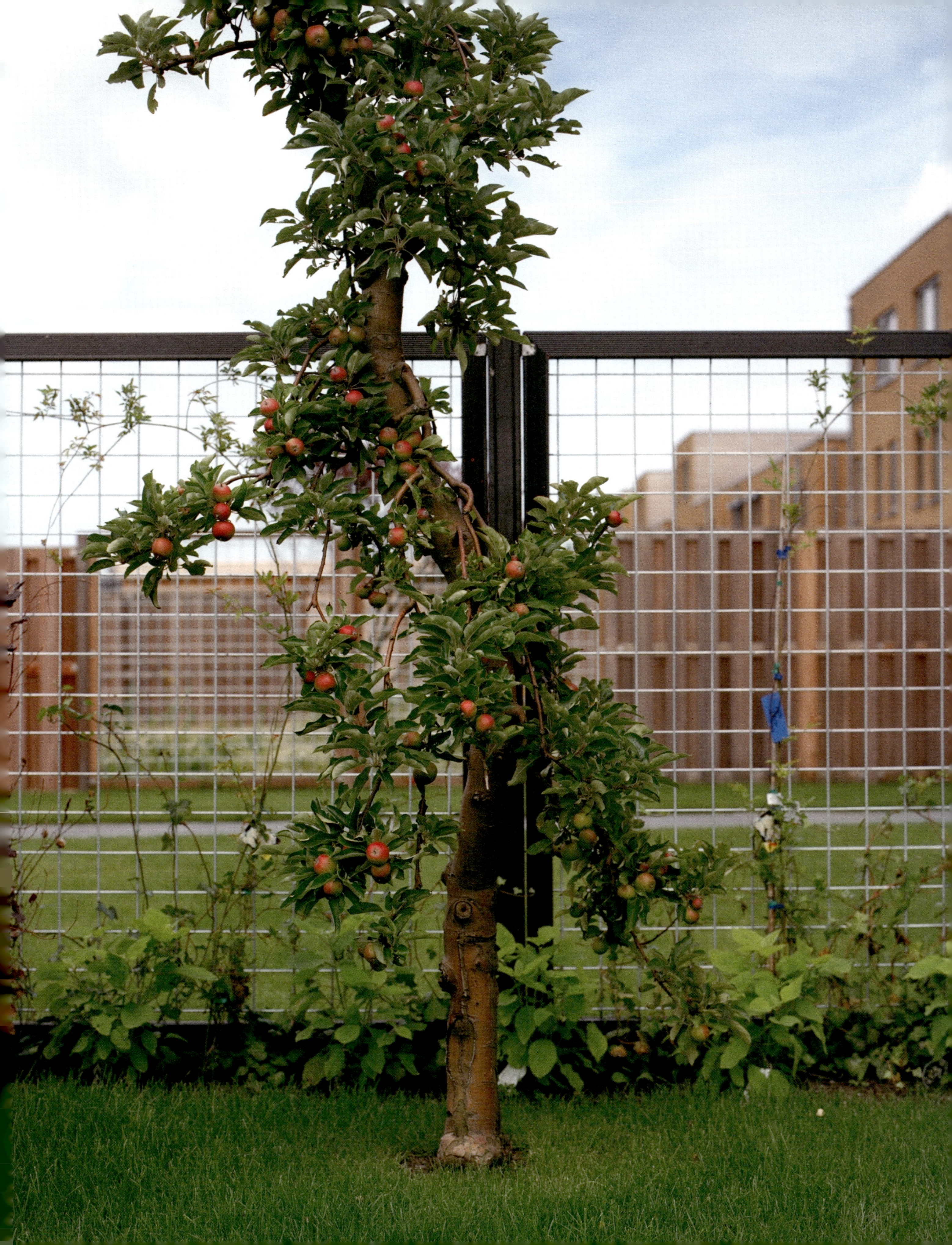

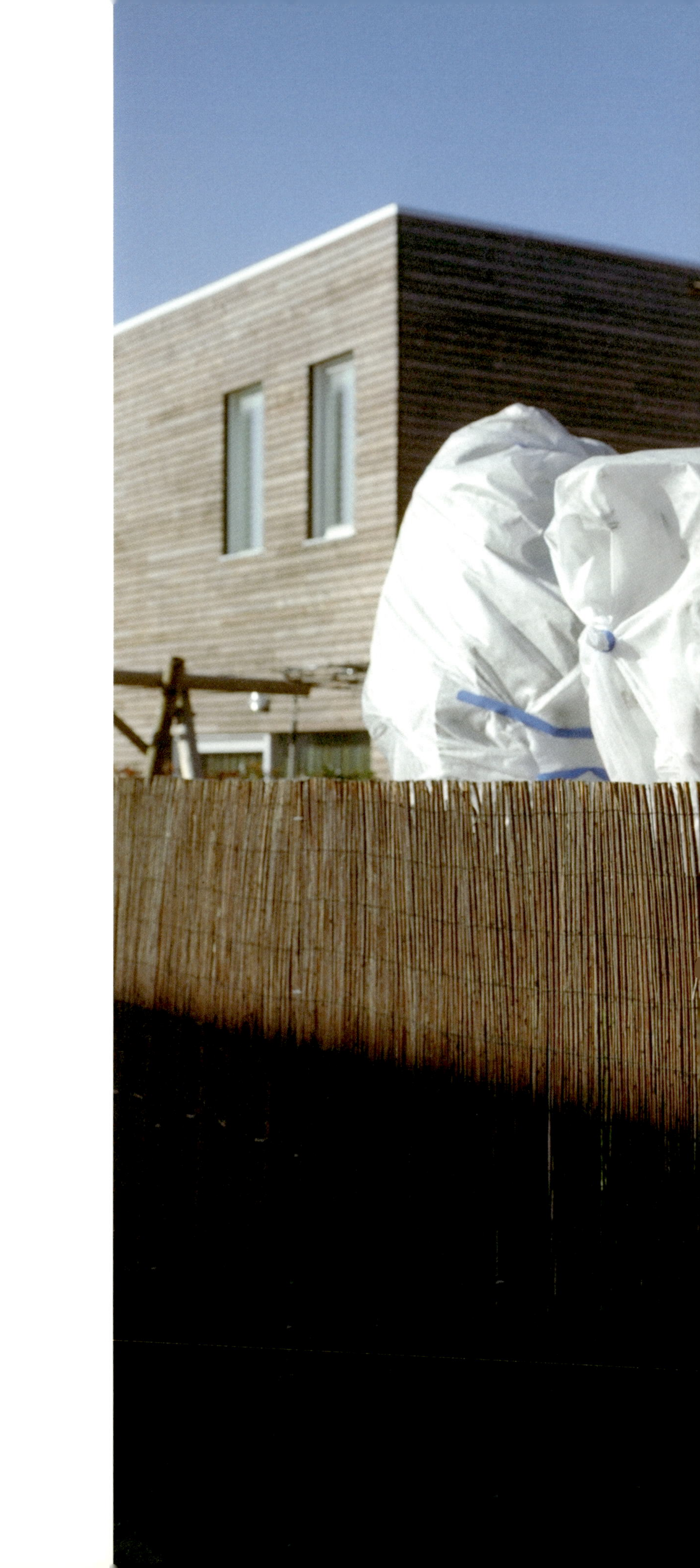

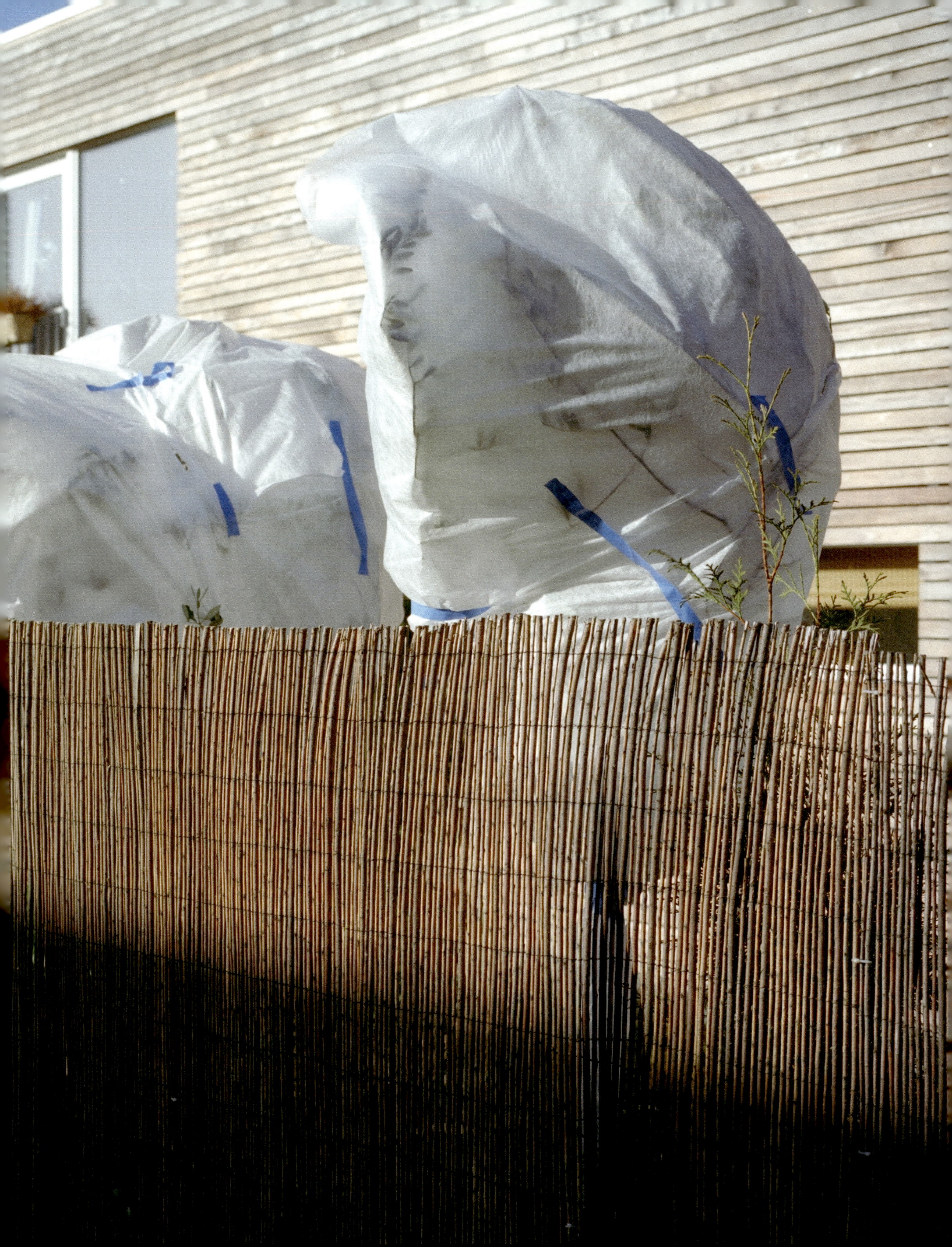

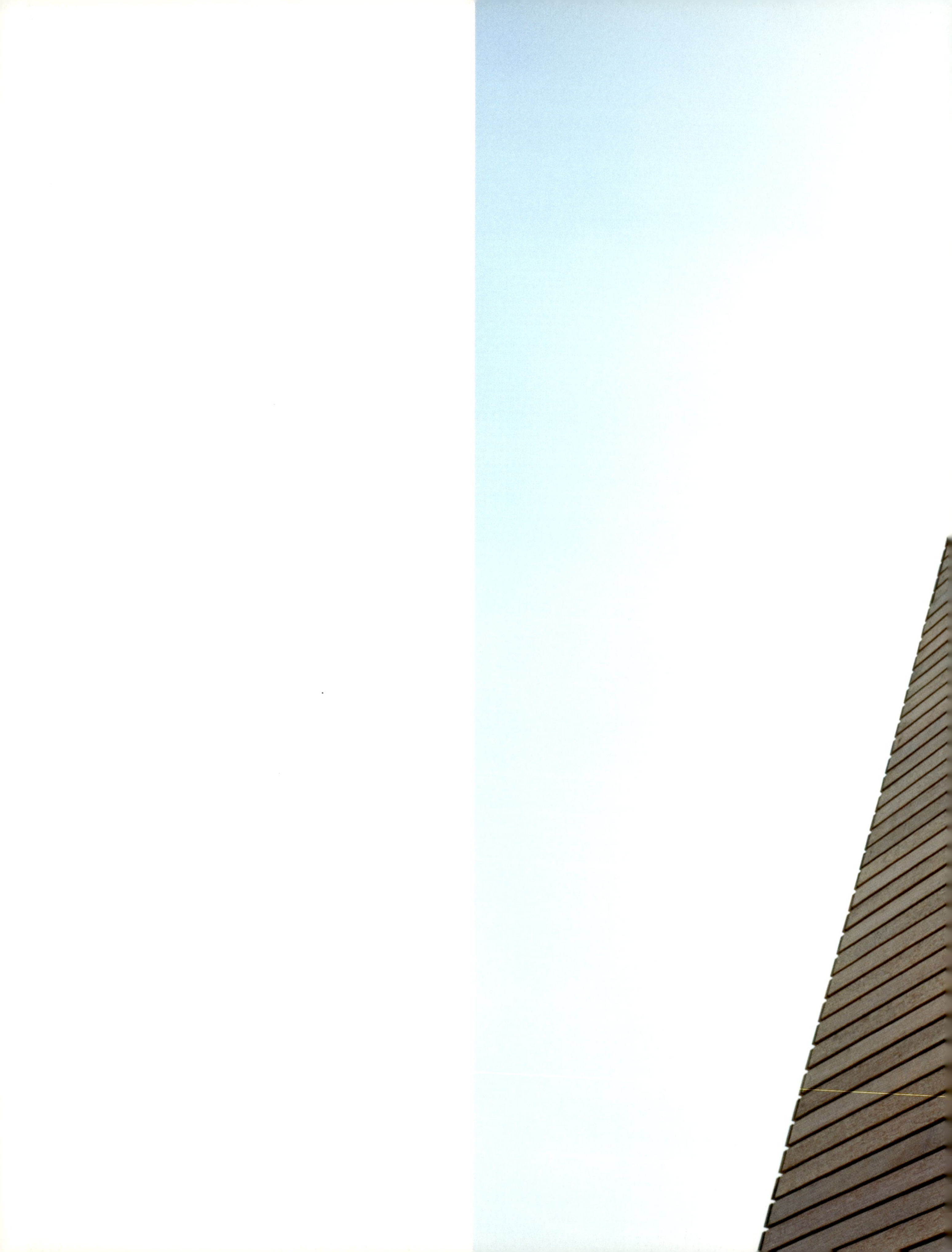

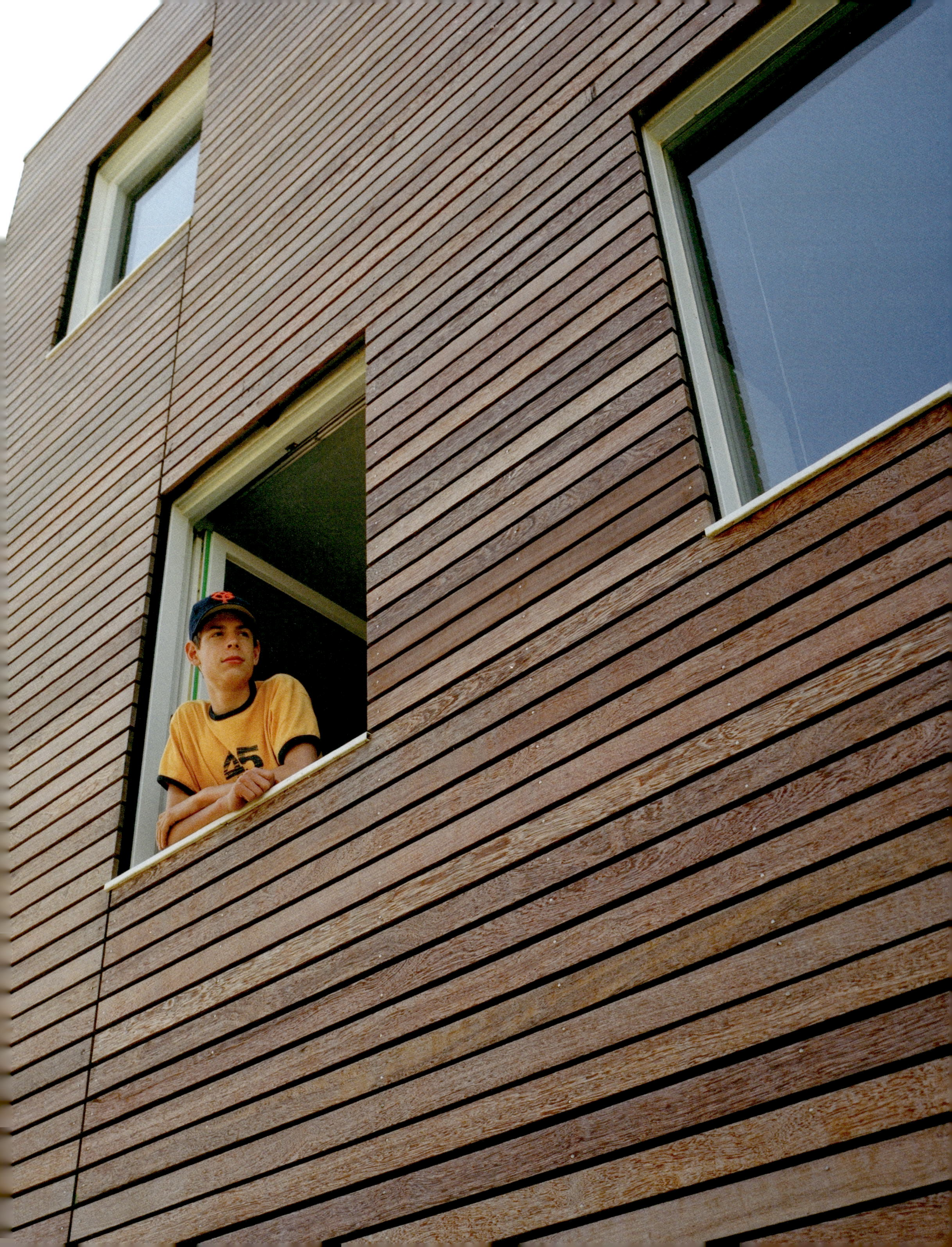

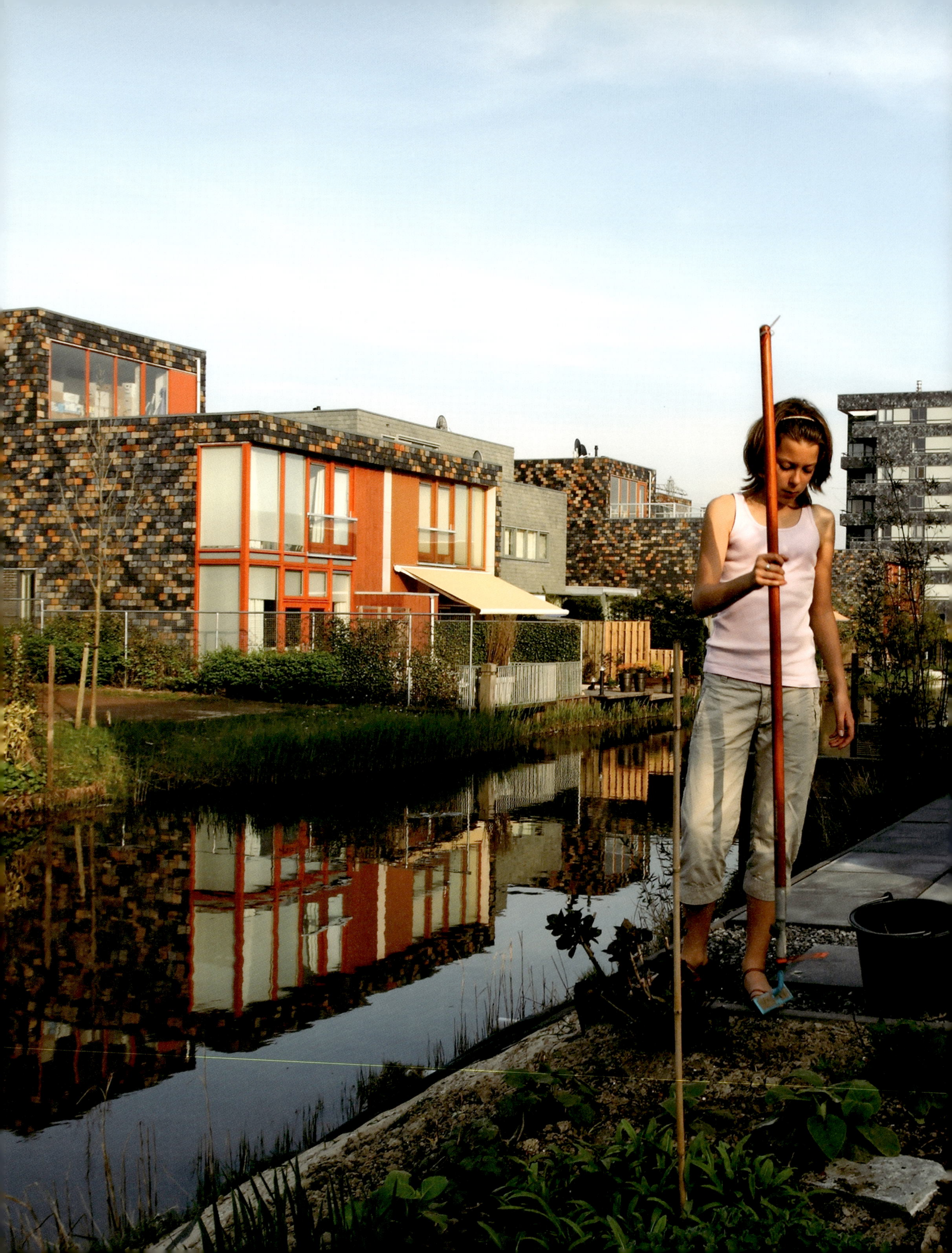

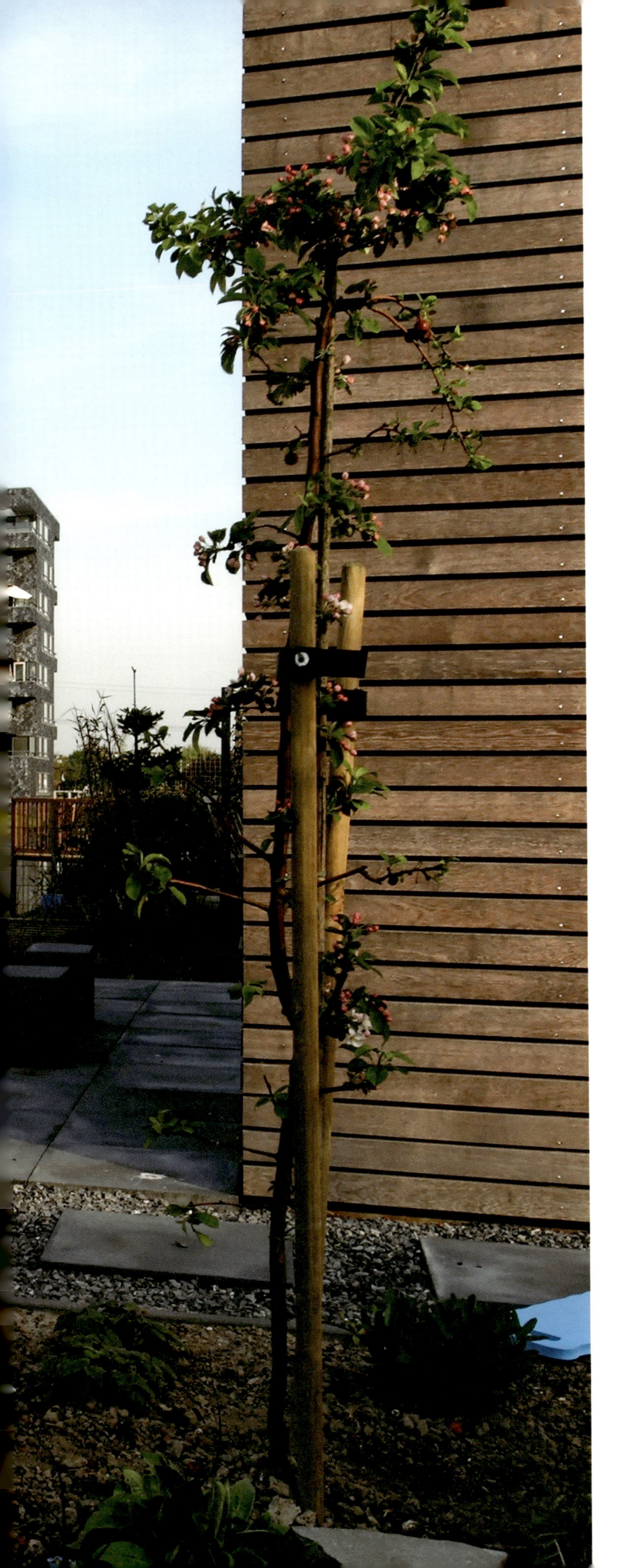

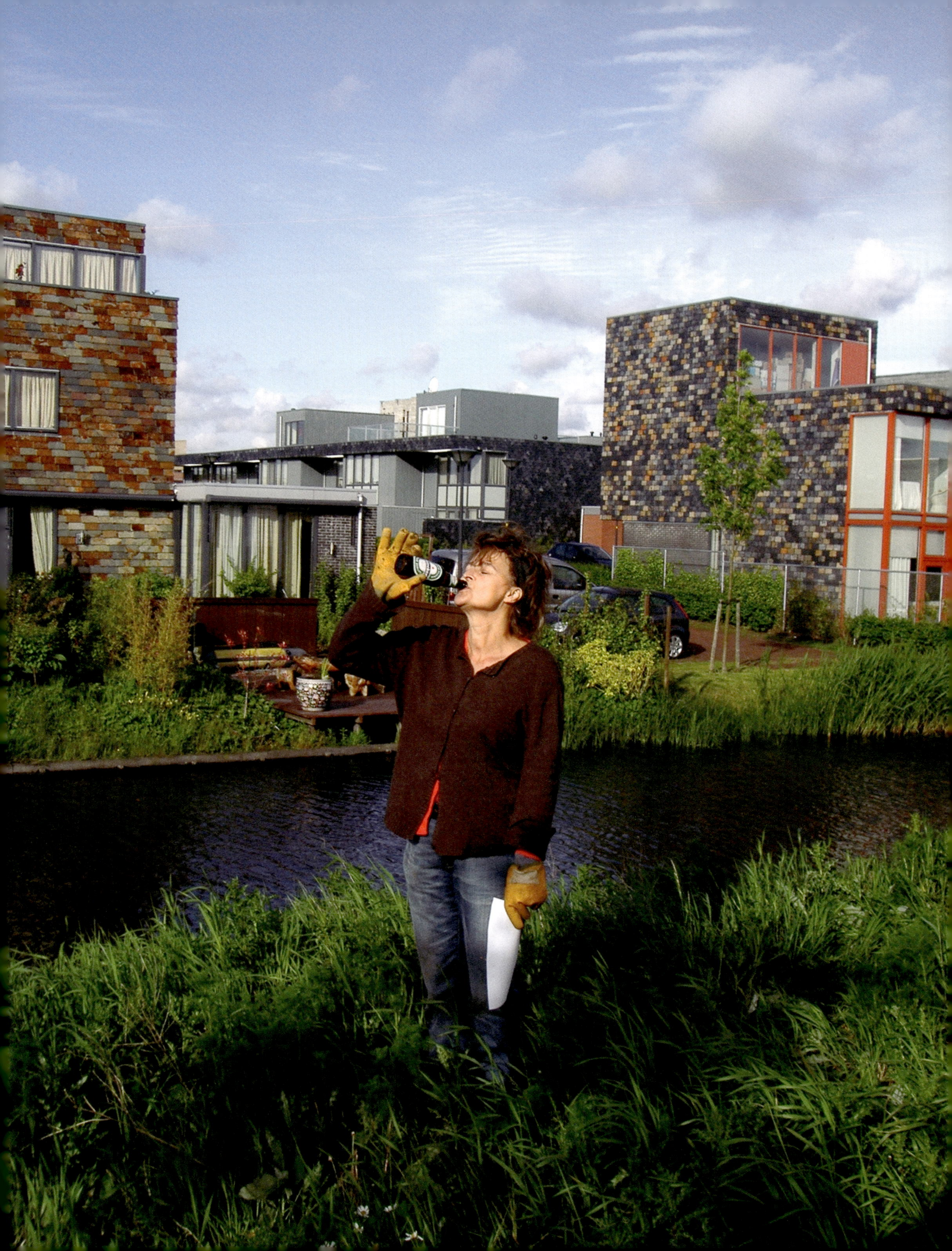

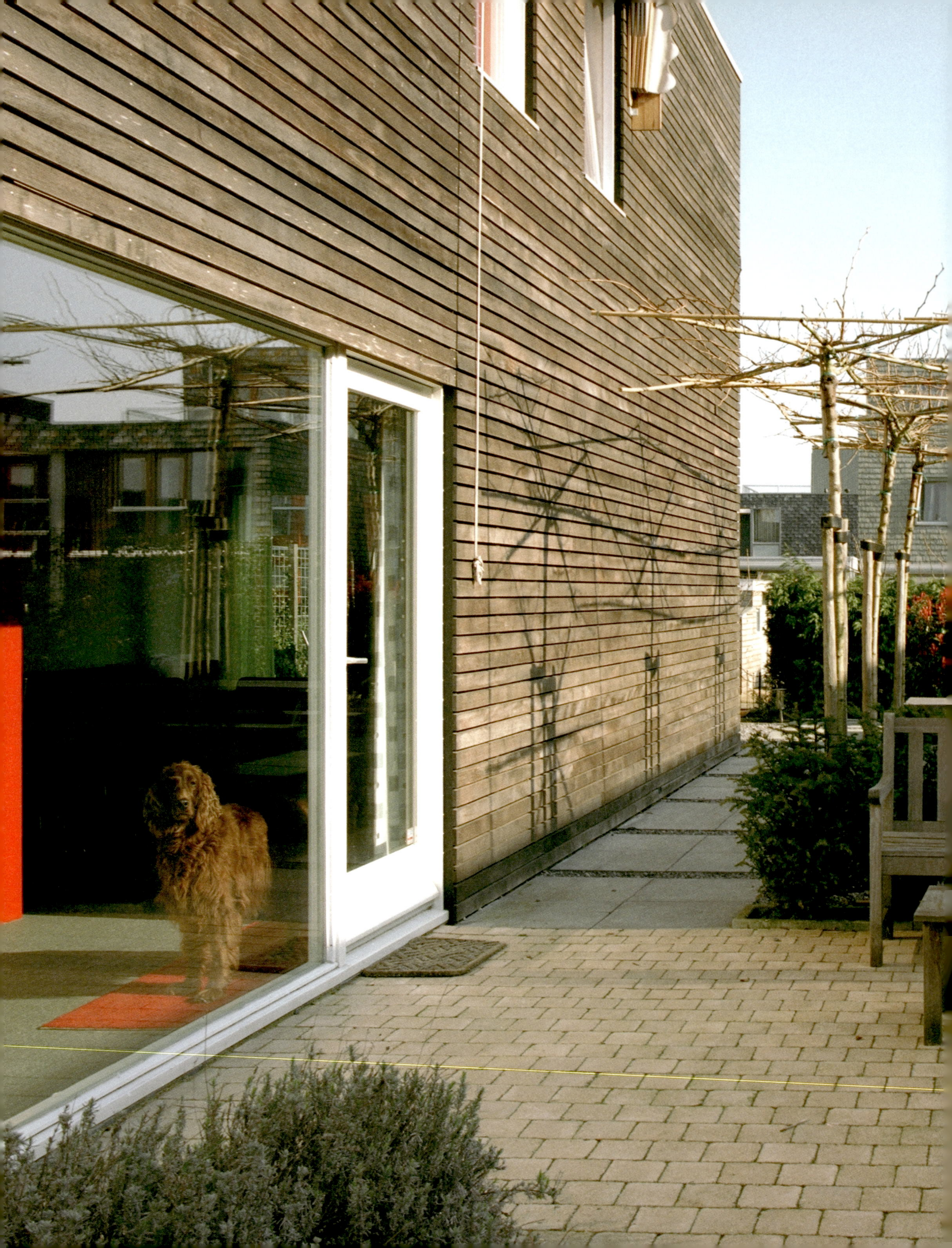

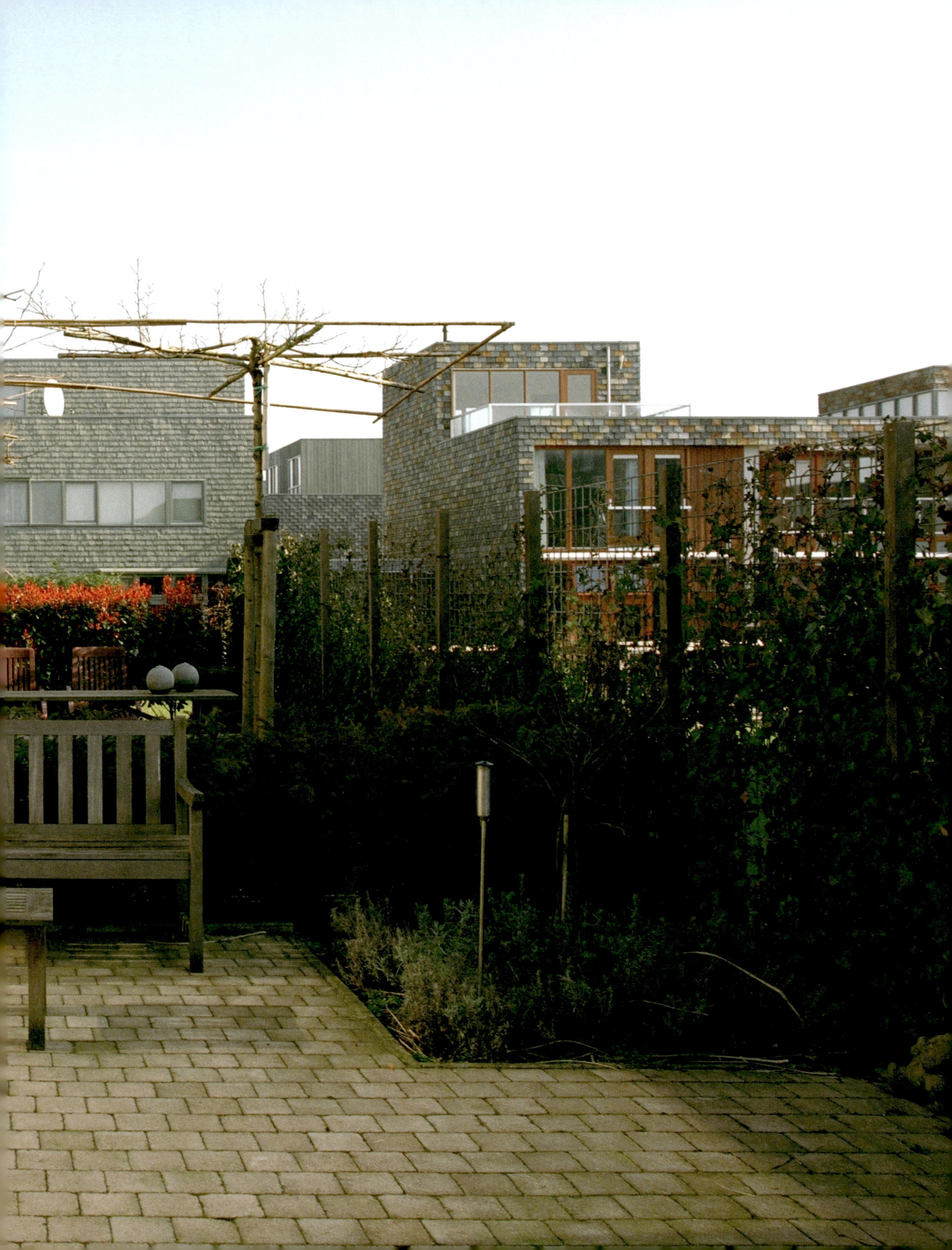

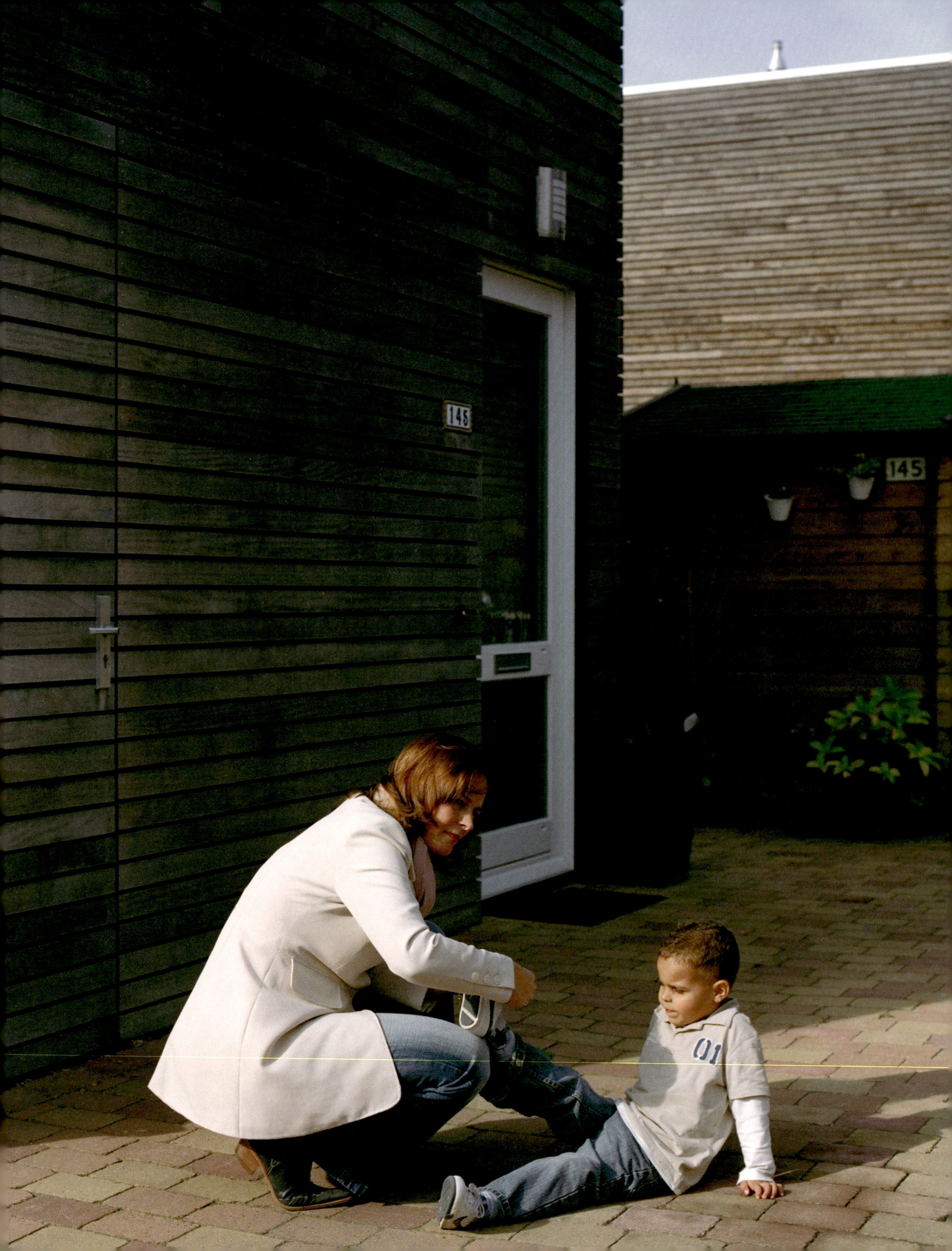

Eiland 7, De Muy
Cynthia (34) mortgage advisor
Redouan (34) supervisor
Yassine (4)
Norah (2)

Cynthia:

It all looked fine on paper. Small, but just right for the two of us. As a buyer, you're totally at a loss. Plans are subject to change. Take the parking, for instance, behind the houses on the green – and next to our house. That was thought up by the project developer only much later, after we had already bought the place. People are poorly informed: too little and too late. After your signature goes on the papers, you just have to accept whatever they do.

Three weeks after we had signed, in early 2003, I got pregnant with Yassine. We did want to sell the house again, since it was going to be too small when the baby came. Then, after Yassine, Norah was born. We went to look at a larger newly built home. And we tried to get on a list for other projects, but that didn't work out. For the time being, no other building is being done in Hoofddorp.

With the sale of the house, they said that an extra level was allowed, but that the foundations had to be adapted for this. When construction was finished, some residents added an extra level. I don't think that all of them adapted the foundations, but we do want to have it done. It costs 10,000 euros, but I certainly wouldn't sleep at night if that hadn't been done. With an existing home, you pay 50,000 to 60,000 euros for an extra room. Here, for that same amount of money, you can build an entire upper level big enough for three extra rooms.

Seeing how the homes with an extra level are selling, it appears to be a good investment. So we've gone to the municipality and applied for a building permit.

We've got the money, and we've found a builder. But still no building permit. A halt has been put on all the requests, due to the new zoning plan that's in the making. All of the extra levels and extensions built by residents up to now were subject to the old zoning plan. And that allowed for just about anything. If the zoning plan becomes more strict and we don't get the permit, then we'll have to move. But we'd rather not, since we like living here.

5

'Are you really going to build this?' Albert Groothuizen could scarcely believe his eyes when colleagues showed him the plans for Eiland 7 in early 2001. He had just started as manager for the project developer AM Wonen. 'It was a time when the market could handle anything. So if we decided to go nuts, for instance, it would be okay,' says Groothuizen looking back. This was the golden age of project development, one that, in the end, lasted only a few years. Ambition and pretensions flourished. The housing market was very tight. Money poured into it. Project developers, architects and municipalities wanted to set a new course, break away from the row house. But after September 2001 all of that changed quickly.

'Here houses are sold from a drawing,' says municipal architect Fred Kaaij. 'The Haarlemmermeer area is practically risk-free.' Bjarne Mastenbroek's plan – very narrow lots, narrow houses and very deep yards – was unusual. Inexpensive homes were to be freestanding. Expensive ones were relatively wide, but not freestanding. 'On the south side of the green, you paid 400,000 euros and still lived in a row. It went against the laws of project development.' The selling price lay somewhere between 2,000 and 2,200 euros per m² of living area. Around the turn of the century, that was common for new housing.

No marketing research was done. 'Why would you? The first information day already drew vast numbers of people interested in Floriande,' Groothuizen recalls.

But on Eiland 7, construction could not yet begin. Könst seed potatoes still occupied the land. This unusual plan would also involve a longer design phase. The design of the first seven islands had started at the same time, but the technical execution and financial aspects of the Eiland 7 plan brought delay.

Meanwhile, the market gradually began to change. In August 2001, a sales event was held for the homes on islands 1 through 7. That had no great success. In the aftermath of that fateful day, 11 September, things only became worse. By late 2001 a 'buyers' strike' had begun, and in early 2002 recession hit the Netherlands. Buyers having more than 300,000 euros to spend were suddenly scarce. And if there were any buyers who had that sort of money and dared to take the plunge, then they evidently had no desire to live in a row house. The homes on the south side of the green weren't selling. Wooden homes, at least the small and inexpensive types, were still doing reasonably well.

In May 2002 the project developer decided to halt the sale of homes on the south side of the green. What remained was the entire north side of the plan, consisting of the residential park with its expensive and inexpensive homes as well as the north side of the brink with its less expensive homes. 'We detached the residential park, with the timber frame constructions, from the homes on the north side of the green,' says Albert Groothuizen. Eiland 7 would now be put on the market in segments. 'And that's precisely when we reached the 70 percent threshold of sold homes.' To the project developer, that 70 percent threshold means having to build. 'We actually wanted to be rid of it, but now we had to go ahead with the construction,' Groothuizen remarks. 'We had indeed sold 70 percent of the residential park, but only the inexpensive homes, on which we took a substantial loss. Not one of the more expensive timber-frame homes, which were to compensate for that loss, had been sold yet.'

There were plenty of reasons for the project developer to slow down production, but the municipality was on his back, having become obligated to produce certain quantities of housing for the national government. The project developer had agreed to produce housing within a certain period of time. And so the construction of Eiland 7 had to begin.

That led to losses for AM Wonen. Sales had never been at such a low point, and now Eiland 7 had to be built. This gave rise to an unusual situation: a loss-making part of the project was already sold and was being built. As far as the other part of the island was concerned, the project developer decided to redevelop, to revise the designs. That was to make up for the losses incurred.

The municipality put pressure on the process of designing, selling and building. 'We agreed on a certain planning from the start, and the financial management is all geared to this. We aim for quality but do want our money,' says Hans Zuurbier, responsible for the municipal budget. 'I assume that I'll get that money at a certain point. The interest continues as compensation, but I also want to receive the actual amount. If that moment keeps on being delayed, I can't go along with that. I don't want the project developer to start thinking, at the expense of the municipality and its inhabitants, about how to go on with a project.'

'In April 2002 we should have started building the homes on the green,' says Albert Groothuizen of AM Wonen. 'Once ground is broken, the buyer's first payment comes in. But because of the redevelopment, we started later. The municipality wanted us, despite low sales and the redevelopment, to pay for the land according to the agreement. We had to generate expenses in order to comply with that agreement, while we had no income.'

The redevelopment of Eiland 7 marks a turning point, according to Bjarne Mastenbroek. Tastes were becoming more conservative in the Netherlands, and the demand for traditional homes rose.

If the market hadn't collapsed, Mastenbroek's total concept would have been carried in full and sold; all parties involved in the project agree on that. But AM Wonen had now become a no-nonsense organization. By 1 April 2003, the housing market had hit rock bottom: a m² of living area was being sold for 1,900 euros.

Mastenbroek's original plan for the homes to the north of the green – ones having eave-like 'overhangs' of 5 m – would have brought the developer, with a selling price of 210,000 euros, a loss of 5,000 euros per home. But that of course was 'a terribly expensive design' with a 'less-than-efficient housing program' in Groothuizen's view. 'A very large two-room dwelling for 210,000 euros.' The design was then adjusted according to the so-called principle of 'Luxury Home Value.' 'That means,' explains architect Mastenbroek, 'that you design a façade for a standardized layout. This has already been established by the accountants years ago and can't be beat as far as efficiency goes.' The 'overhang,' an extension of the second floor, under which cars could be parked, was made smaller. The housing layout was made more efficient. 'The meter box was put right behind the front door, since that reduces the amount of wiring. And from the meter box, the wiring should be as short as possible: so the kitchen, and the bathroom upstairs, need to be located as close to the meter box as possible,' says Groothuizen, who wanted to sell practical and affordable homes. At that he did succeed. 'Mastenbroek made the basic home so efficient that it even became possible to get four bedrooms on one floor and, within the scope of the project, he gave the homes their own look.'

With this revised design AM Wonen was able to reduce the selling price as far as 199,000 euros. It was no longer taking a loss on those homes. 'In fact,' remarks Groothuizen, 'we were even able to compensate for all of the double sales costs – double expenses from previous designs, deals with the municipality on temporary infrastructure and land excavation, as well as internal expenses – with that selling price. Because the building costs, including sales tax, were reduced from 120,000 to 80,000 euros per home.'

'But the quality of the plan went up in smoke,' laments architect Mastenbroek, who nonetheless took part in this redevelopment.

In February 2004, the redeveloped houses on the north side of the green are put up for sale. AM Wonen ultimately sets the prices for the smaller homes at 206,000 euros and for the larger ones at 250,000. 'We didn't dare go higher,' says Eric van Oversteeg now. When Van Oversteeg goes to his office at six in the morning to begin preparations for the sale, the prospective buyers are lying at the door in sleeping bags. That's what usually happens when a *Vinex* neighborhood goes up for sale. By then Van Oversteeg realizes, of course, that he has probably set the price a bit too low.

Meanwhile, AM Wonen does everything it can to sell the expensive timber-frame homes. The aftermath of 9/11 was remaining evident in the market. These homes would require extra effort on the part of the sales department. And so a model home was built – this being very exceptional for a *Vinex* neighborhood – on a lot that remained bare for the rest.

Eric van Oversteeg was part of AM Wonen's sales team. 'It was a tough product to sell. The island was initially portrayed as a "vacation island" with freestanding wooden houses and lots of greenery. But people didn't see them as freestanding houses, since it wasn't possible to walk around each

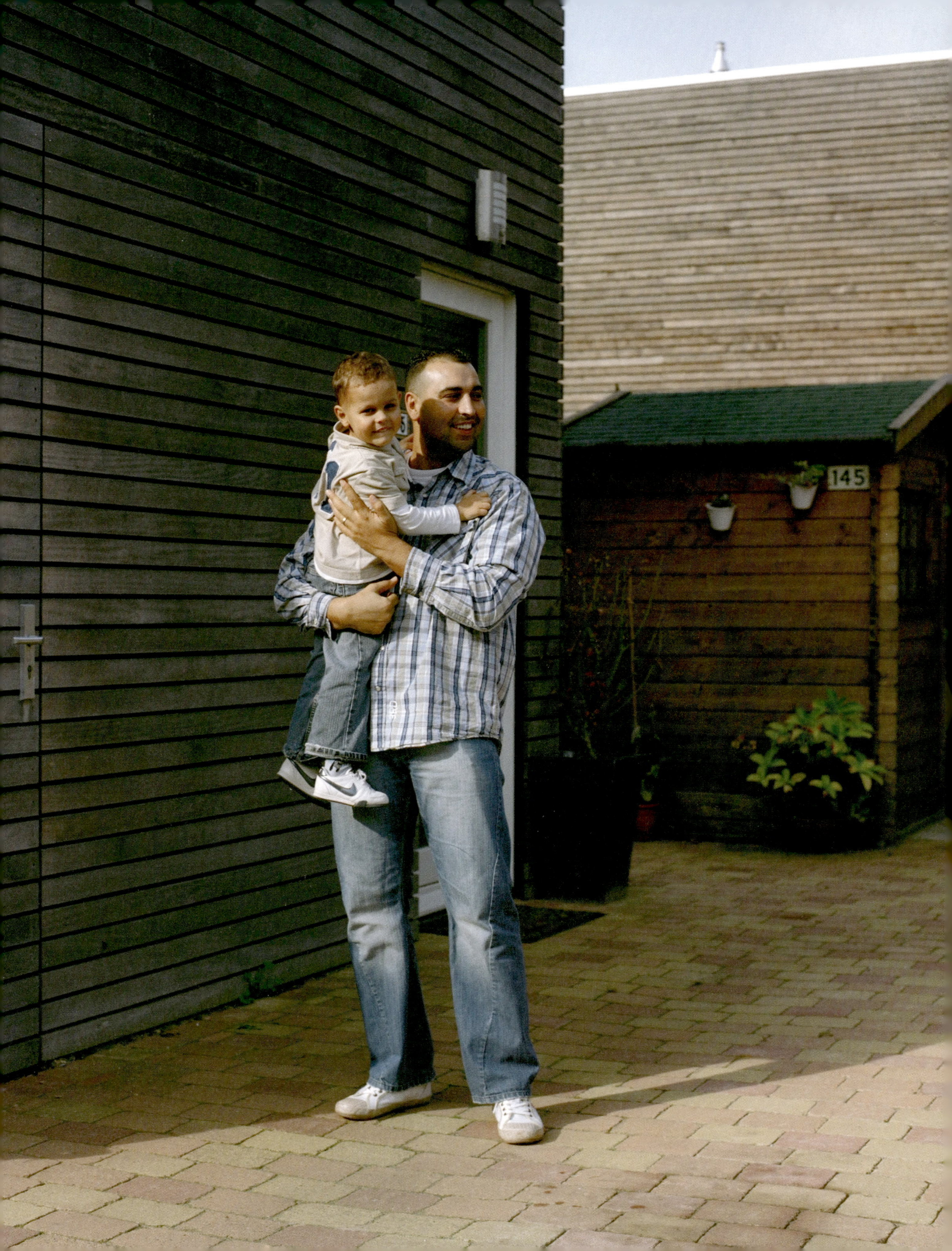

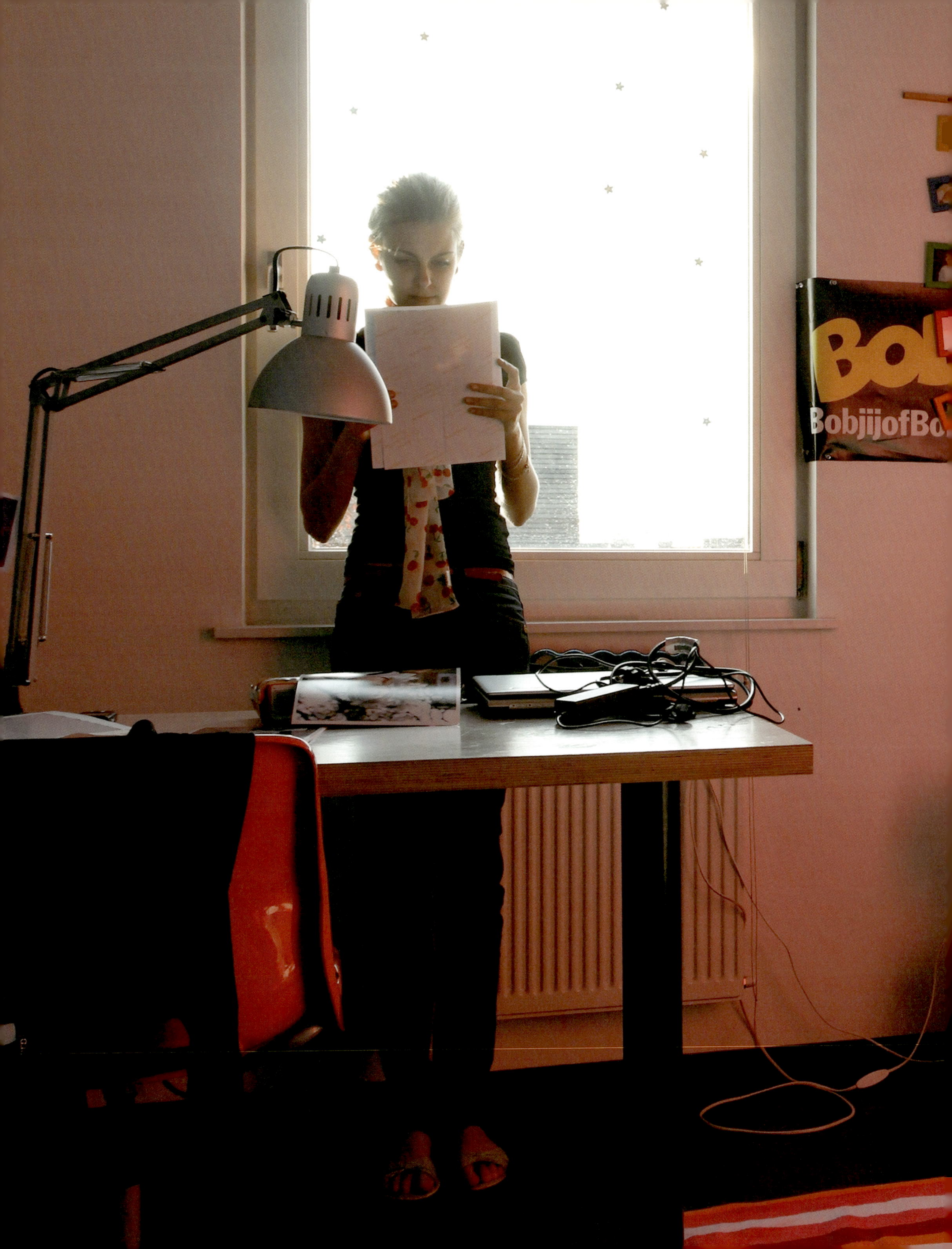
BOL
BobjijofBo

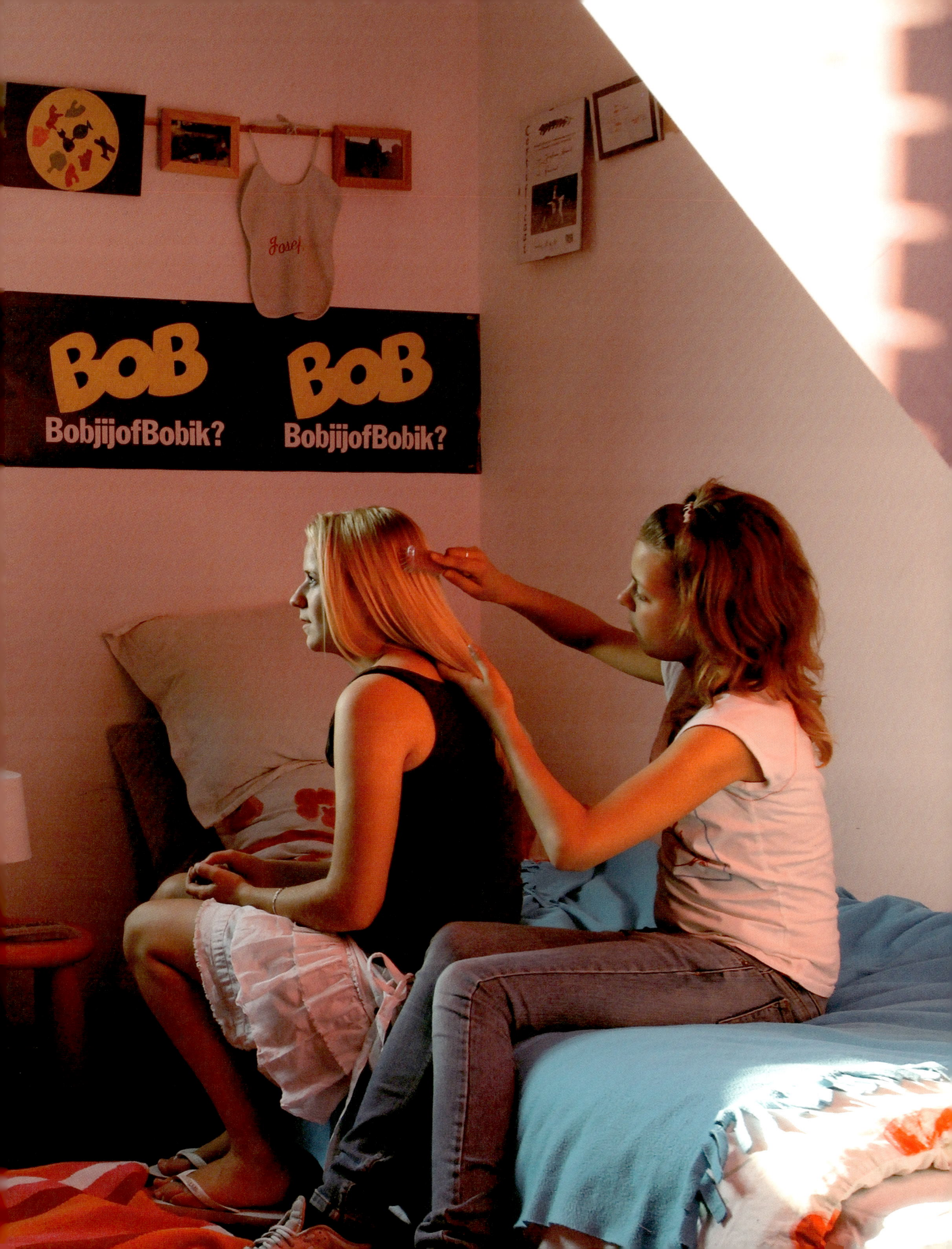

BOB
BobjijofBobik?
BOB
BobjijofBobik?
Josef

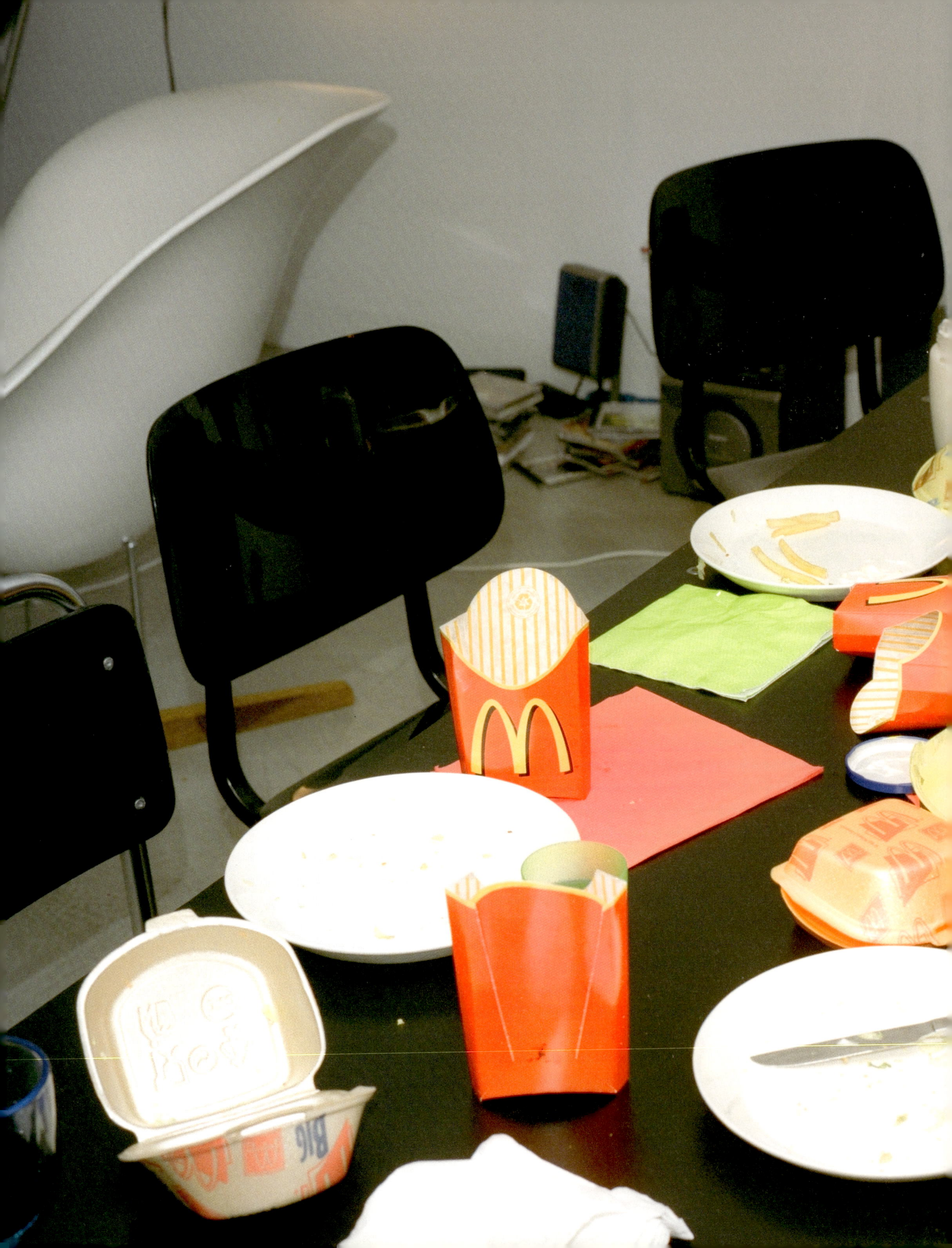

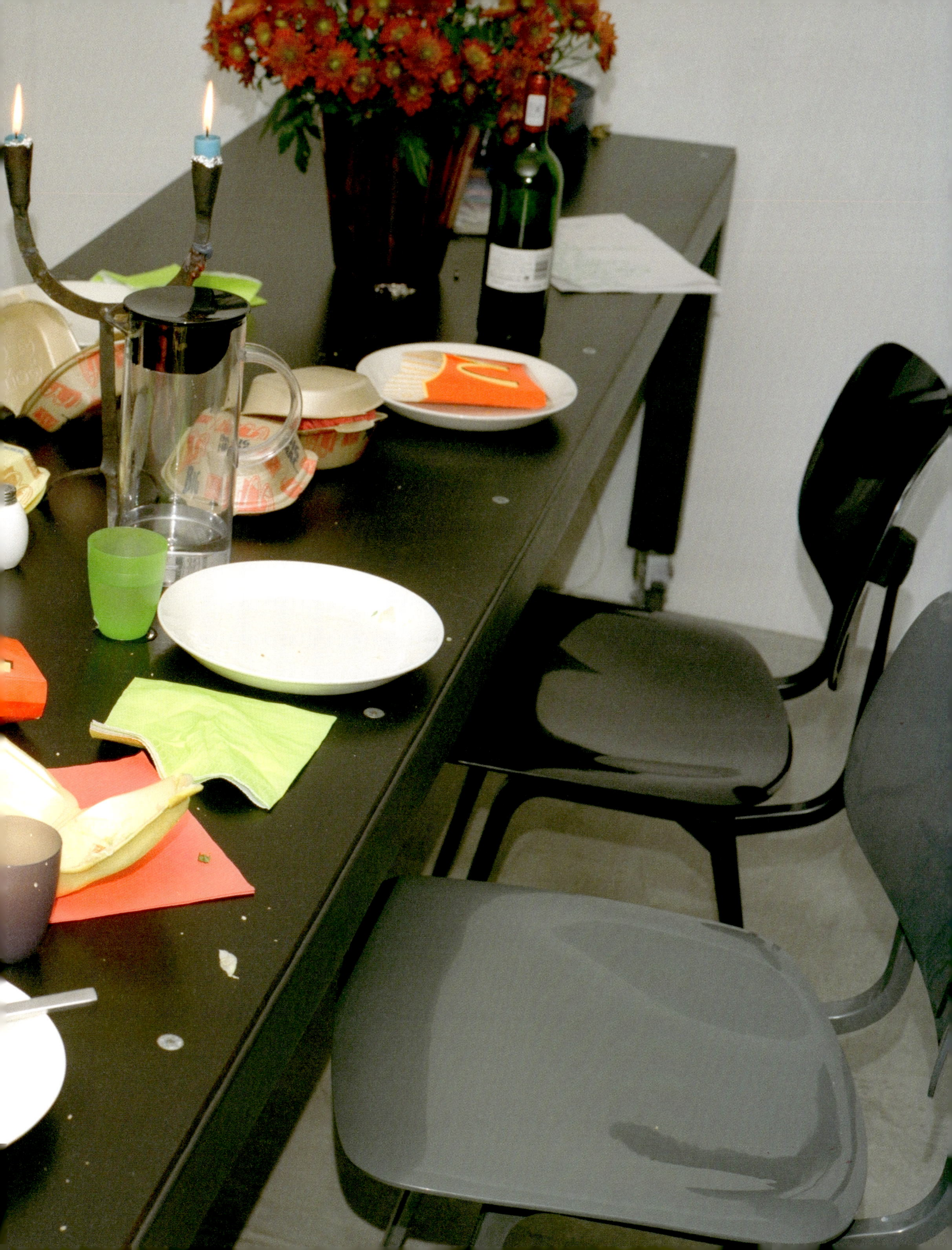

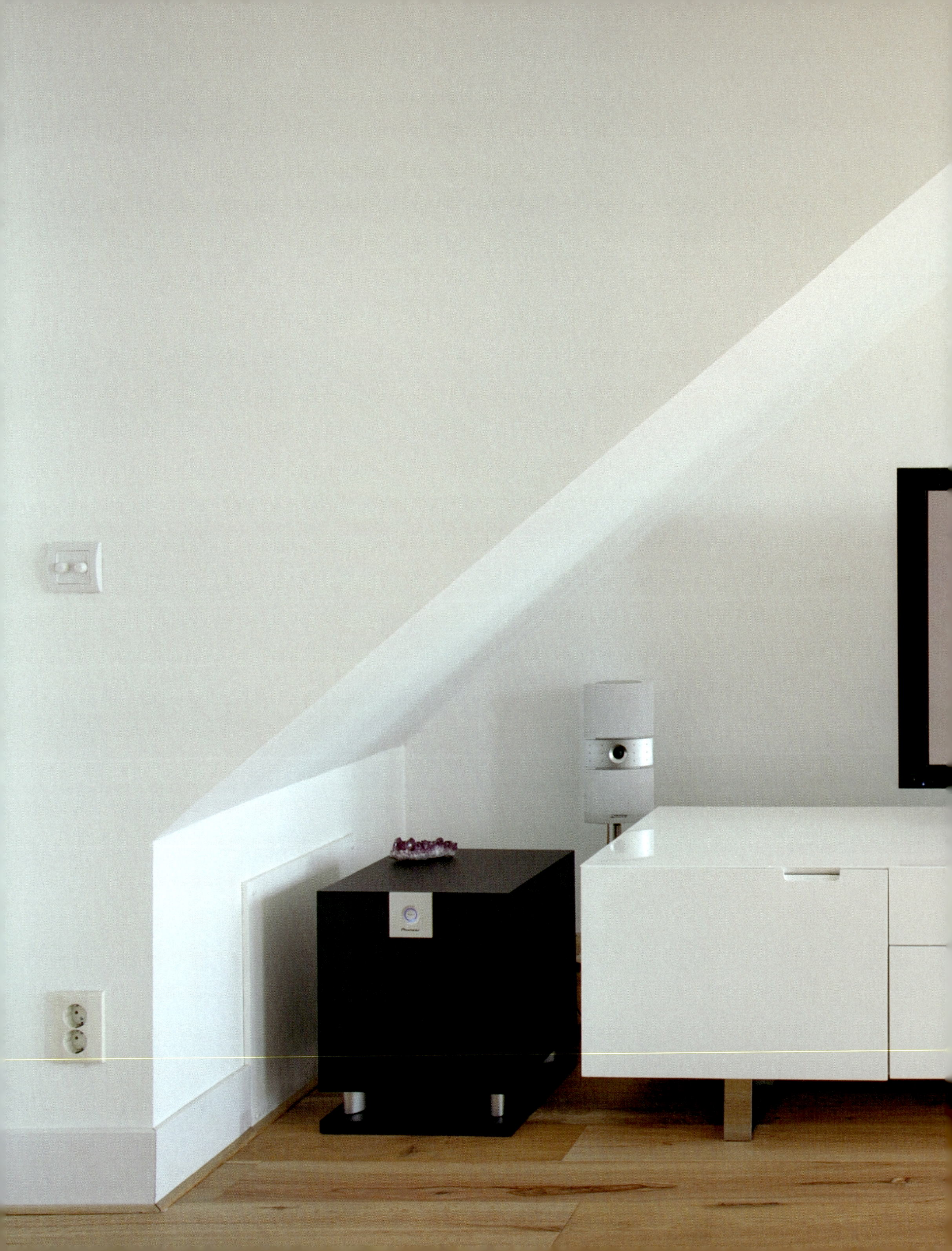

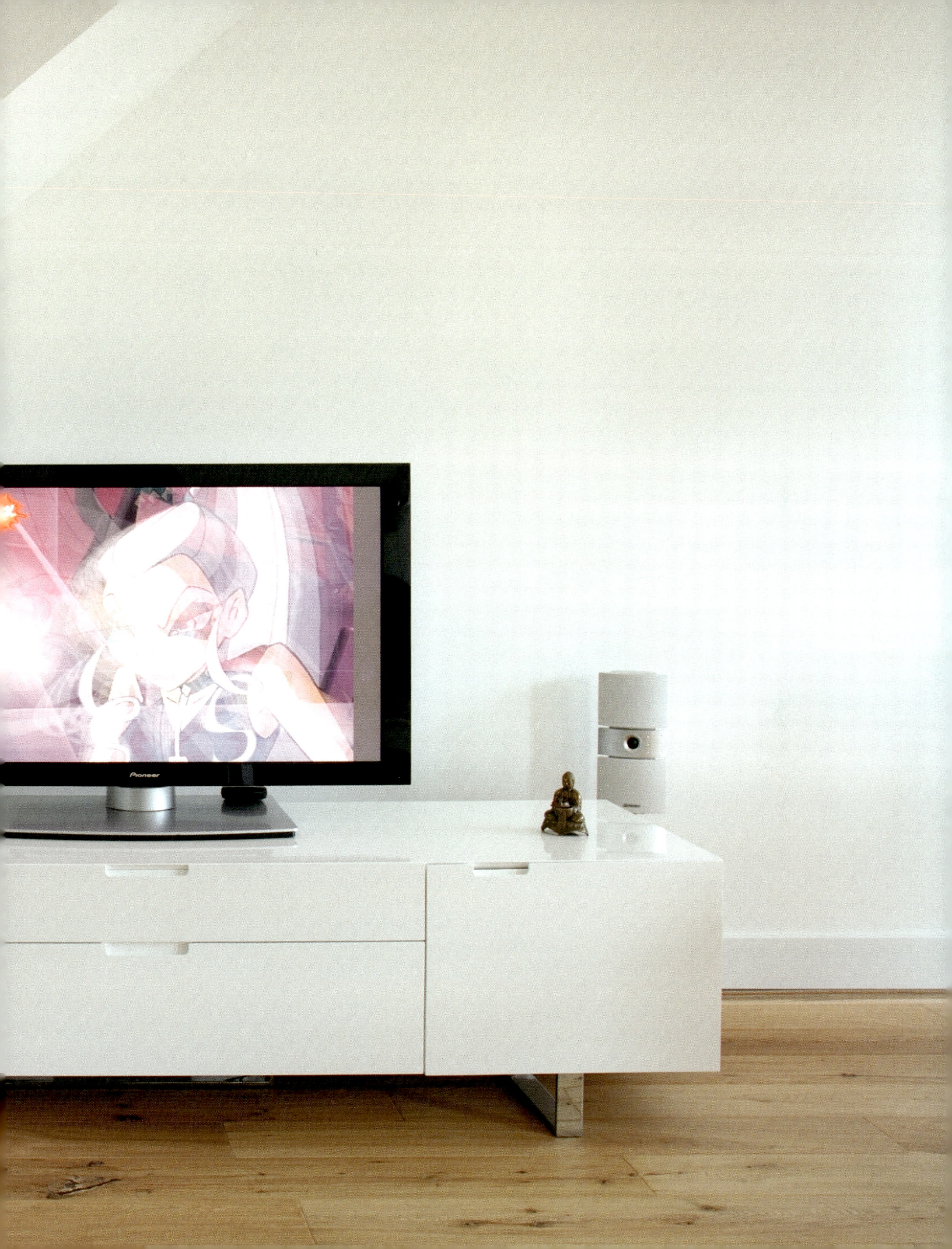

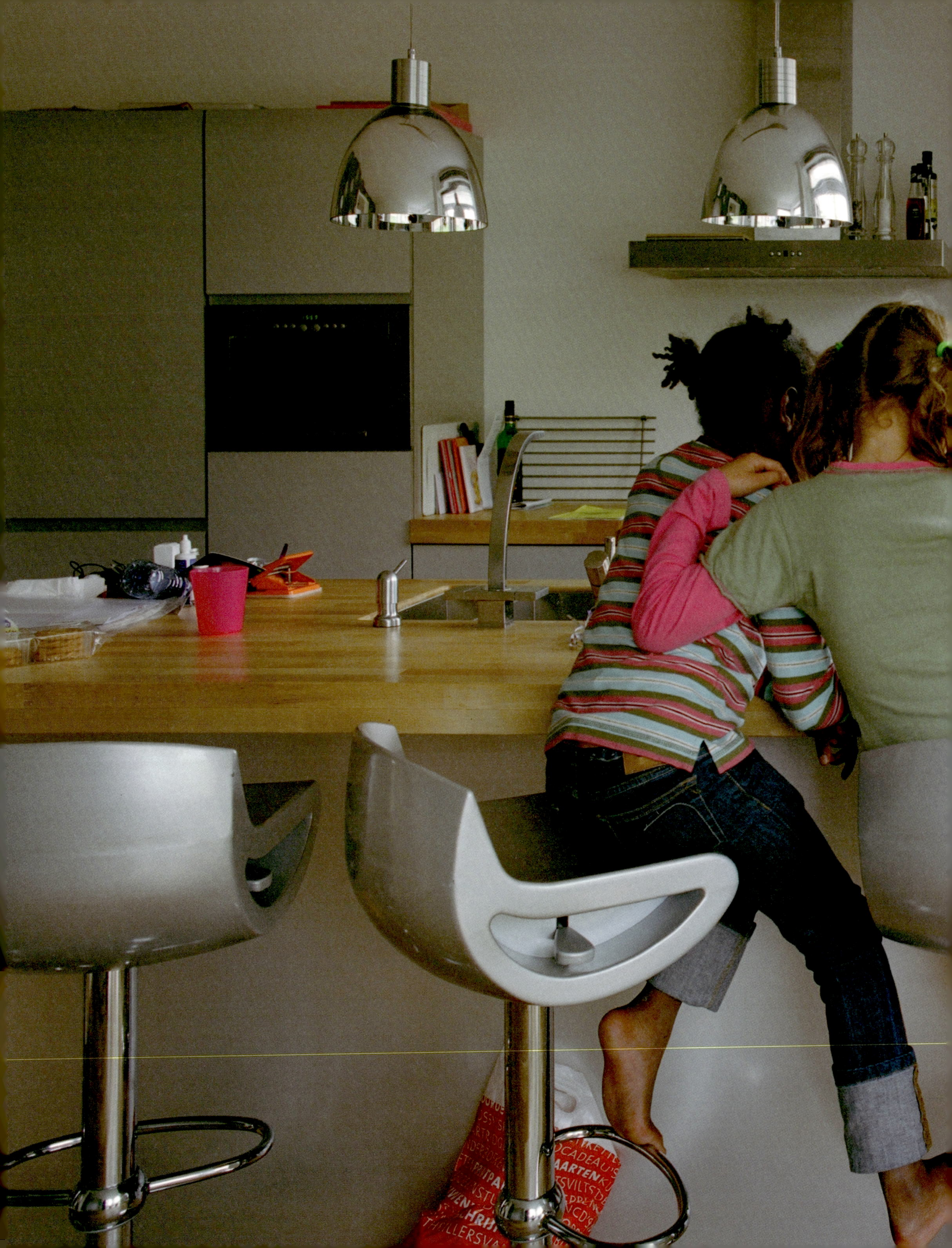

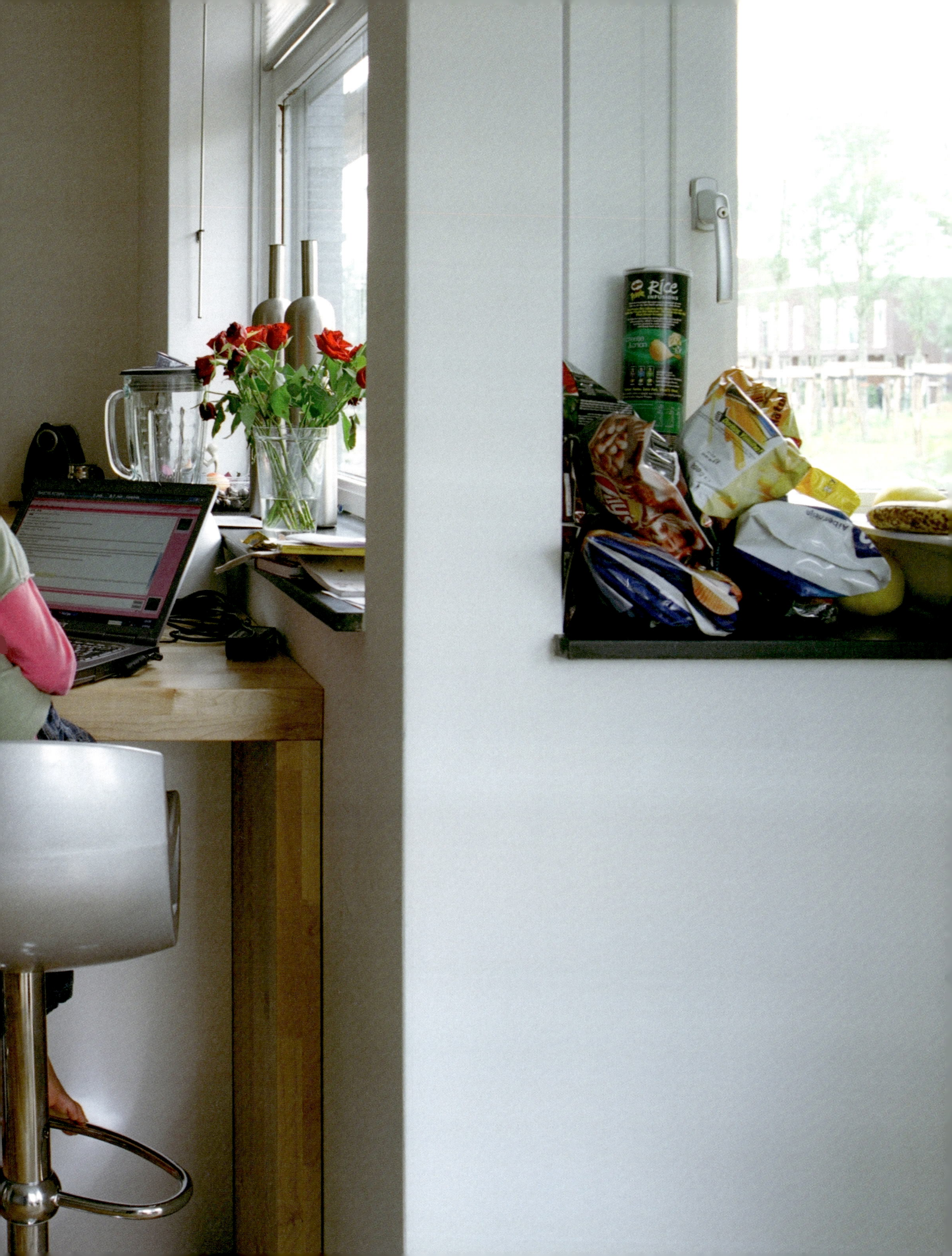

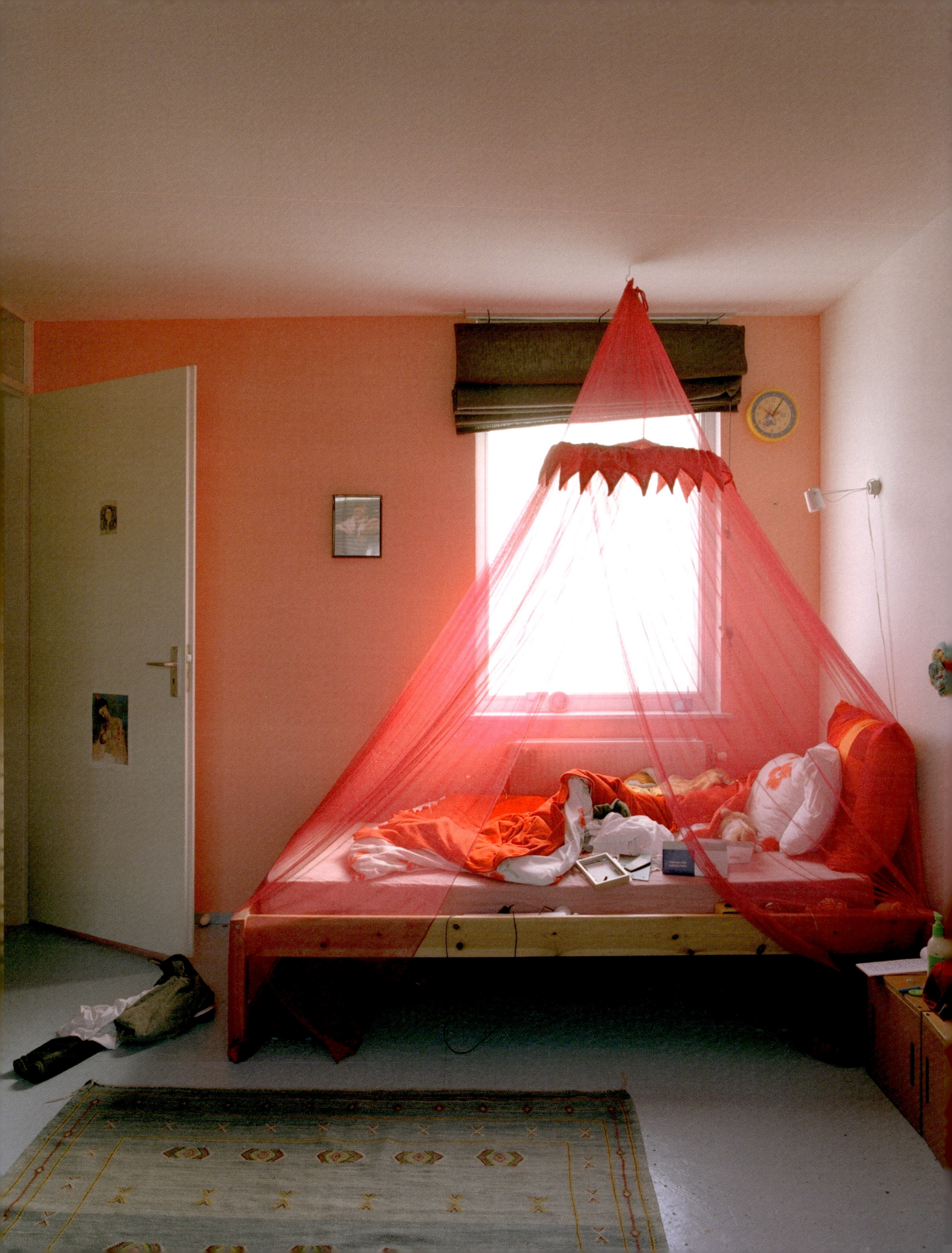

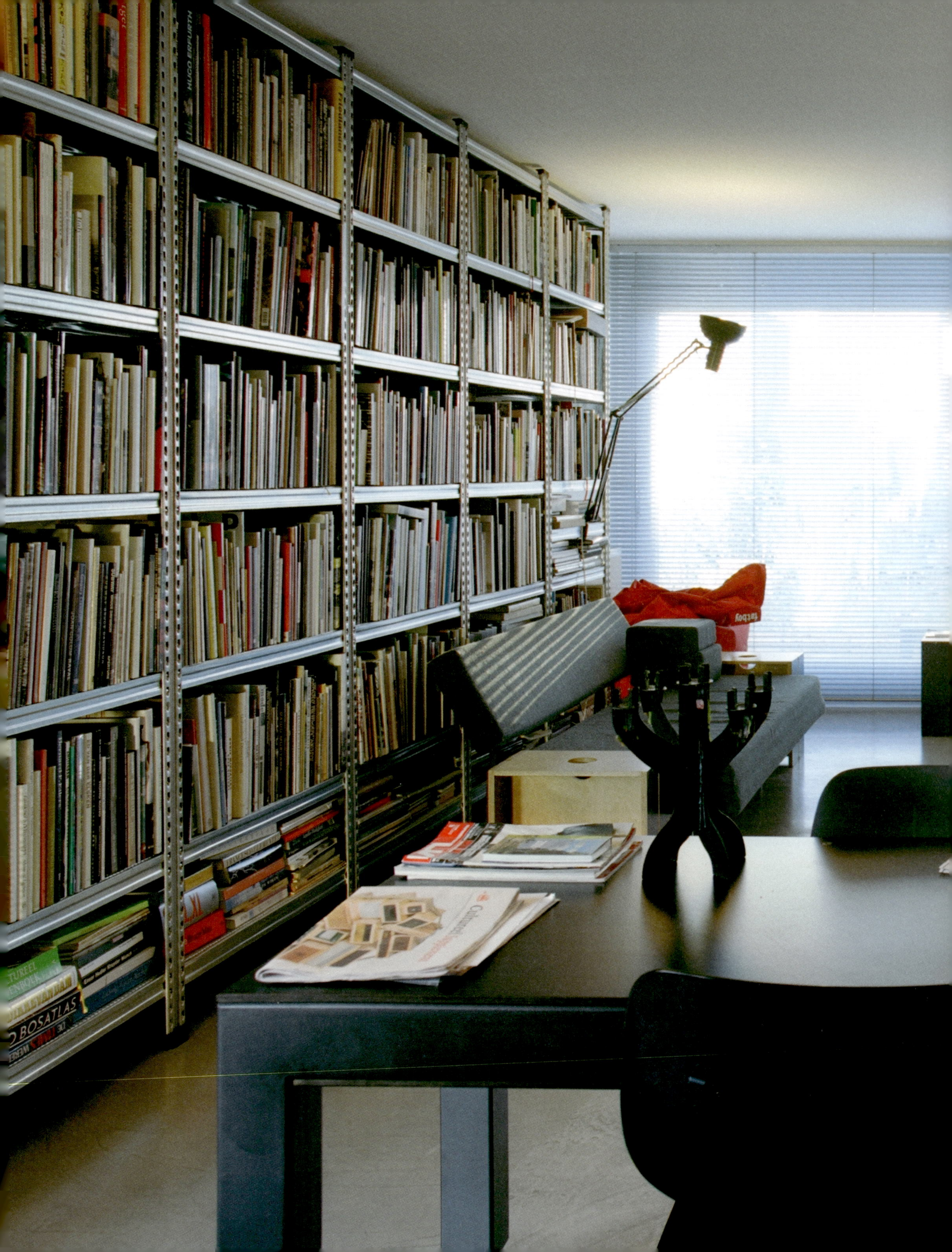

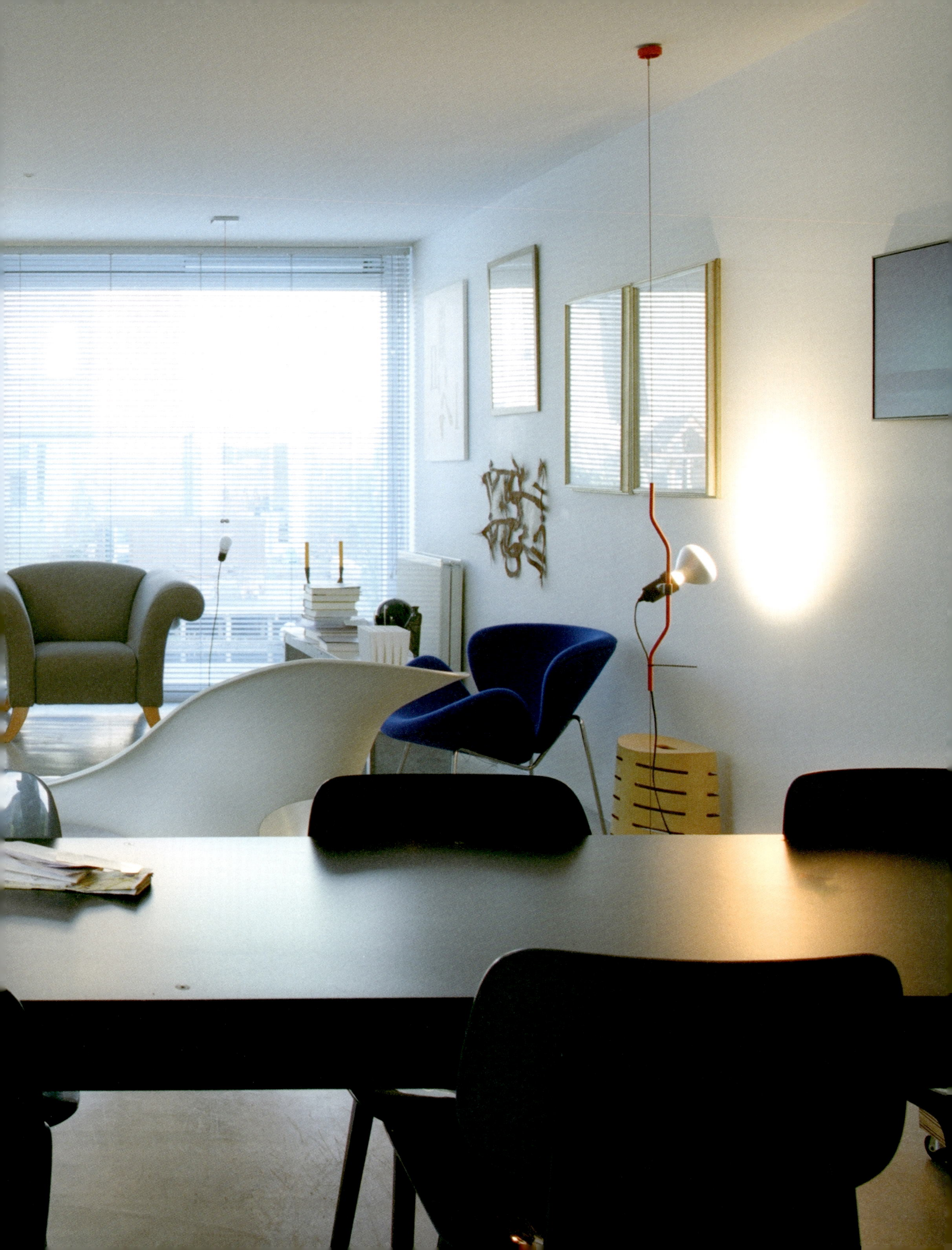

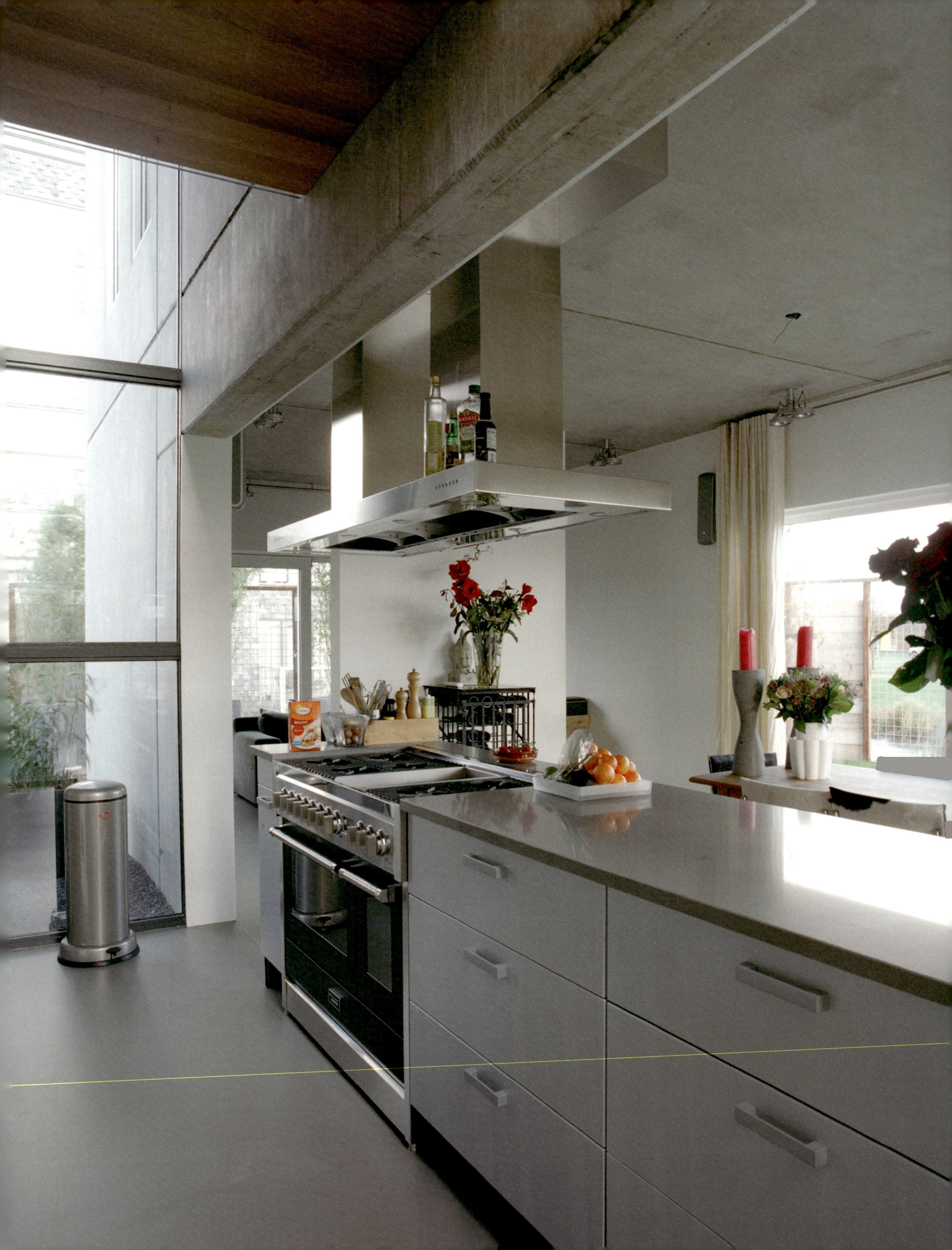

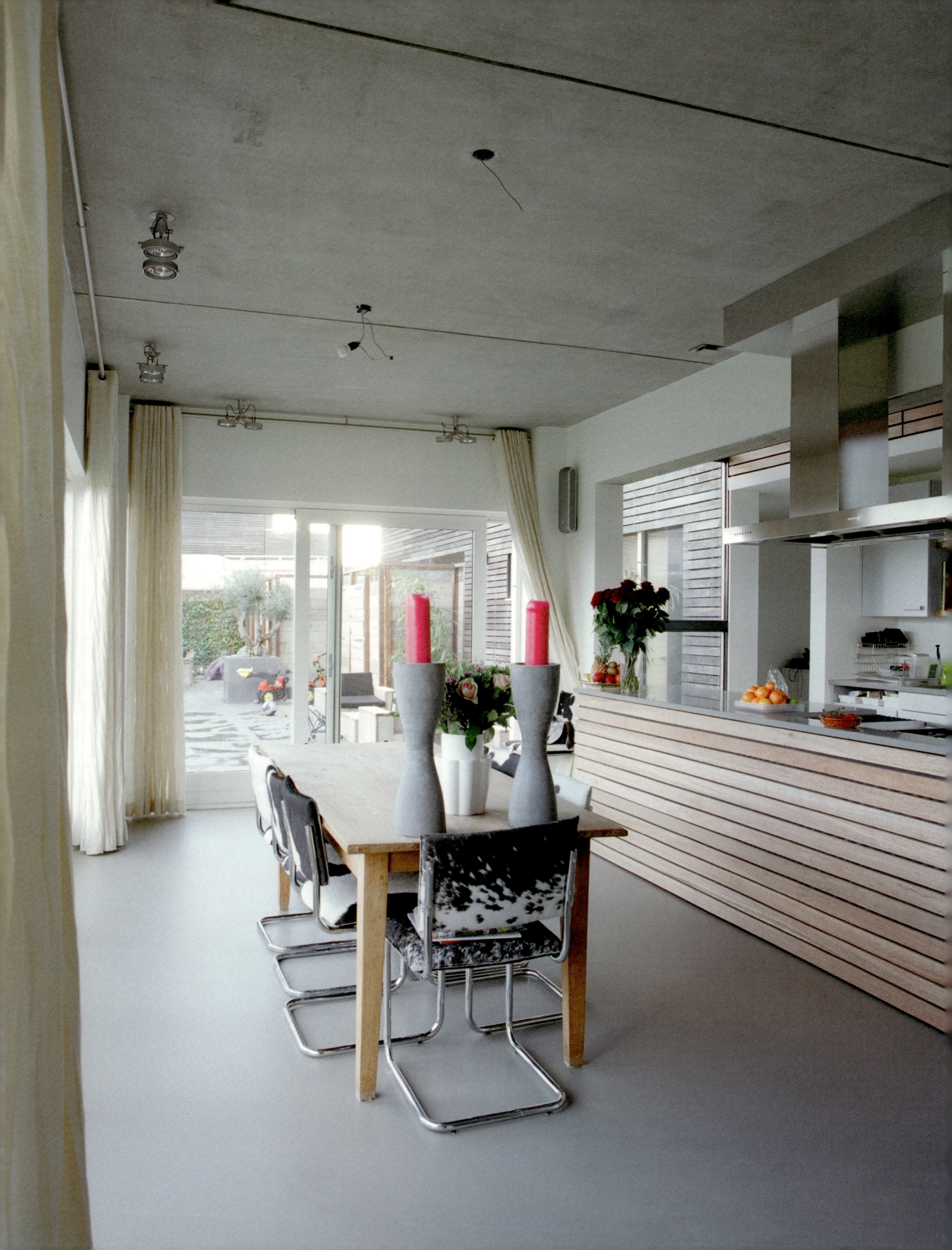

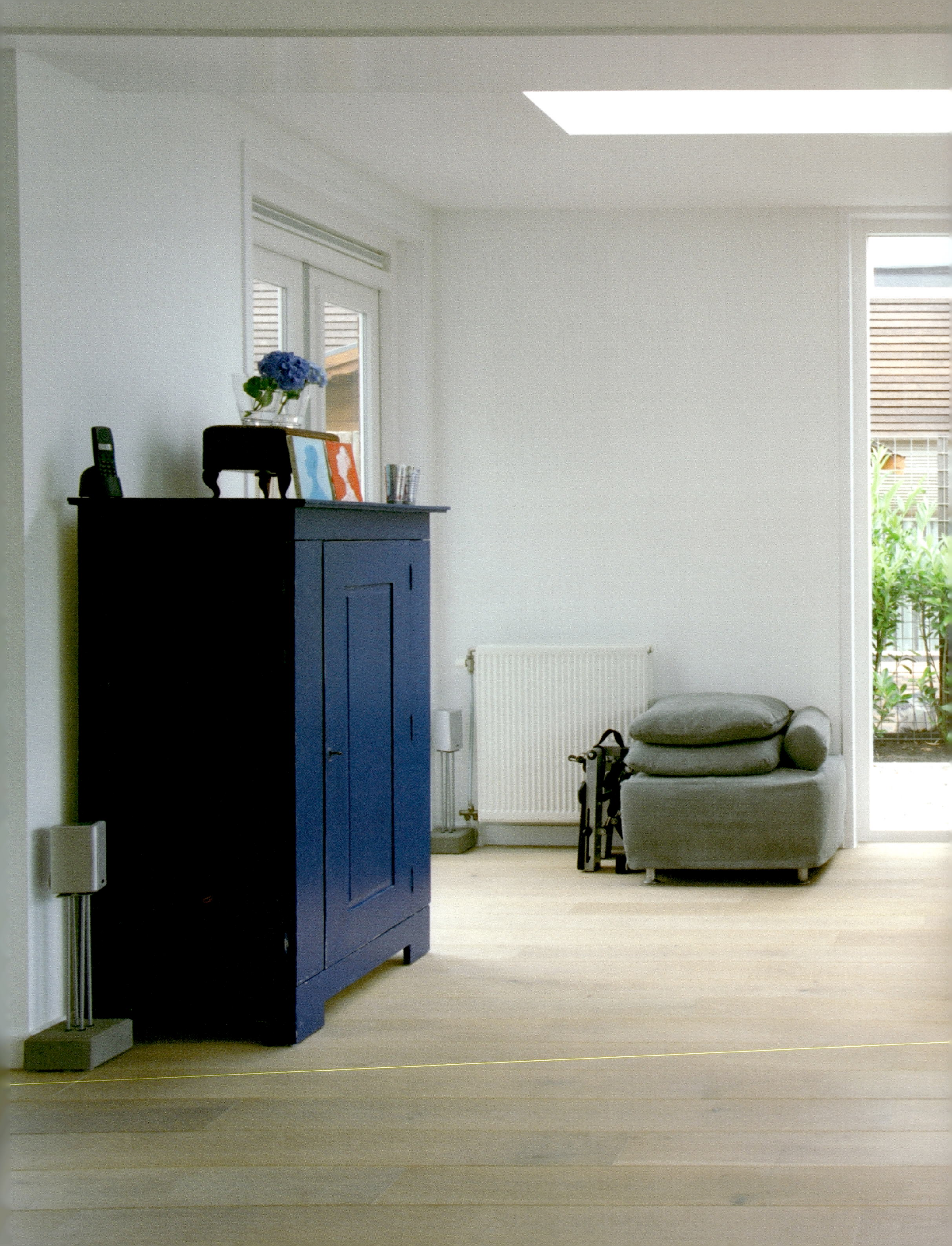

house on its own property. The houses are narrow and deep. The downstairs level is relatively small and upstairs, with the more expensive ones, it gets considerably more spacious due to the 5-m extension.' Aside from this, the Dutch public's unfamiliarity with timber-frame construction and the highly unusual division of lots made buyers somewhat reticent. Thus the sales strategy had to change. A staff director of sales suggested, 'You know what'll work? Because it *is* wood after all . . . that idea of American living. That's what you've got to call it: that'll sell.' This new outlook brought no significant rise in sales.

Not only were homes for sale being built on the island. Low-income rental housing had to make up 30 percent of all the construction. That meant: rent ranging from 350 to 650 euros per month. As the owner of all the land, the municipality was in a position to impose that requirement. The distribution of the homes for sale had also been established by the municipality: 40 percent would be inexpensive, 30 percent expensive.

In 1999 AM Wonen asked housing corporation Ymere to carry out the low-income housing program. 'If you add it up,' says Betty Oderkerk, project developer at Ymere, 'it isn't possible to rent homes for 350 to 650 euros. You'd have to sacrifice money, about an average of 35,000 euros per home. A housing corporation is then expected to invest that unprofitable segment by way of its own means.'

Housing corporations have a social purpose. Like ordinary project developers, they do make a profit on the homes that they build. But they invest that profit in low-income rental housing. Another difference with respect to project developers is that corporations own the homes for a very long time. Because of that, they can profit from the housing's rise in value.

The economic recession that began after 2001 brought the corporation an unexpected advantage. Things were not going well in the construction industry, and that led to lower estimates from builders than those originally calculated into the budget. In this case the difference amounted to 8 percent, not inconsiderable for a project where the total organizational cost (land, construction and additional expenses) came to 9,800,000 euros including sales tax – for 34 landed residences and 35 apartments.

Aside from that, there was another squaring of accounts. In the development of low-income housing, there are generally no funds for property partitions or other quality-related additions to the urban-developmental plan.

It had been agreed that these items would be paid for with the profit from sold homes. On Eiland 7, AM Wonen had put aside 2,269 euros per low-income home for this purpose. The low-income homes were given garden sheds and decent fences. Buyers of expensive homes had indeed paid for sheds and fences, but they had been placed somewhere else: at the low-income rental homes.

'There was an urban-developmental plan for Eiland 7; a couple of things were left to us. At the time when the *Vinex* projects began, we weren't contributing any land, and then you don't have much influence,' explains Betty Oderkerk, developer of the rental homes.

Bjarne Mastenbroek had done a design sketch for the houses on the green; some would be sold by AM Wonen, and others low-income rentals for Ymere. 'We couldn't give our approval to the design for homes on the green,' recalls Betty Oderkerk. 'This design failed to comply at all with our view of sound construction. Not getting anywhere with Mastenbroek's firm SeARCH, we decided to call it quits with them.'

At this point Ymere brings in architect Maartje Lammers. Together with Boris Zeisser, she runs 24H architecture in Rotterdam. The firm is asked to design the program for low-income housing. Despite the limited budget, they opt for spacious entrances to the apartment buildings.

Nor is the façade allowed to become an afterthought. Apart from the 'village green,' there are few other landscaped areas for the public on this island. They compensate for that somewhat by coming up with an architectural solution. Since the budget won't allow for natural green, they collect sycamore leaves and place them on the scanner. These are converted into a pattern of pixels, and that pattern is then punched into gold-colored sheets of aluminum. The exterior wall is covered with those sheets.

Having become restless due to disappointing sales on Eiland 7, AM Wonen asks Maartje Lammers's firm to produce a design for the buildings on the south side of the green. Bjarne Mastenbroek's original idea was to situate a row of large and expensive homes along that south side. Using the changing market as its excuse, AM Wonen comes up with the trusty Dutch variation on the duplex. Both 24H architecture and SeARCH produce designs. AM Wonen wants to offer both designs and considers an even distribution of these throughout the area to be developed.

At the sales event held in late May 2004, Bjarne Mastenbroek of SeARCH and Maartje Lammers of 24H architecture each present their designs. Soon enough, there appears to be more interest in the design by 24H architecture. AM Wonen withdraws the design by Bjarne Mastenbroek and sells only the design by 24H architecture.

The idea proposed by 24H architecture involves creating a counterform to the form of the eave-like 'overhang' on the opposite side of the green. A defined front yard, a stone façade and properties divided by hedges provide clear differentiations between private and public property. Maartje Lammers resists 'the terror' of the duplex, with its extra width (5.4 m) and its semi-detached garage. She approaches it with a scale of 3 m for the garage, 6 m for the house, 6 m for the house next door and then 3 m for its garage, with a path leading to the back between the two garages. The breakfast kitchen is 'shifted' to the front, and the living room toward the backyard. 'We included all the options in the sketch right away,' Lammers says. 'The residents could choose: an added level on top of the garage, on top of the roof, and so on. Many of the options were carried out right away, and that set a trend for possible add-ons by owners in the future. The message being: things have to be done as we designed them, not otherwise.'

Due to the difficulty in selling the timber-frame construction, AM Wonen was a bit hesitant about incorporating wood in the houses, Maartje Lammers comments. 'But we stood firm.' Concessions did need to be made on cost – and therefore on quality – with respect to the types of wood used. Maartje Lammers tries to guarantee the design as much as possible by stipulating as much detail as possible in the construction order; 'otherwise, with the realization of the design, you haven't got a leg to stand on when faced with the project developer.'

When the design was finished, it was contracted out. Various construction companies make a bid on the realization of the design. For 127,000 euros the standard version can be built. But AM Wonen wants this amount to be reduced to 110,000 euros. The recent losses that came about during the development and redevelopment of the island need to be balanced out as soon as possible. 'We had to make small cutbacks wherever we could in order to find that 17,000 euros,' Lammers explains. 'Toilets became smaller, since that would reduce the tiling. Stone, only 20 percent more expensive than standard brickwork – hardly a big difference with such an amount – was eliminated. We opted to put as much visible quality on the front, as that contributes to public space. In the back we did have to compromise.'

Local realtors and the marketing department of the project developer provide some indication as to the selling price of duplexes on a market now picking up to a degree: just under 400,000 euros for a standard home on a lot measuring 410 m². The project developer takes this advice: the 'beginner's' model will go for 399,000 euros.

How does such a price take shape? I ask Hans Kranenburg, developer for the project developing firm Bouwfonds and thereby closely involved in the development of the *Vinex* location Floriande. 'On the whole, things are calculated as follows. With a selling price of 400,000 euros for a newly built house, there should be a land price of about 120,000 euros. The builder's fee should be roughly 55 percent of the selling price. The additional external costs, including hook-up charges and loss of interest on preparation expenses, come to 8 percent,' Kranenburg explains.

In 2000, landscape architect Ben Kuipers was approached by the municipality Haarlemmermeer. His assignment: to execute the urban plan conceived by Bjarne Mastenbroek. 'It was an interesting urban-planning concept,' Kuipers says. 'All of the Floriande islands tend to be based on the pattern of streets with houses. In this plan that idea is tossed out the window. Mastenbroek turned it into a real island by broadening the canals. And due to the village green, it truly became a residential park.' The French village served as a model for this idea. 'Semi-hard paving' with wall-to-wall gravel and 400 trees, acacias. Anything goes on a village green – except parking.

'Mastenbroek's stance was a good one. We've gone too far in the Netherlands with all our rules about the organization of public space,' comments Kuipers. Semi-hard paving was considered out-of-the-question by the municipality. If cars would drive over it, tracks would show. If it rained, puddles would form; the place would be a mess within six months. And then it's not the architect they call, but the municipality: that's how they figured it.' The semi-hard paving soon gets shoved aside. Ben Kuipers looks for ways to adjust the plan. The idea of a 'floor' (extending across this central area, between opposite exterior walls) does remain, but he uses other materials. Kuipers produces a definitive design and submits it.

Three years later, in 2003, Kuipers is again approached by the municipality. This time the design for the green needs to be revised. The atmosphere has changed: between the architect, the municipality and the project developer, it's now a fight to the finish. By now Eiland 7 has been redeveloped. Many of the original ideas have been abandoned in favor of the no-nonsense approach that the project developer now deems necessary.

'We started all over with the "village green" idea,' says Ben Kuipers. The points of departure were now being articulated by the administrators, the municipal department of public works. The department was refusing to accept any plans that went beyond their standard budget. 'The original idea of a wall-to-wall "floor" had to be tossed out the window. It did become a village green (or common) from wall to wall, but with a transition from hard to soft. It hasn't turned into something rock-hard and that seems arbitrary; but it does comply with all the standards for distance, scale and radius. No semi-hard surface, but grass and stone. A smart-looking steel edge sets off the grass and keeps cars from parking on it. A nice kind of stone was used, a fired cobblestone. The grass makes it more a Dutch *brink* than a French square. It creates a pleasant impression of greenery, and it's better for the trees.' Instead of acacias, which end up getting blown to shreds, silver maples are chosen. The planned cobblestones, to control parking, were kept.

Ben Kuipers serves as ambassador for the plan and has managed to win considerable support for it. As he sees it, there should be some understanding for the position of the civil servant. 'It's great to think up new concepts together with architects and urban planners, in a kind of experiment. But if you don't involve the people who need to realize it and maintain it, then it will never get off the ground. The maintenance department has to be part of it from the start. With a plan like this, higher budgets are available for the construction, but not for maintenance. So the maintenance people can't do much.'

Due to the redevelopment of the housing on the north side of the green – leading to the removal of parking beneath the 5-m 'overhang' on the front – parking is situated behind the homes. But that which is 'the back' for homeowners on the green happens to be the entrance for residents in the streets with timber-frame houses. Cars being parked at the back disrupt the car-free idea of those streets. In the end, though, Mastenbroek wishes to keep the green intact and agrees to have parking at the back.

Rik Bolderheij, who dealt with most of the development and construction of Eiland 7 as the final director of the *Vinex* project office, says that the relations between the municipality and the project developer were so strained during that phase that nobody wanted to pay for this solution any longer. They had arrived at an impasse. Buyers, some of whom had signed a contract three years before, were informed at a meeting of buyers. None of the buyers wants this solution. After all, another picture had been presented in the sketch when the homes were sold.

The parking places are ultimately situated behind the houses. Two rows of concrete tiles are placed on the dirt. It doesn't really work: the paving stones slide out of place once a car parks on them. Now it's up to the residents, say the project developer and municipality. And that's how it goes. On private property, according to individual insight and with the budget available, part of the outdoor space will be organized.

Just before the construction industry's summer vacation of 2004, the first homes of Eiland 7 are completed.

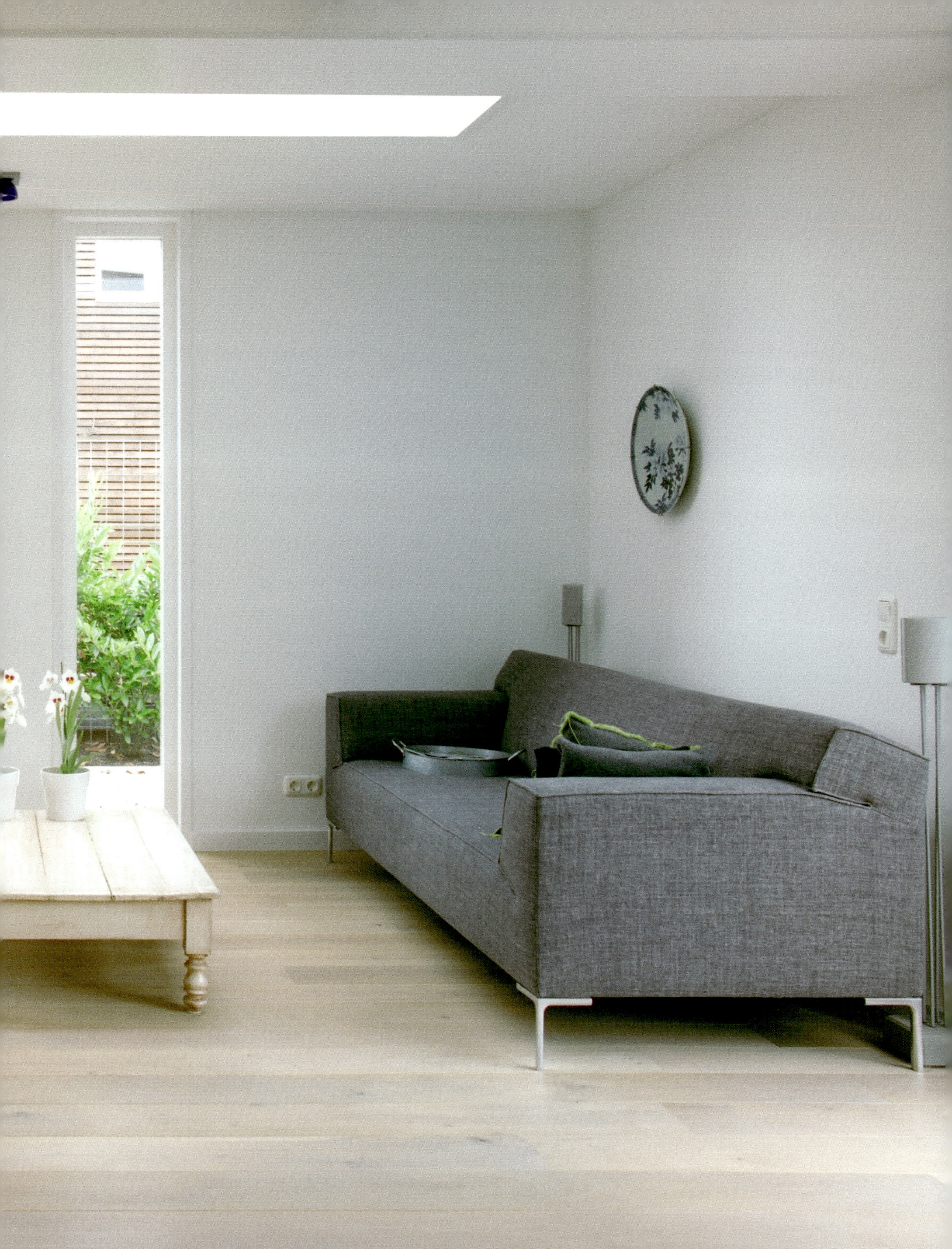

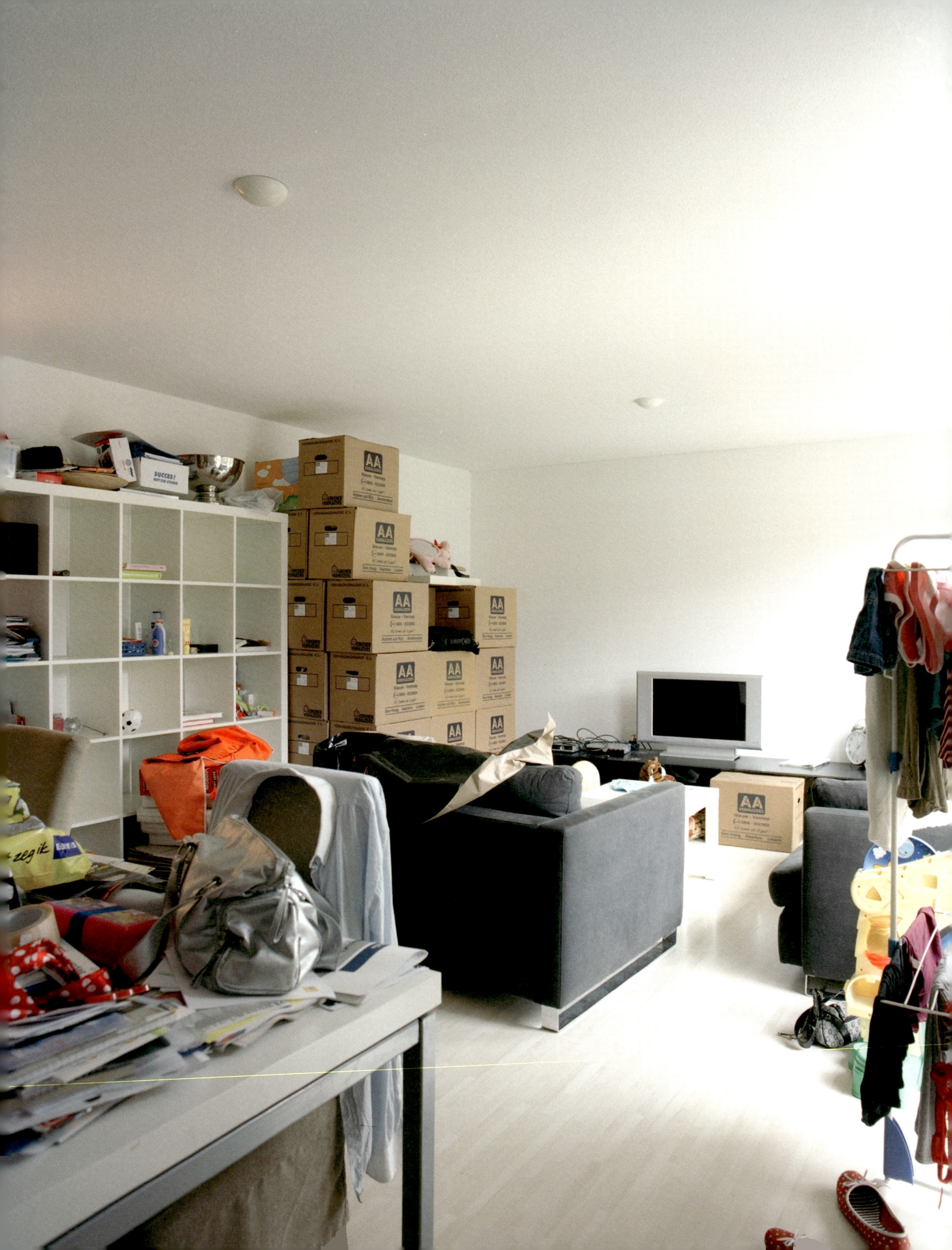

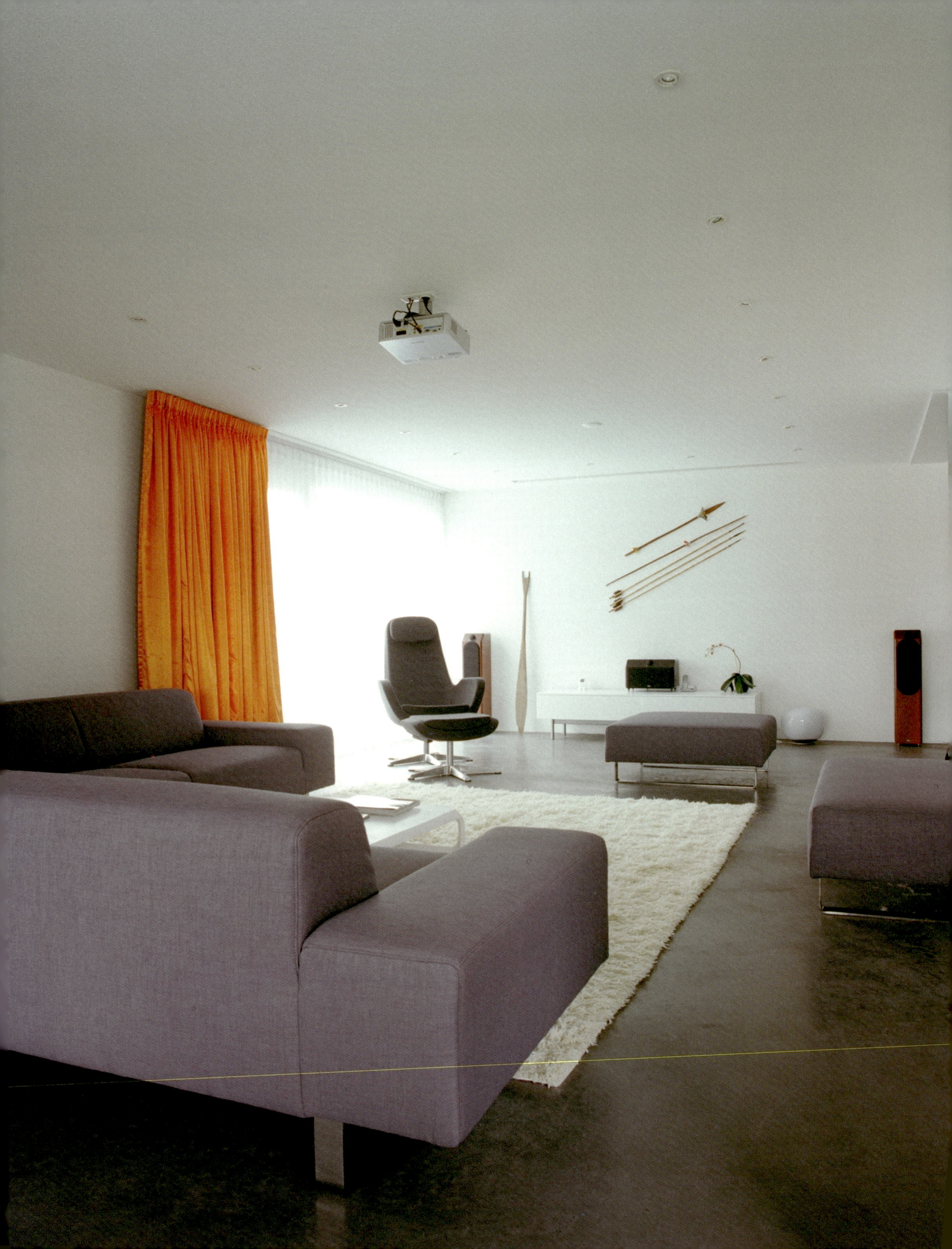

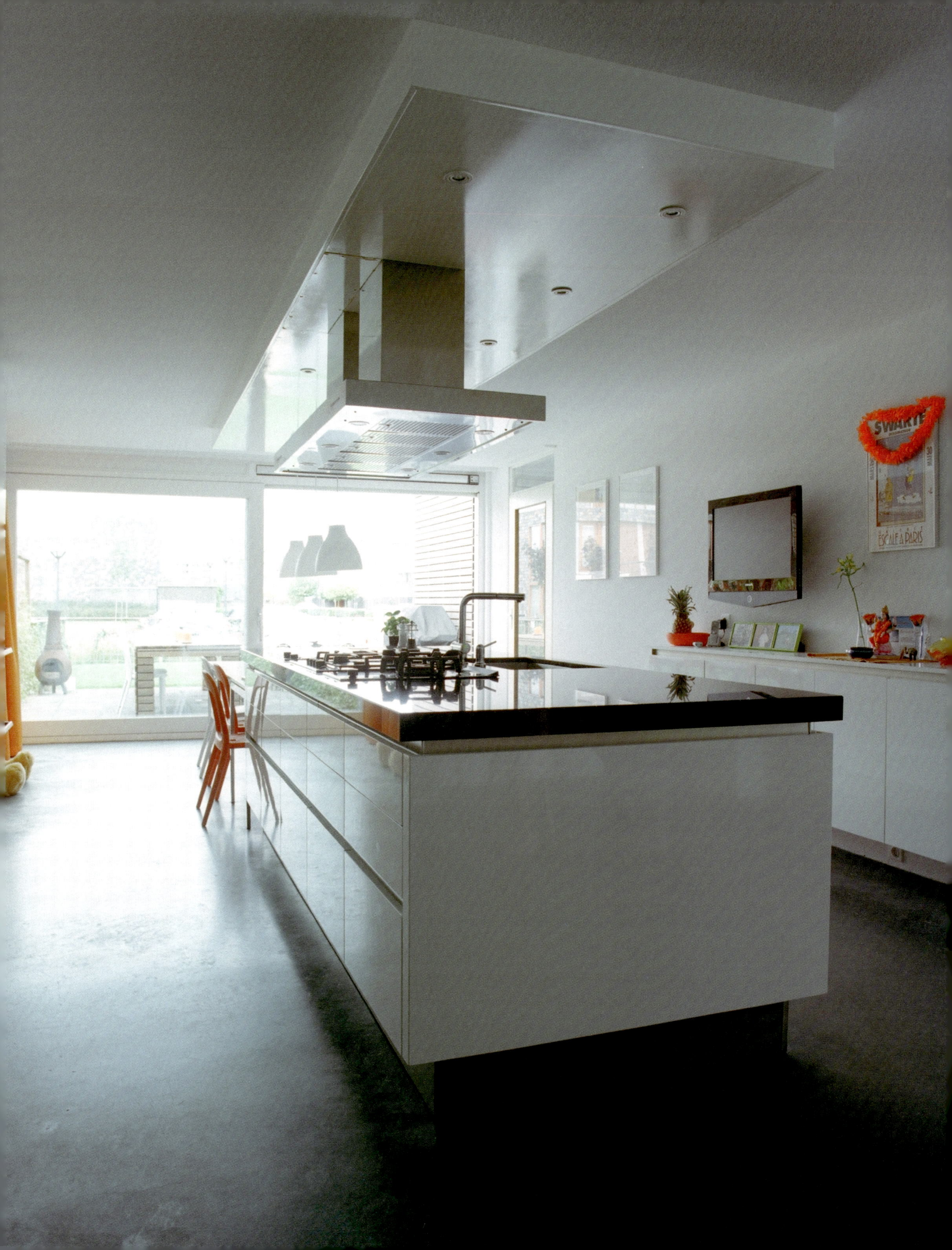

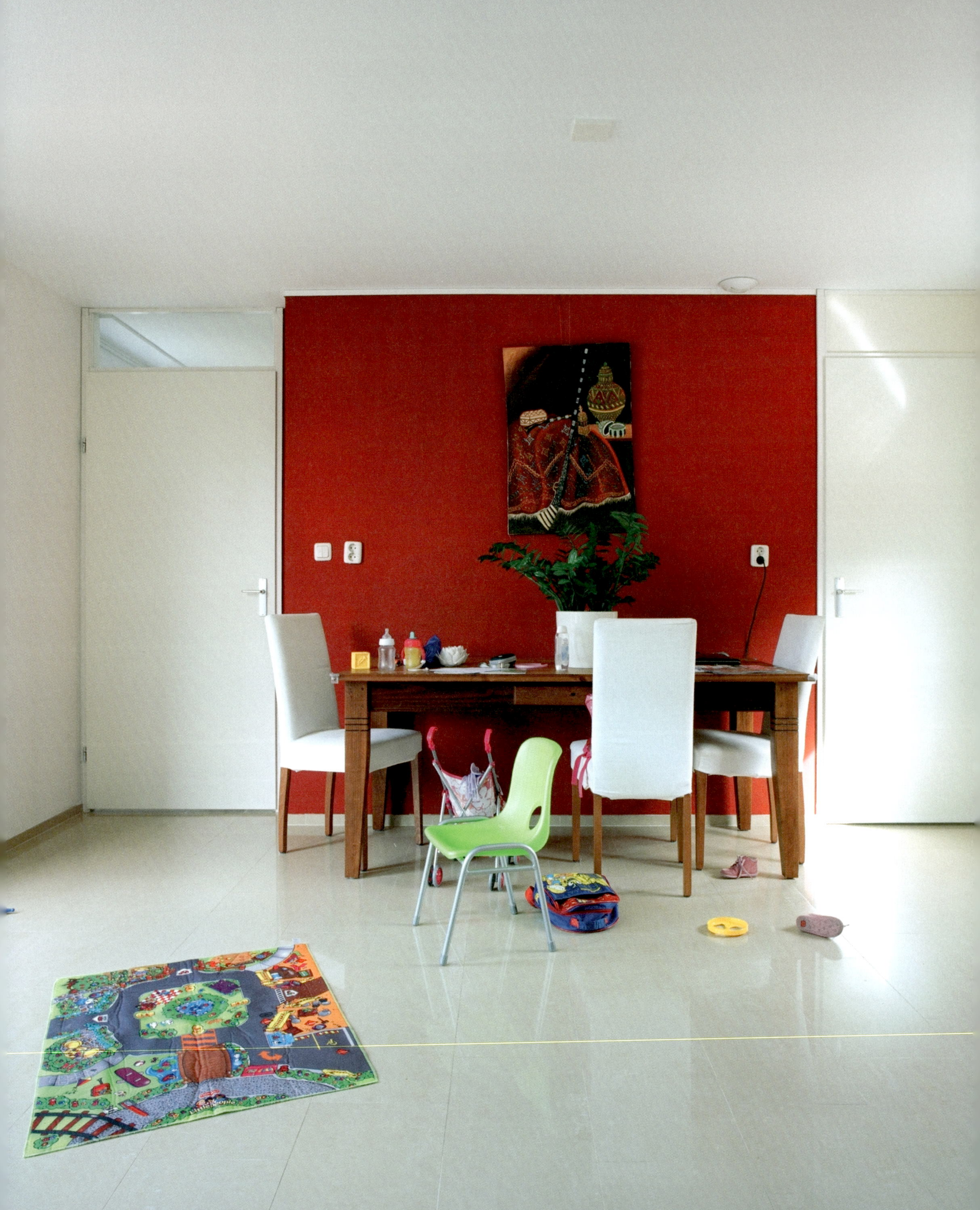

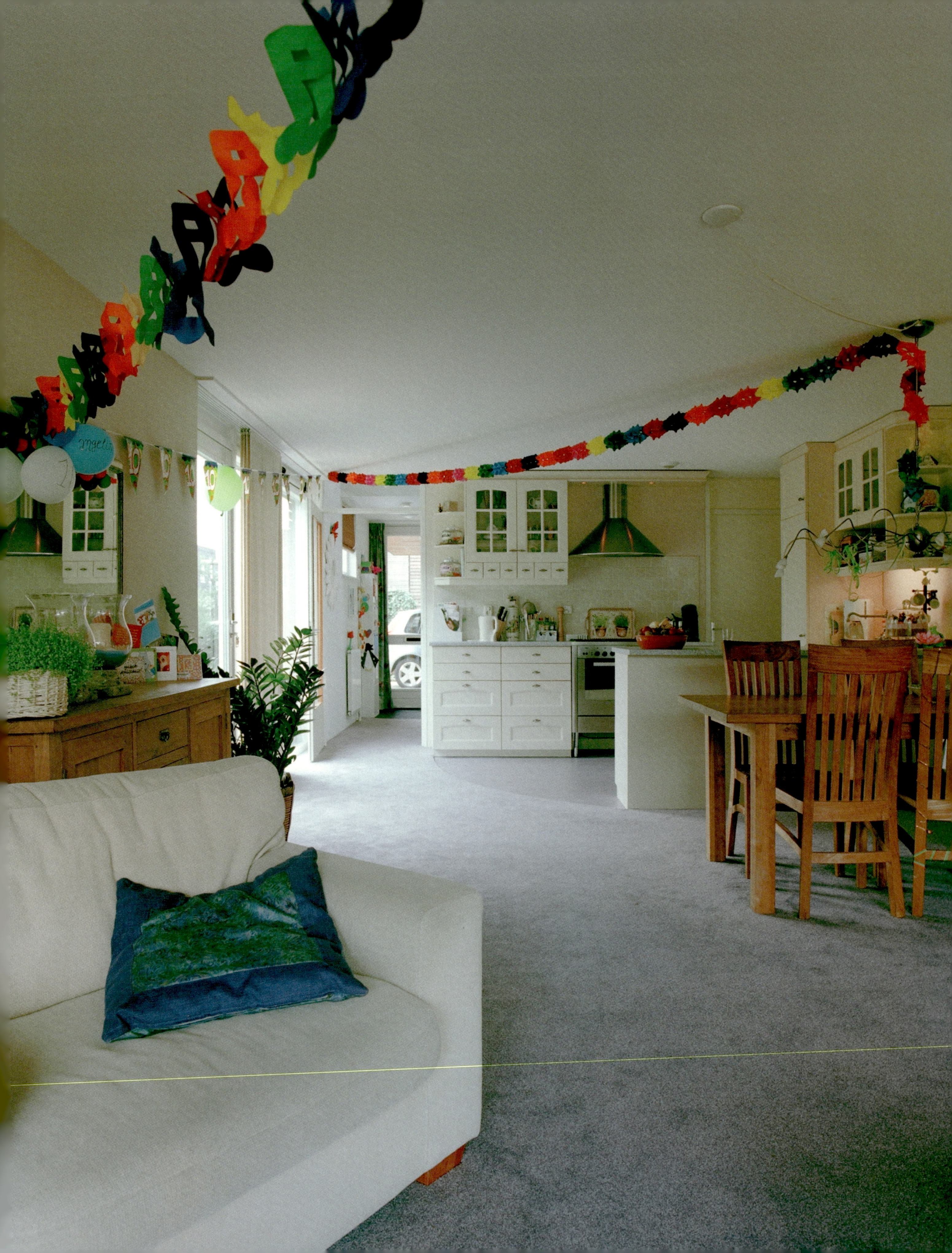

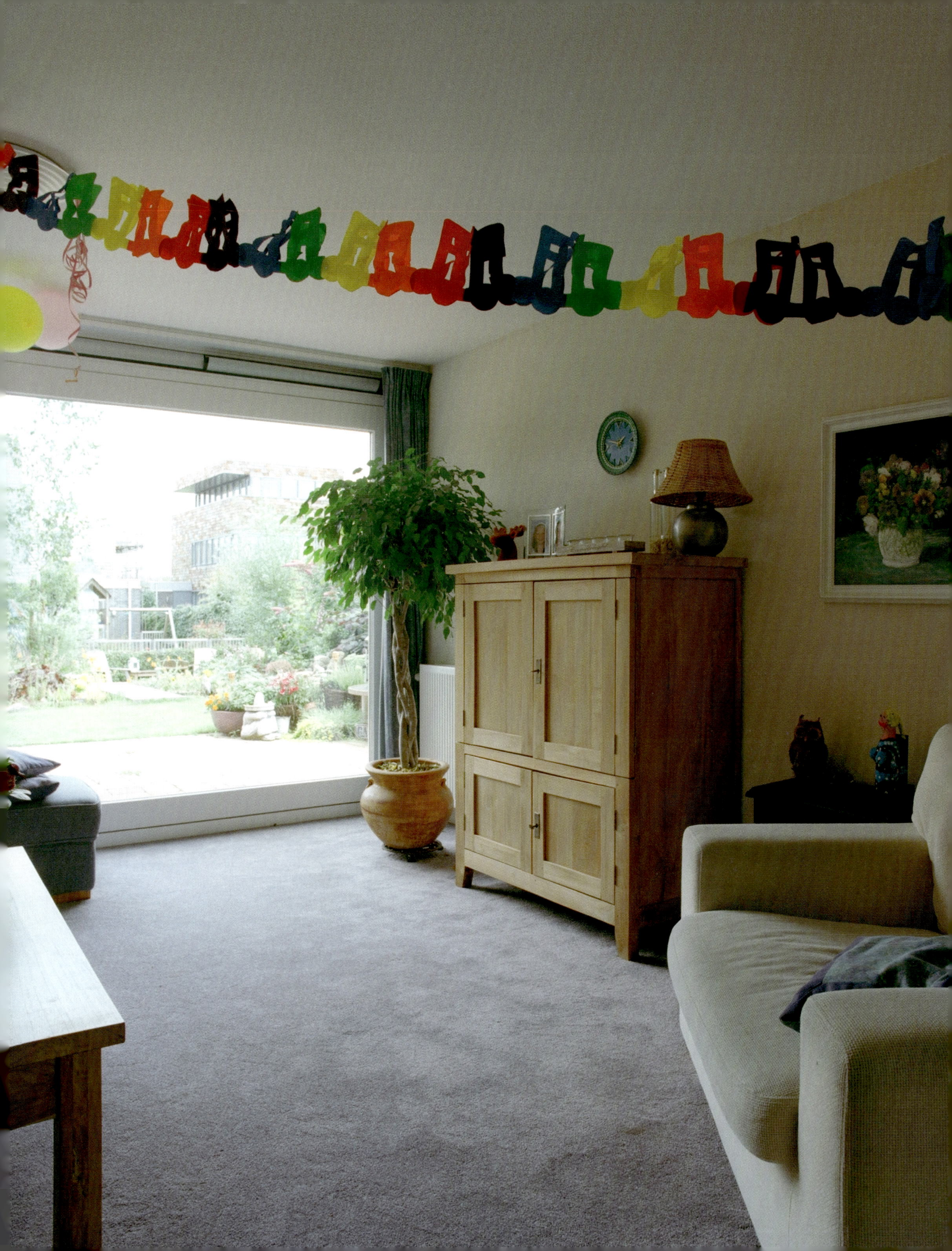

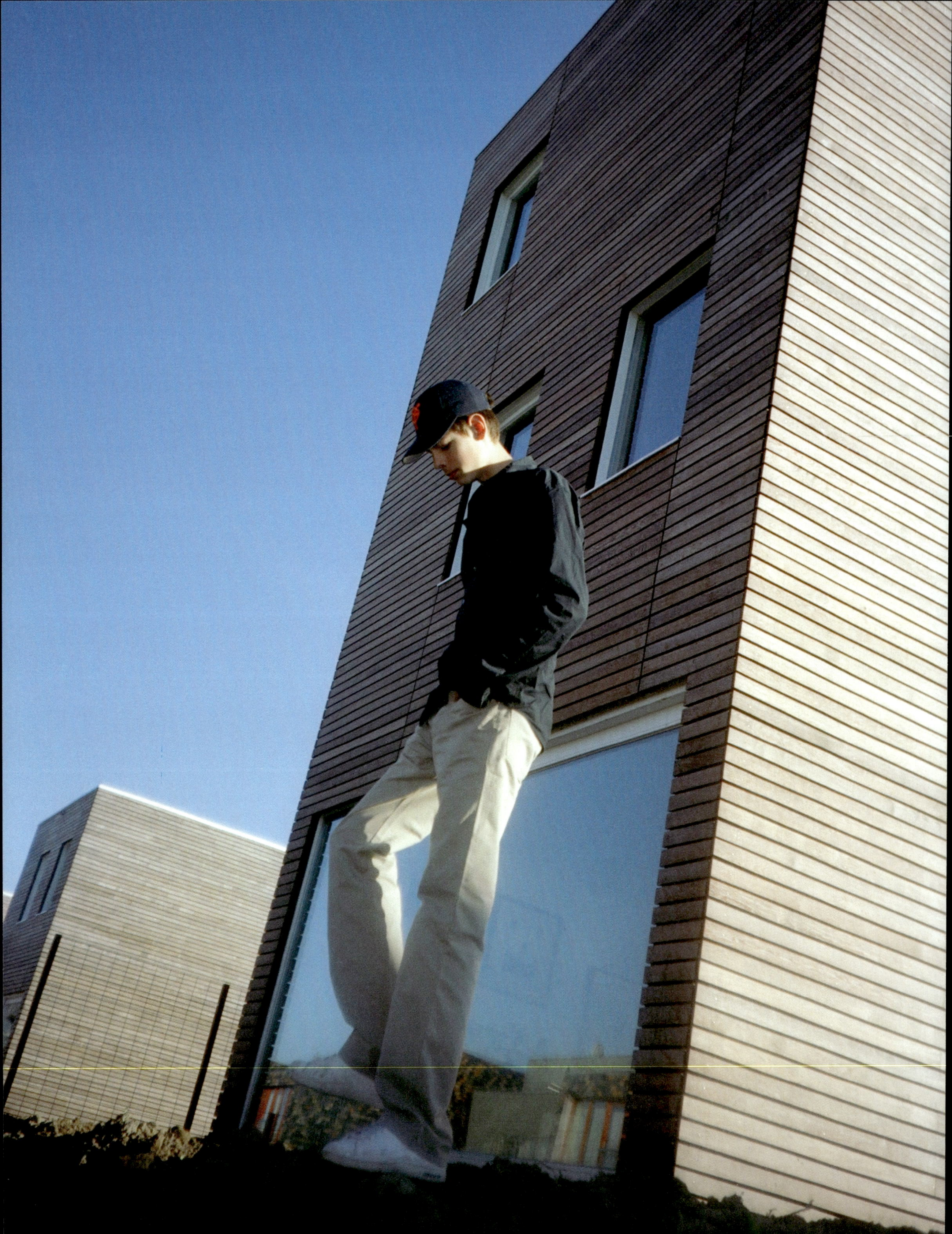

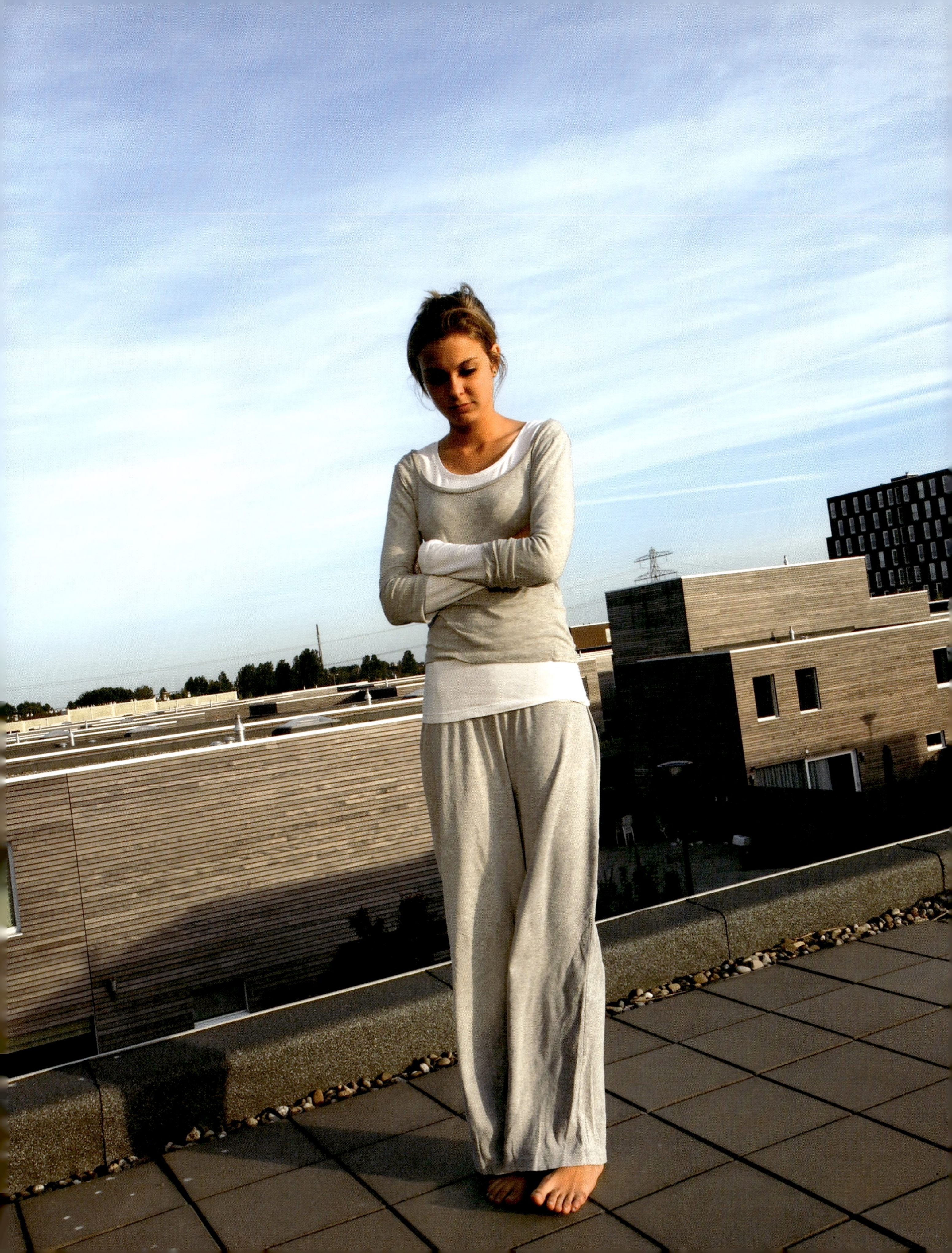

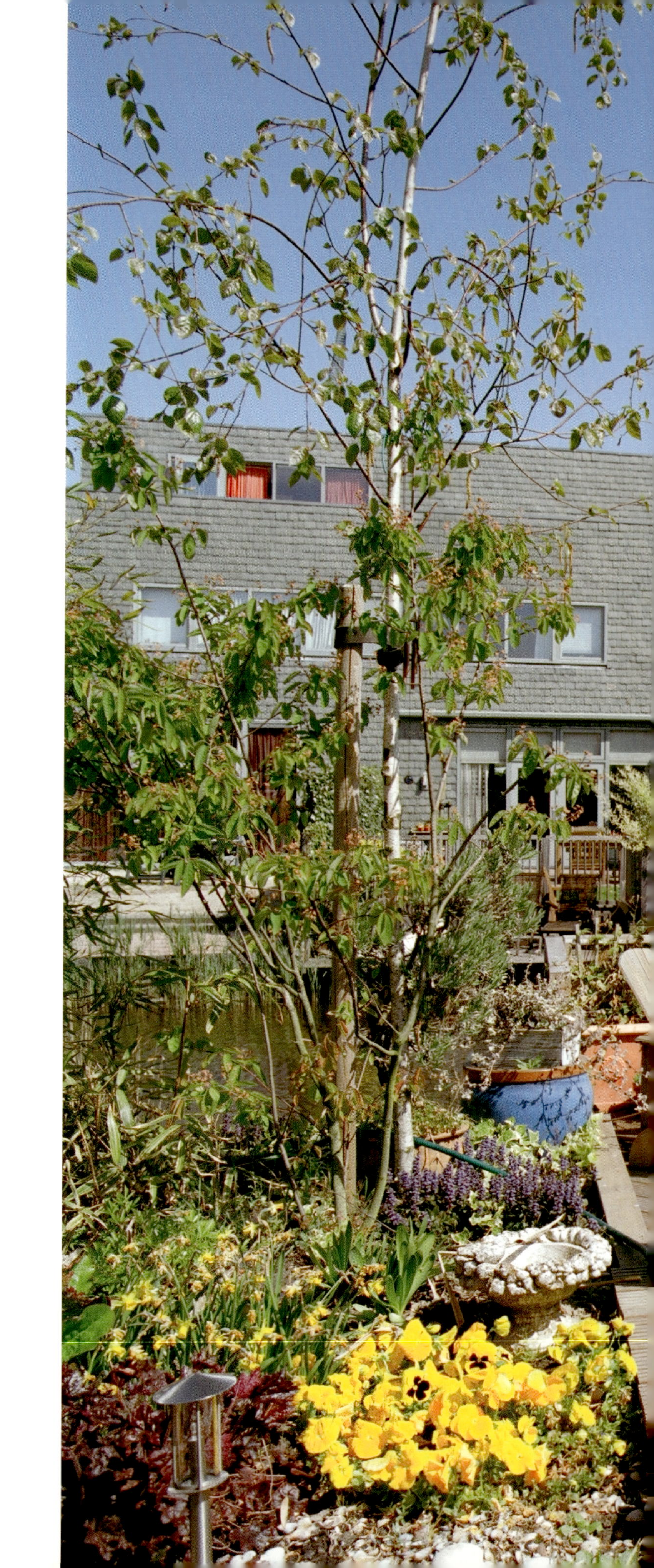

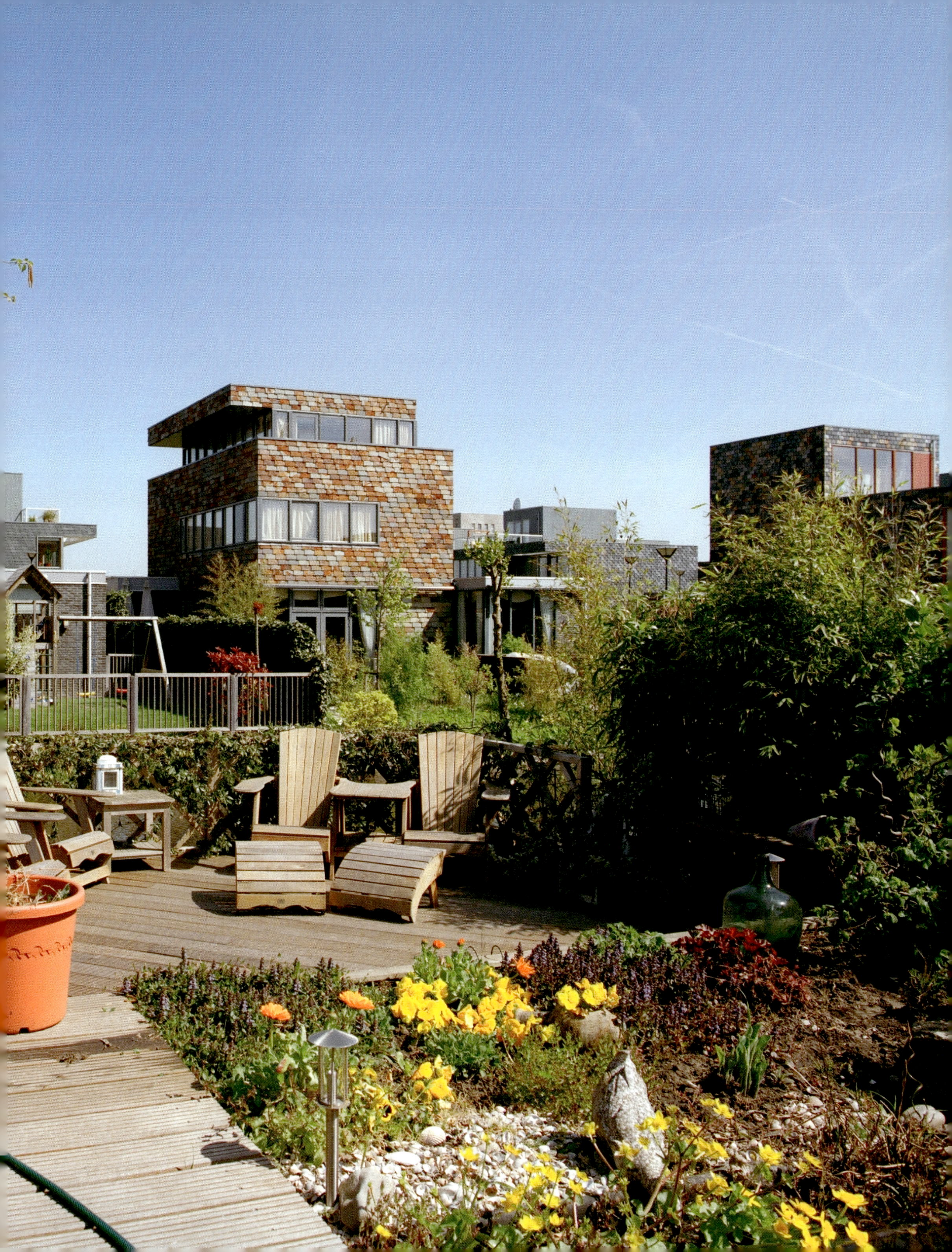

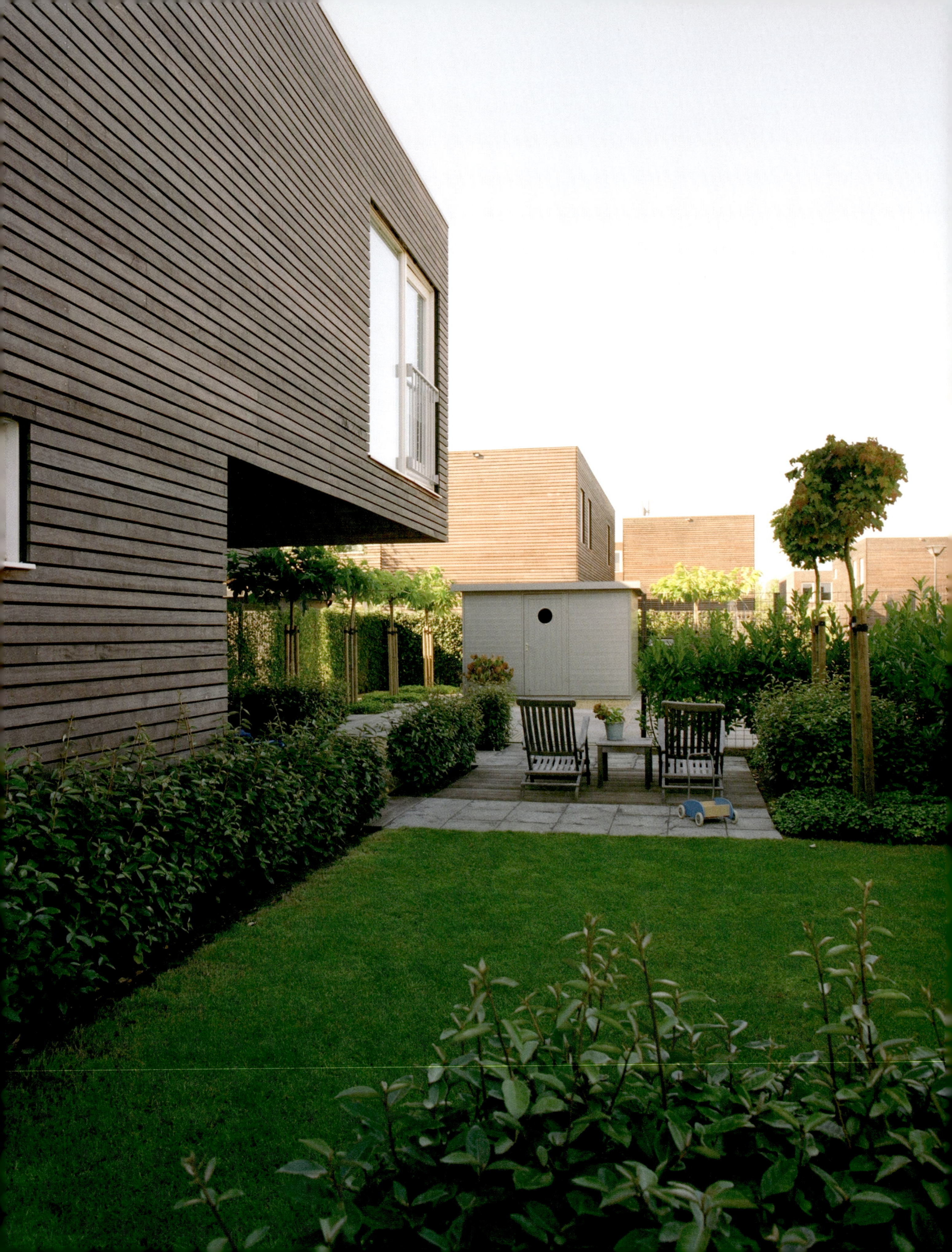

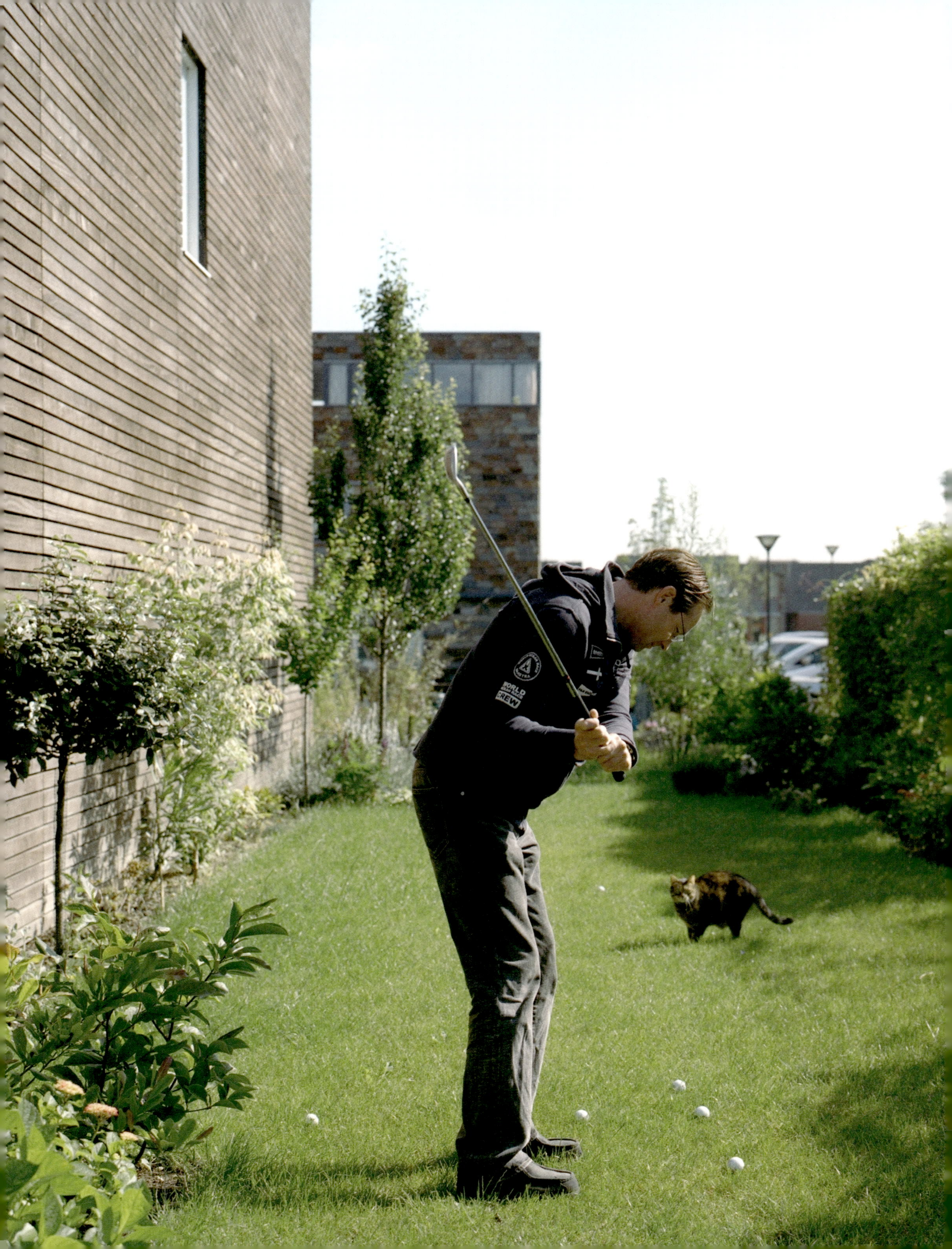

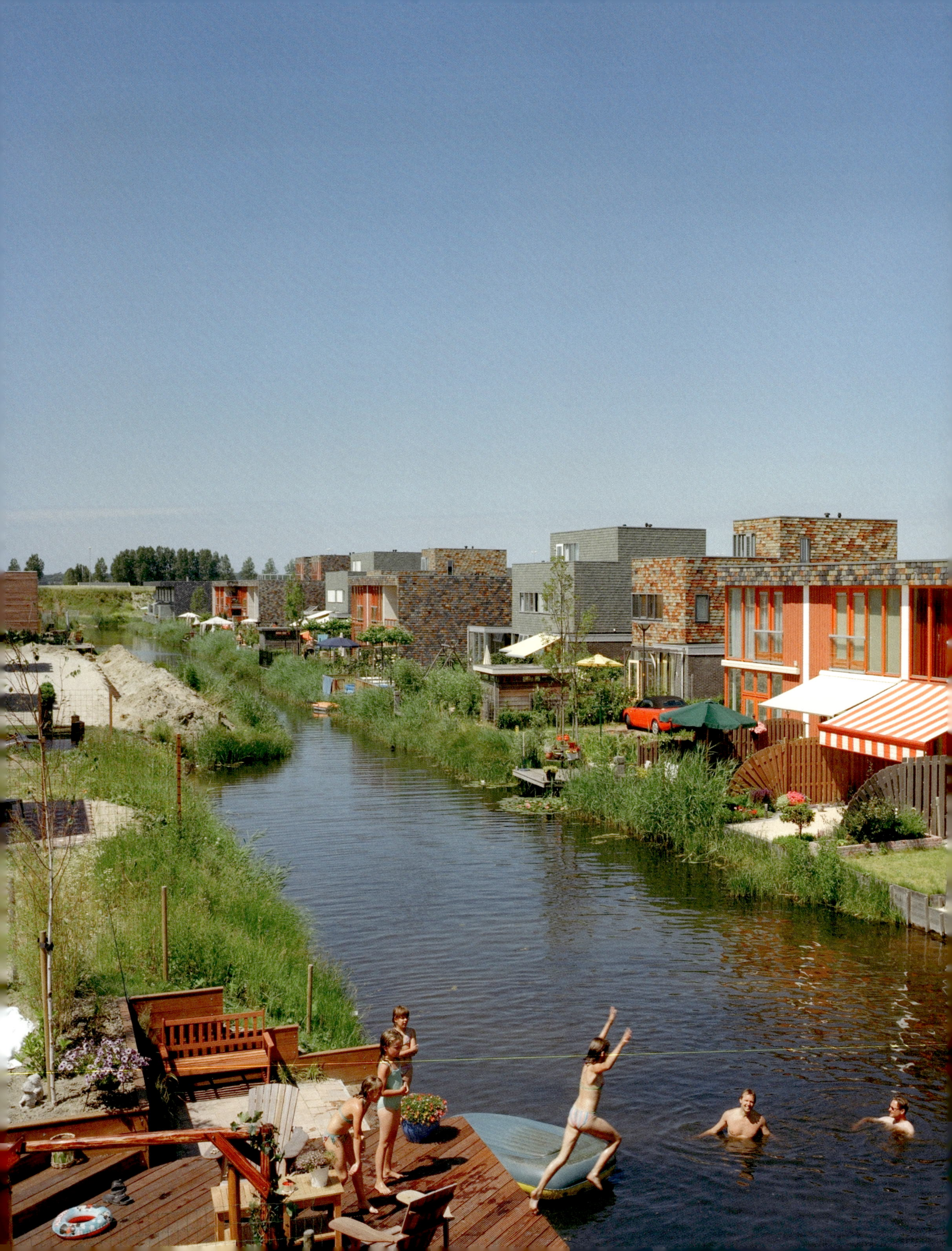

6

In the spring of 2007, the island is finished. The duplexes are the last to be completed. After that, the municipality begins landscaping the green. Nearly 300 silver maples have been planted. Delay has done them no harm: for a few years, they were able to keep on growing at a nursery. Now we have a veritable forest.

Looking back, architect Maartje Lammers says that the development of Eiland 7 'has been a monstrous process.' Her firm, 24H architecture, came into that process at a late stage. It aimed to adapt what it considered weak points in the urban-developmental plan. But a 'gentlemen's agreement' had already been made previously, and new arguments no longer had relevance. 'After all those years, everyone was beaten to a pulp; and the result shows it,' says Maartje Lammers. She mentions the organization of public space, the execution of the original plan and the enforcement of rules. 'You could say there was little backbone here; nobody dared to make choices.'

Ben Kuipers, the landscape architect responsible for the 'village green,' says that the placement of every component in the residential area, such as sheds and fences, should have been included in the plan from the start. He is not in favor of drawing up the plan first and *then* telling the residents how to do things – so that they fit into the plan. That isn't realistic in his view. 'Design the options, such as the added levels and extensions. Then it becomes complicated to do things differently; now it's complicated to do it right. The architect has been too concerned with aesthetic purity; everyday use thus becomes subordinate to this. As an architect, you have to examine those kinds of things.' He points out the garage as an example of this: a car can fit into it, but there's no extra room for a bicycle. 'So what happens then? The bike ends up in the garage, and the car gets left out on the street somewhere.'

Albert Groothuizen, project developer during the redevelopment of Eiland 7, was no longer closely involved in the final stage of the process. He remarks that the situation was unusual, due to the fact that the architect also happened to be the urban planner. The idea of having a village green came from Bjarne Mastenbroek as well. 'The project developer grants the assignment for the creation of an urban-developmental concept; the urban planner produces the design, and the municipality should carry out the planning of public space. Here an unclear situation arose, because the question was: who, in fact, has given Mastenbroek the assignment? We granted the assignment; we told the municipality that this was the concept. It eventually became a kind of 'double pass' situation, where Mastenbroek ended up being sidelined.'

Not only do responsibilities become unclear and subject to change over such a lengthy period. There are a few definite boundaries that form a barrier to new insights or necessary adjustments. The sacred all-inclusive selling price is one of them. 'You can't go a penny over this amount,' says Ben Kuipers. Everything is stripped from the design in order to remain under this price. Driveways and property partitions could be put in right away, for instance. That might add 1,000 euros to the price. Then it gets done. But this is often out of the question due to the rigid system of the all-inclusive price.' Kuipers refers again to the parking spaces that were situated in the back as a result of redeveloping homes on the north side of the green. Something like this should have been part of the design and its execution, but every component was subject to cutbacks. 'AM Wonen says that they couldn't afford to do that, and evidently this became accepted during the negotiation process. Now the shabby result of pine fences has determined the look of the residential park.'

According to Rik Bolderheij, the last *Vinex* program director for the Haarlemmermeer, it hardly makes any difference whether someone has a mortgage of 230,000 or 235,000 euros. From that point of view, the municipality or project developer could indeed design and carry out components such as fences and parking spaces. As it stands now, the project developer clings to his established price, and the municipality says: 'but then we won't pay for that hedge in front or, as with Eiland 7, those parking spaces behind the houses.'

Rik Bolderheij argues for greater flexibility among project developers, but also on the part of municipalities: 'If the selling price could have been a fraction higher, and the municipality wouldn't be greedy with its quote on the land – by not allowing the profit from land to rise along with everything else – then, where Eiland 7 is concerned, the municipality could have put in fences and parking spaces. Control and maintenance could then have been handed over to the residents. That would have raised the quality. You need that kind of freedom. But when you do that, you deviate from the policy with regard to land pricing. And that means going back to the town council for permission.'

In Mastenbroek's opinion, there isn't a great deal of mutual trust to be found among the parties involved in construction in the Netherlands. 'The municipality doesn't trust the project developer and says: this is the deal, this is the price you quoted us. That leaves little leeway for the project developer.' And conversely, the project developer has no trust in the municipality. Everything gets nailed to agreements. According to Mastenbroek, there is no collaboration in terms of spirit, only according to the 'dollars and cents' of an agreement.

That sounds very plausible. A municipality has its interests at stake in getting the highest (all-inclusive) selling price possible, since that yields the highest profit from the sale of the land. And those proceeds are, in turn, needed in order to balance the municipal budget. The project developer also has an interest in getting the highest selling price. That yields greater profit. At the start of the process, therefore, the interests of the project developers and the municipalities are the same. Later on interests begin to conflict, since the profit of one party happens to be earned at the expense of the other.

Bjarne Mastenbroek believes that the money goes everywhere except into the construction material. 'There's money involved in the construction costs, in the costs of the entire plan and in the time that we take to carry it out. In the Netherlands we spend seven to nine years on formulating the plan. Three years would be enough. Do you think that difference of six years doesn't cost anything?' Rik Bolderheij also thinks that it should be possible to finalize the idea within three years, but that it won't happen due to a lack of trust between the developer and the municipality. Building that trust takes time.

Aside from a lack of trust, the lack of expertise and memory also play a significant role in the length of the process. That pertains to both municipality and developer. The municipality hardly has any experts on its staff. 'When there is an intensive period of building, as with the *Vinex* projects, many temporary people are hired. They stay for about six months and then move on to another job. Memory no longer plays a role,' says Rik Bolderheij. Changing players in the middle of the game leads to a loss in quality, certainly where such an out-of-the-ordinary plan as Eiland 7 is concerned. 'A new person shows up and simply says, 'Well, now I'm the boss and we're going to do things this way, even if that wasn't the original idea,' tells Mastenbroek, among the few who underwent the entire process of building Eiland 7.

Ron Blomaard, project developer at AM Wonen, oversaw the final phase of Eiland 7 after its redevelopment by Albert Groothuizen. As he sees it, such an unusual plan requires a special approach from the start. 'This urban-planning concept could have been carried out successfully if it had been developed in its entirety, all at once. With adequate care and means for the landscaping of public space. But the money ran out, and you can see that.'

Rik Bolderheij says that, at the project office, there had never been much awareness as to the plan's vulnerability. The total plan consisted of 12 different islands, each with its own distinct style, from traditional to modern. It was expected that buyers would deliberately opt for the Eiland 7 concept, and that led to the assumption that 'the design's integrity wouldn't have to be upheld.'

A general kind of zoning plan took shape during the construction. According to Bolderheij, that has advantages. Nothing had been arranged in that respect for Eiland 7, except for the stipulation that 'gutter height' could be no higher than 9 m. 'Only once everything has been built can a definitive zoning plan be drawn up, and then it can be maintained,' comments Bolderheij in defense of the usual procedure. Creating a zoning plan for each island would not have been very convenient in his view. It was the moment when the entire *Vinex* project was finished that everyone awaited. For Eiland 7, that meant delaying the definitive zoning plan until three years after the first houses were finished. Rather late for a project that was so deviant and thereby so vulnerable. 'The consequent loss in terms of quality could be discussed here at the town hall at some point,' admits Bolderheij. As of 2001, the political decree advocating 'fewer rules' went into effect. Now that the consequences of that outlook have become evident, the municipality has reversed its policy.

Fred Kaaij, the city architect, was proud of the original plan. The homes and layout conceived by Mastenbroek were breathtakingly beautiful. 'But in our euphoria we never carried out a risk analysis. If you look at the way some residents are now dealing with this vulnerable design by putting up sheds and fences everywhere, you could say that we never actually envisaged the consequences of experiments – and we should blame ourselves for that,' says Kaaij. 'It's okay to experiment, but then the plan has to be guided intensively and maintained intensively. Doing that is relatively difficult in a municipality like this one, where a great deal of building is going on. Being naive, I thought this was such a specific kind of island – only people who read the [highbrow newspaper] *NRC Handelsblad* would be buying here. And that they would treat it with respect.'

Landscape architect Ben Kuipers believes that there has been some misunderstanding. In this housing market, people don't buy because of the concept, but because they can afford it. The concept is basically just part of the package. 'And that's how you get a painted roof tile against the exterior wall. No amount of aesthetic regulation can stop that.'

One afternoon I wait for the newspaper boy and ask him how many households on the island are subscribed to the *NRC Handelsblad*. 'Five.'

The painted roof tile on the exterior wall hasn't really damaged the appearance of the island. But the rampant proliferation of wooden fences, storage sheds and random parking spaces *have* done that. Along the edges of the island, one resident has made large concrete extension that is visible from the main road. This has changed the face of the island.

Every request for a building permit must be submitted to the external-appearance committee for approval. Minor alterations require no approval or permit and are thereby not eligible for a permit request. Many residents found that the 'understated' property partitions put up by the project developer provided too little privacy. These were replaced with high fences. That's not allowed, it says so in the regulations. But who's going to enforce them?

The institution of the 'external appearance committee,' formerly referred to as the 'beautification committee' has been in existence for some 100 years in the Netherlands. Such committees advise town authorities on the outward appearances of building plans. Maartje Lammers is not only employed as an architect on Eiland 7; she also heads this committee for the municipality Haarlemmermeer. 'There's little you can do to prevent damage to these vulnerable types of designs. The committee isn't concerned with whether something is beautiful or ugly, but with deciding whether a change or an addition is acceptable in terms of external appearance. That means looking at whether a design fits in its surroundings and, secondly, whether the design is consistent,' explains Lammers. Eiland 7 is a special situation. 'Generally speaking, what people build in their gardens does not require a permit.'

The idea is that the garden, traditionally situated behind the house in the Netherlands, should give the inhabitant a great sense of freedom. But as the lots of Eiland 7 have been planned, the garden lies not behind the house, but often in front of it or along the street – except with homes situated along the water.

'It's a nail in my coffin,' sighs Mastenbroek on entering our house after surveying the island in the spring of 2007. 'I could protest,' he says with regard to all the extra levels and additions, 'but I've got no chance. Whatever I say, it's pointless.'

With regard to the part of the island owned by the housing corporation, the problem of vulnerability plays a more minor role. As the leasing agent for 30 percent of the homes on Eiland 7, Ymere has an outlook on the freedom of its tenants. 'We want storage areas, we want property partitions and we want balconies. These are standard demands of ours. We don't leave much to the residents. Owners have a bond with the house, but renters frequently haven't made any specific choice for a home. They're on a waiting list and, all at once, they're allowed to come look at a place,' says Betty Oderkerk, at

Ymere. 'We've often owned and maintained housing complexes for 50 years or more. That's why we take an increasing interest in the residential environment. We develop schools, and we get involved in parking management. Those are the lessons we've learned from urban innovation, which we apply to newly developed neighborhoods. It contributes to the enjoyment of a home, and it helps to develop the value of our property.'

It is also easier for a housing corporation to address residents. A lease makes that simple. 'Anything can be put into a deed of purchase, but who's going to uphold it? The municipality has to do that, but usually it doesn't. When government starts taking a backseat, the rules of the game need to be clearly established beforehand – just as on a camping ground,' explains Betty Oderkerk.

Maartje Lammers believes that the architect's position becomes marginalized by the project developers. But this is partly their own fault. They produce a design sketch and avoid a deeper investigation of the tentative and definitive designs. 'If it suits him, the project developer will toss the architect's design in the bin,' says Lammers. 'Project developers say that architects produce lousy drawings. As far as that goes, there is indeed a gap between the actual practice and the professional training programs.' According to Bjarne Mastenbroek, architects aren't given the opportunity to produce detailed drawings. All of that is contracted out; architects do only a design sketch. Mastenbroek would like to see legislation requiring an enforcement of the architect's supervision with requests for construction permits. 'One person draws A; the other calculates B; the third grants the assignment for C; and the builder constructs D. How can it ever amount to anything like that? An architect has to be made responsible for the entire building. As things stand now, everyone walks off before the project is even finished. Where are good buildings being built? In Switzerland, Germany or Denmark. That's where architects are given full responsibility for controlling the entire construction process, from start to finish. No wonder,' he concludes, 'any Dutch architect with a big reputation gets pushed out of the market and opts to work abroad.'

Rien de Ruiter, the architect who came up with the idea of having 12 islands and who designed one of them, believes that architects are beginning to seem unnecessary with housing construction. 'You're allowed to design a façade with a few windows in it. There is a tendency toward mediocrity in housing architecture. This is how things are in the Netherlands. I never get to meet a resident, only the salesmen: it's all business.'

A great deal of quality could be gained, believes Maartje Lammers, if builders would be allowed to make a bit of profit. When that isn't the case, they start cutting back on all sorts of components during the construction process. Endless discussions are held about how many nails will be used in the walls of a timber-frame home: one or two nails per meter? With 80 houses, that can amount to a quite a difference in cost.

Many complaints concern the quality offered by builders. 'A lot of mistakes are made, but on the other hand, the builder isn't given the time to finish something properly,' says Mastenbroek. 'A construction worker gets 20 minutes to install a window or door frame. He hauls that thing off the pallet, whips it in, and if it doesn't fit right away or he spends a half hour on it, then he gets hell from the foreman.' They all put each other through the mill, and that has to do with the price development of the land and the municipal "skimming" of profit,' Mastenbroek continues. 'The part of the (all-inclusive) selling price used for construction costs shrinks in relative terms, while the cost of material and wages goes up: so things get tight. The money goes into the cost of land, interest and planning.'

And the earnings? In this plan the municipality's income was guaranteed. The redevelopment, of course, brought some delay with regard to land proceeds, but that was compensated by earned interest. And perhaps a few (all-inclusive) selling prices were lowered, but presumably these were negligible. The project developer took a far greater risk. Ron Blomaard, the successor to Groothuizen at AM Wonen: 'If a project isn't selling, all eyes are focused on you. It became a disaster for us. But we were able to set things straight by developing the rest of the island.' By having success with the duplexes, in other words, and due to a recovering housing market.

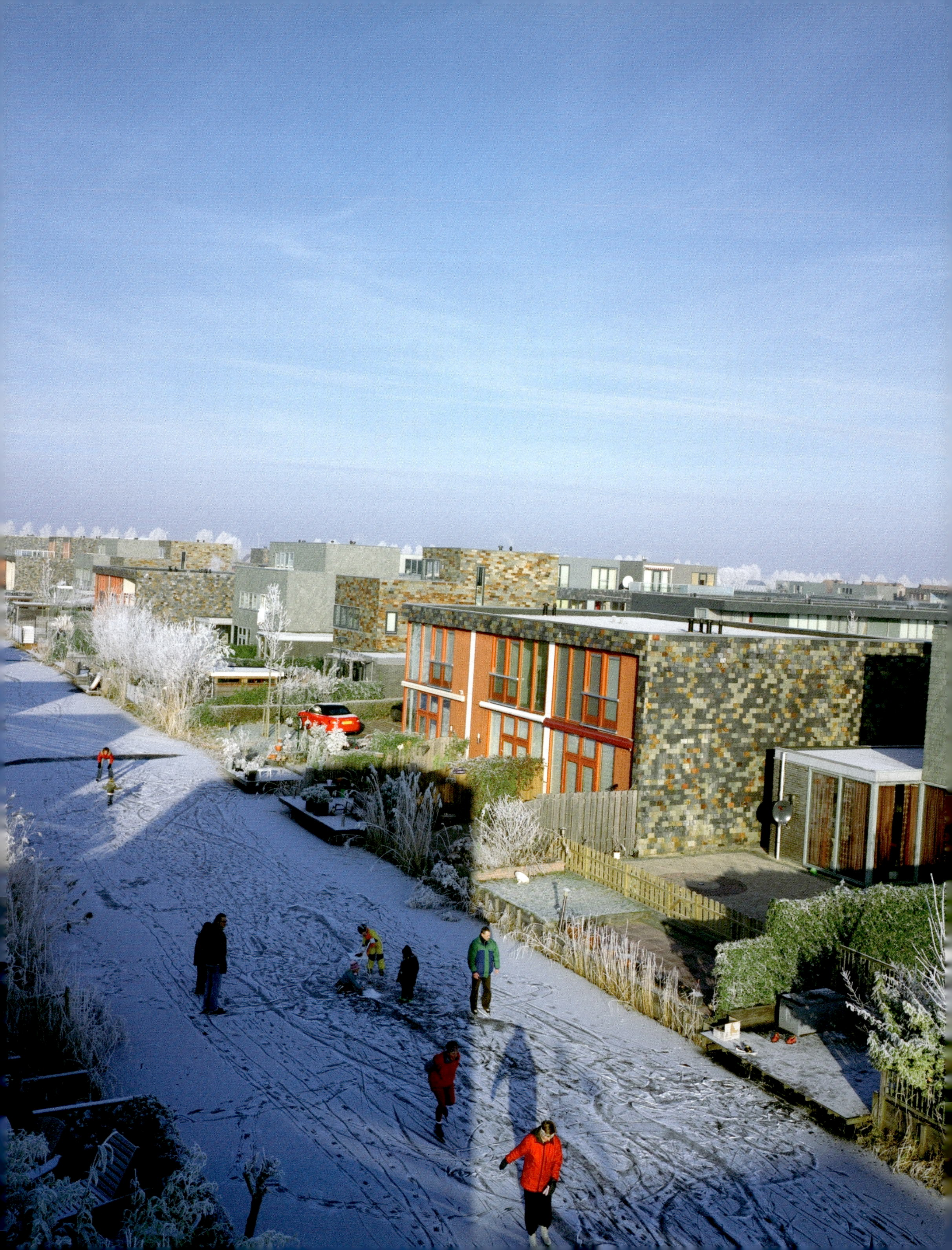

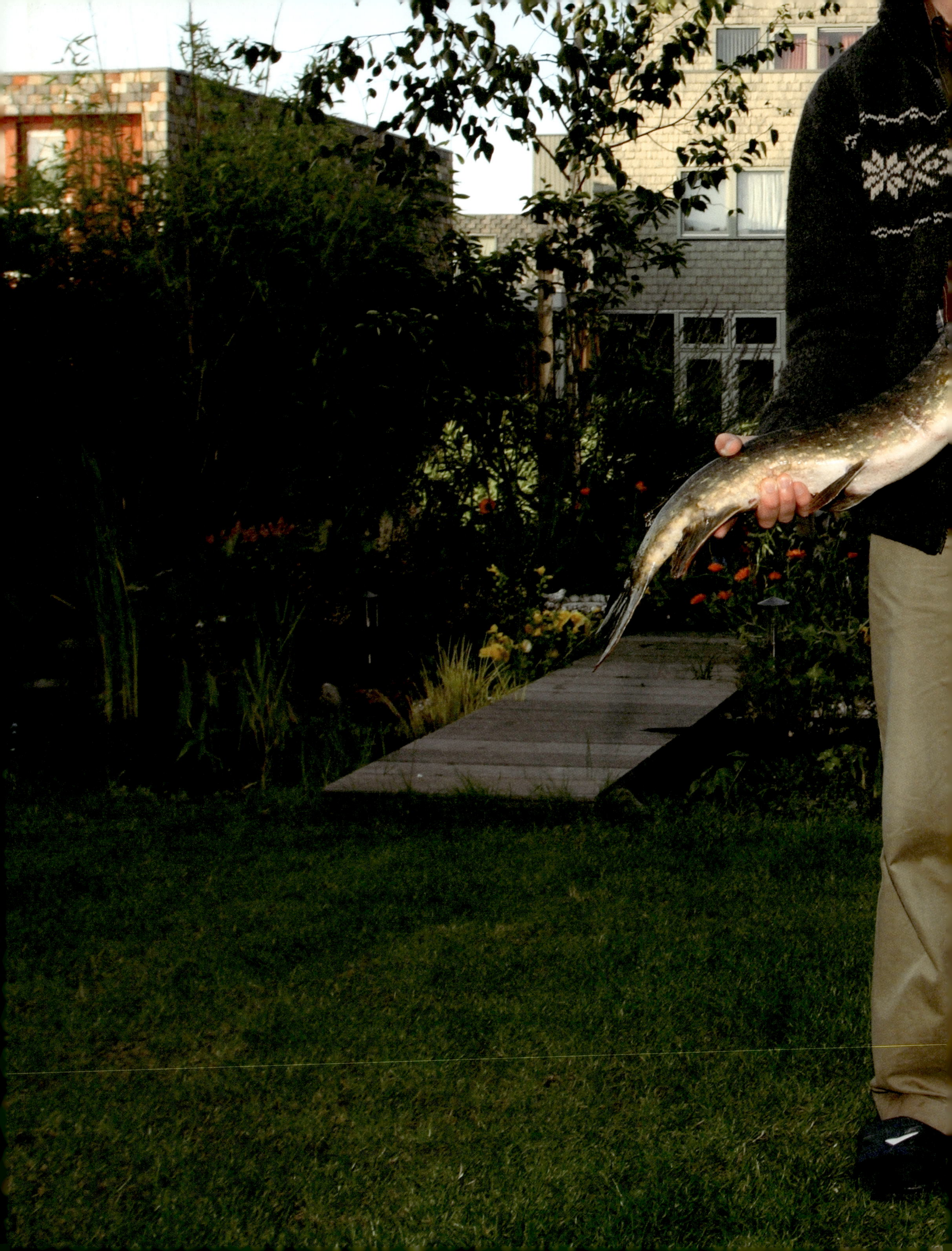

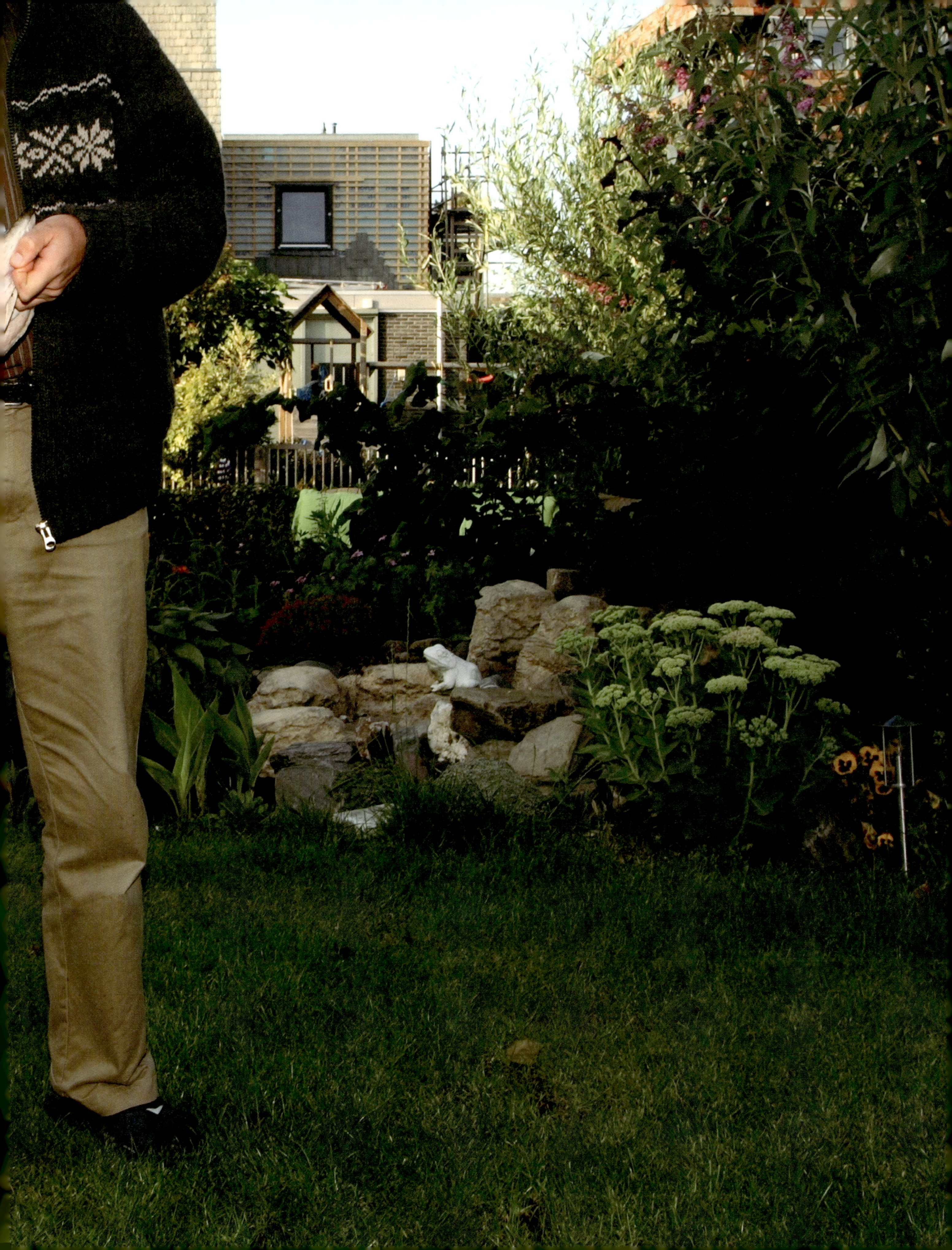

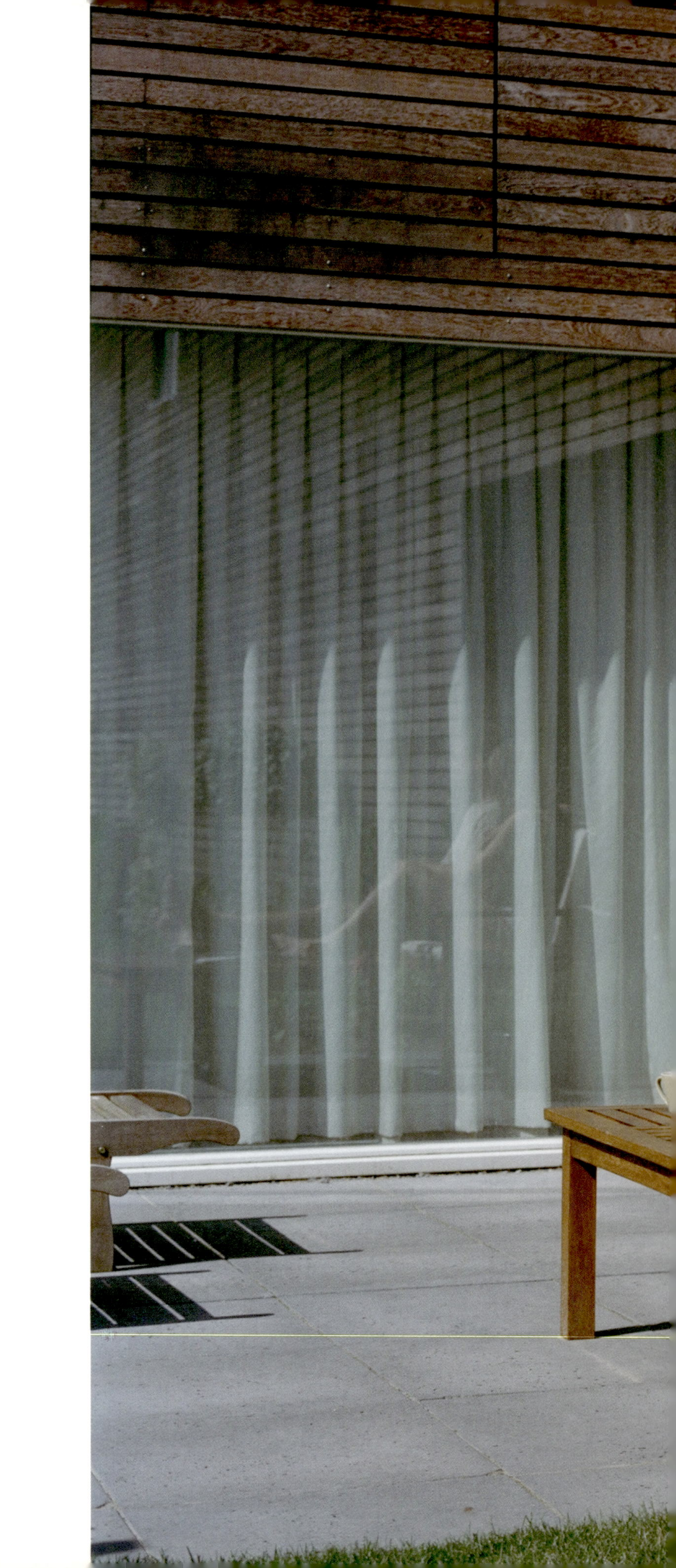

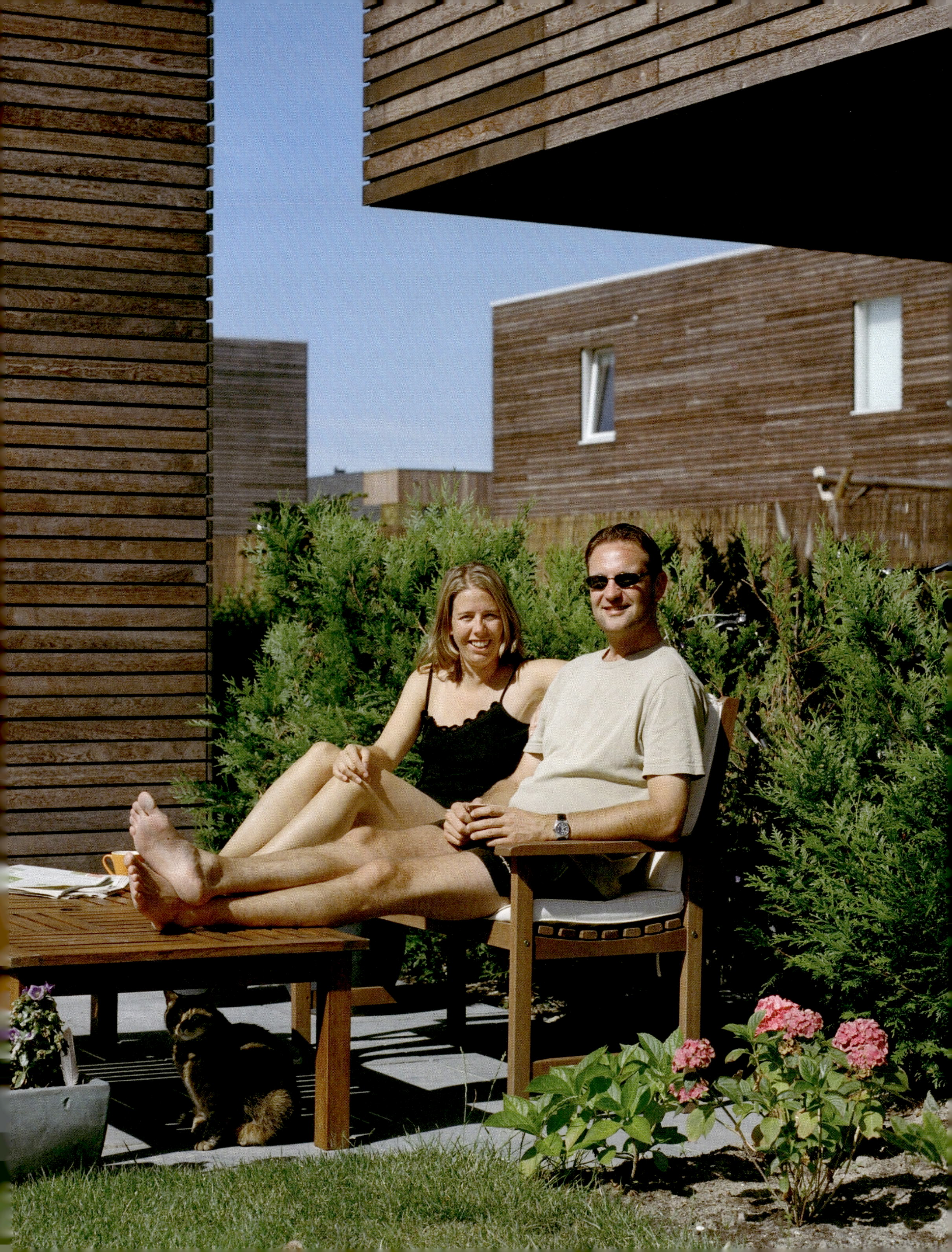

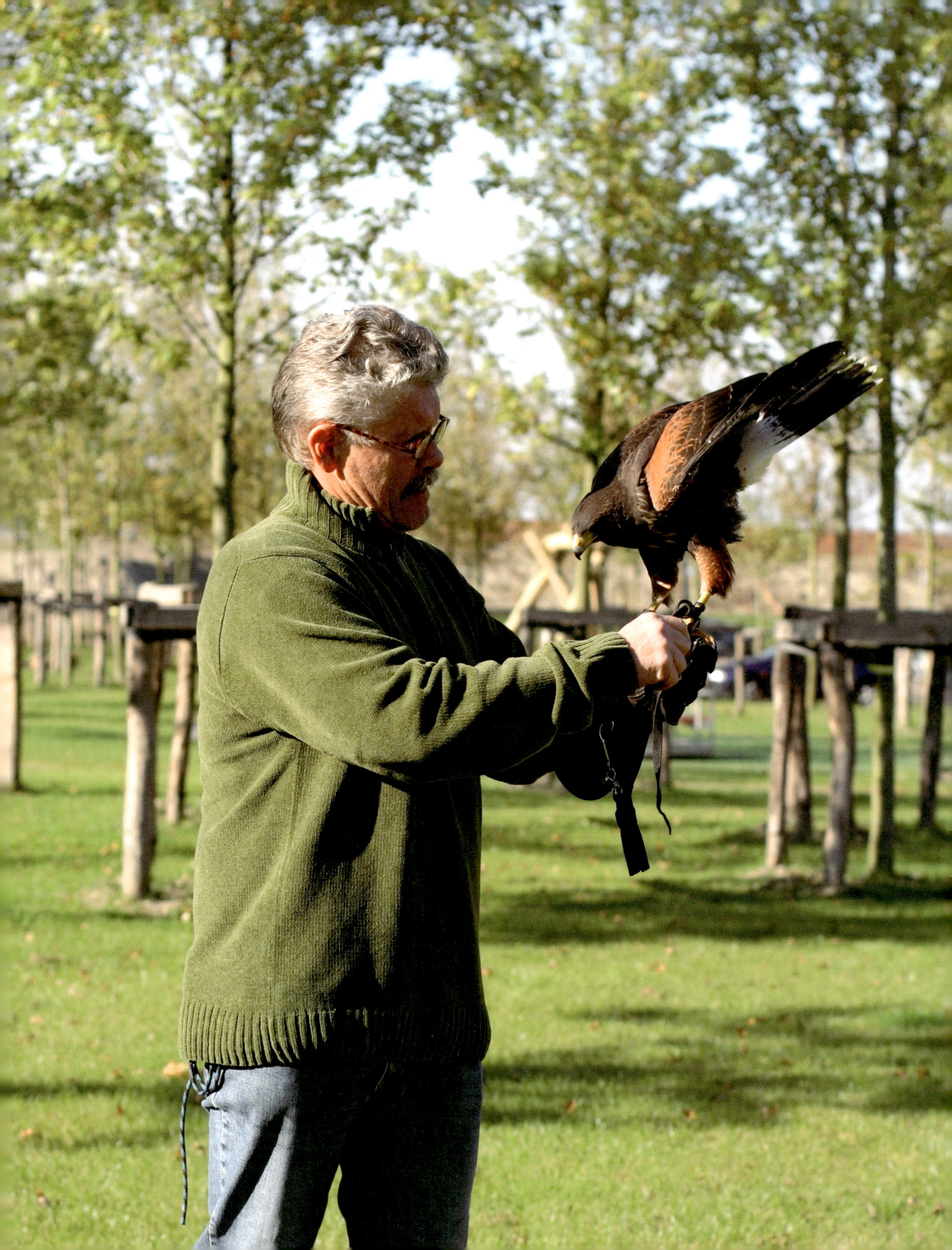

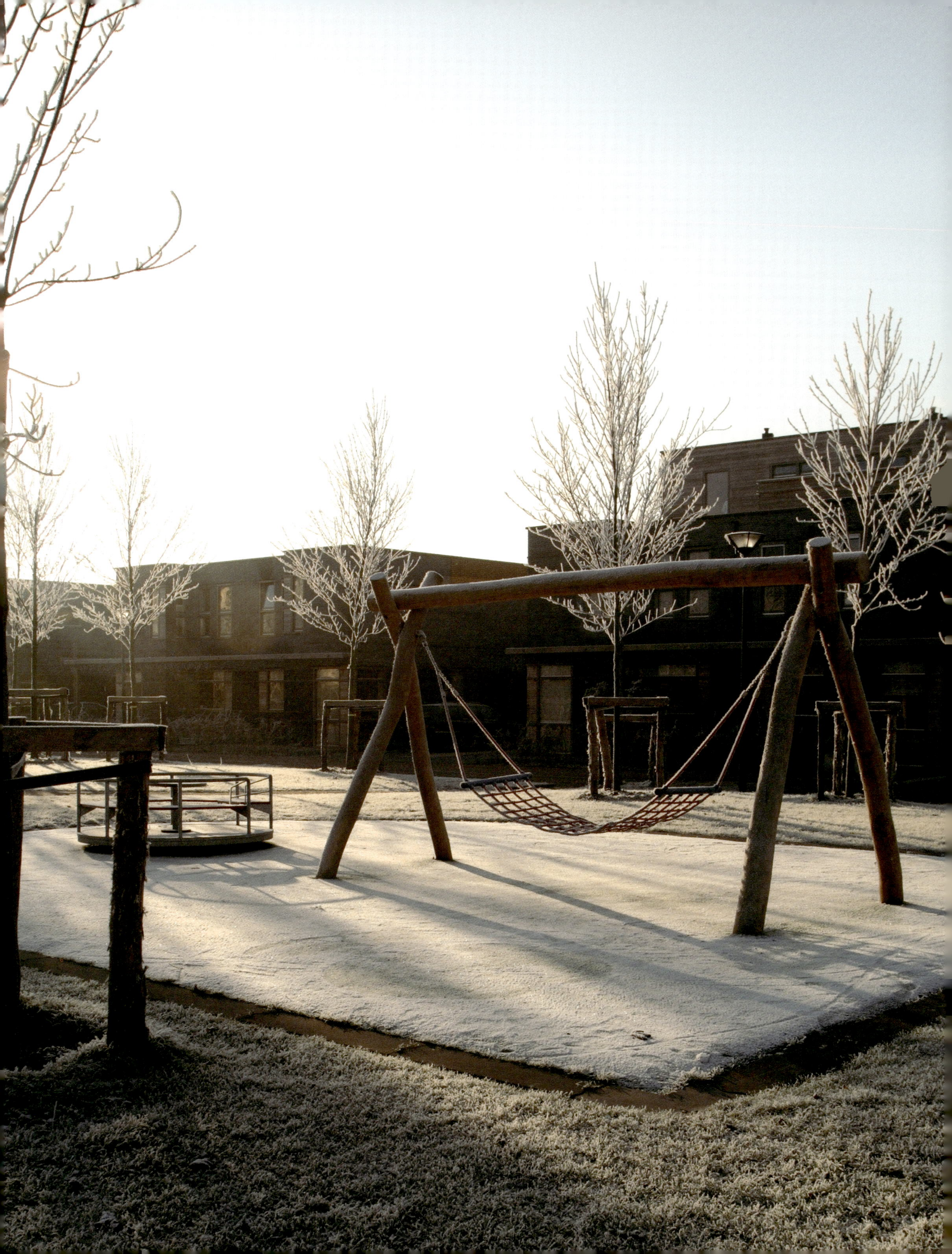

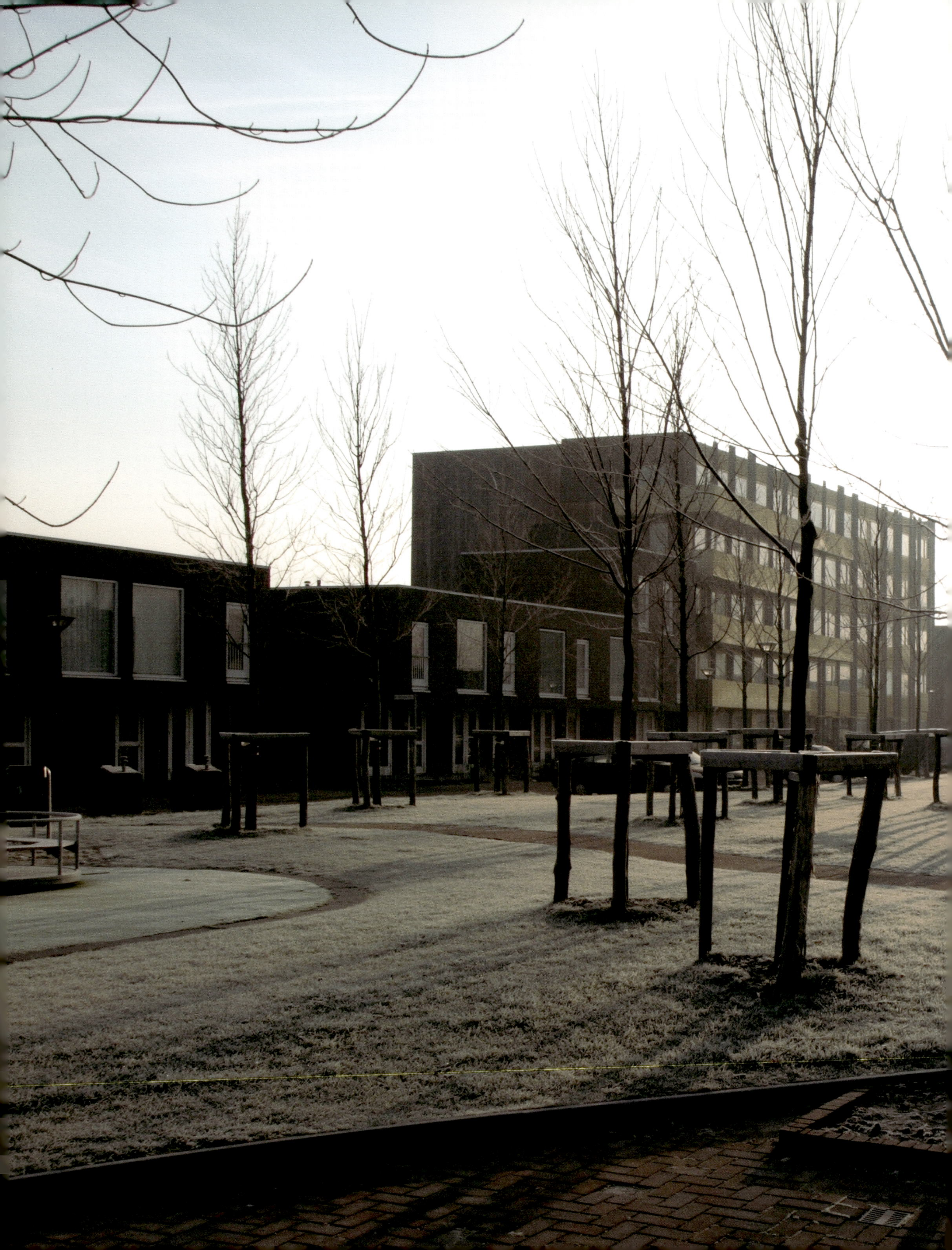

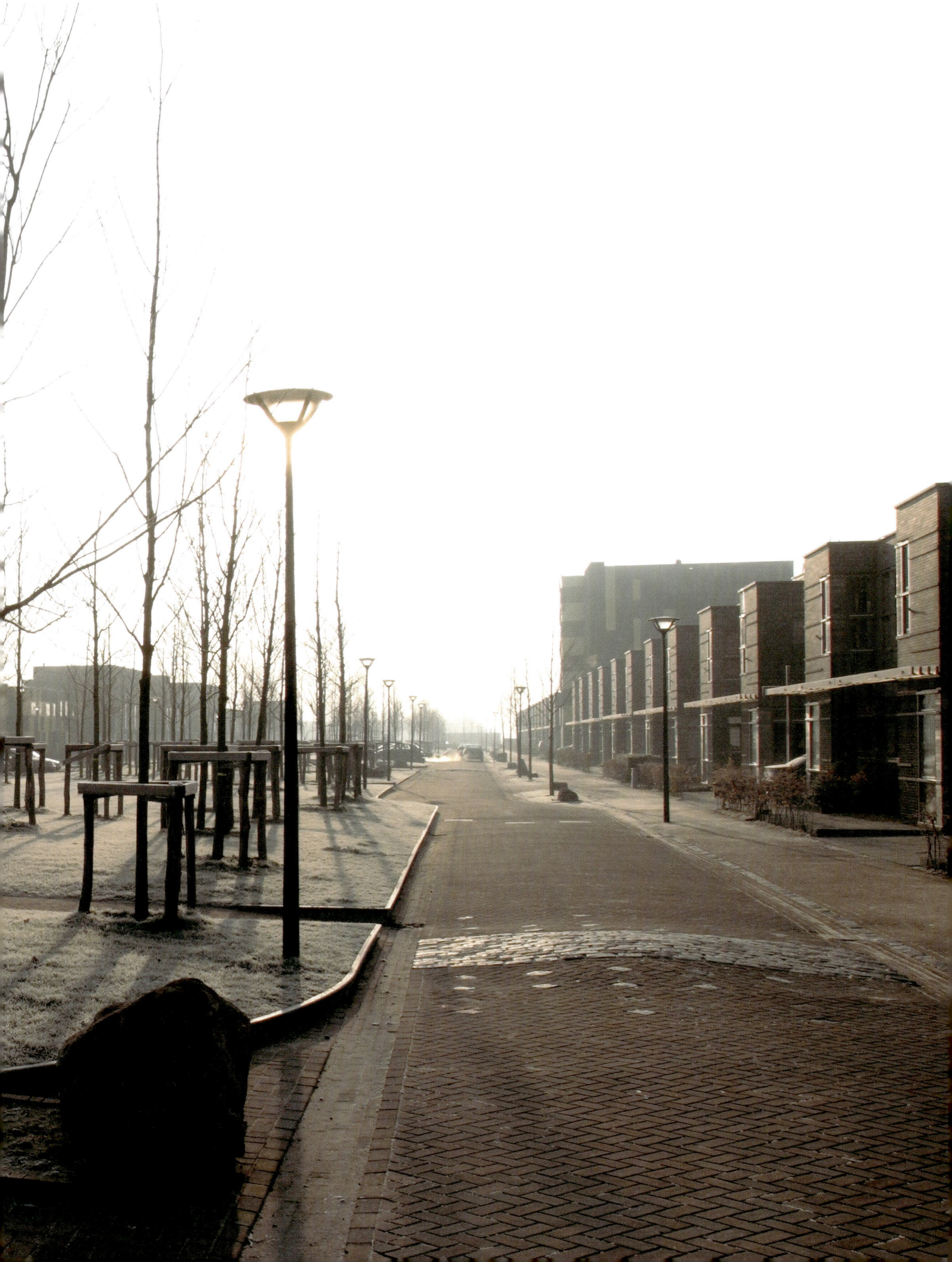

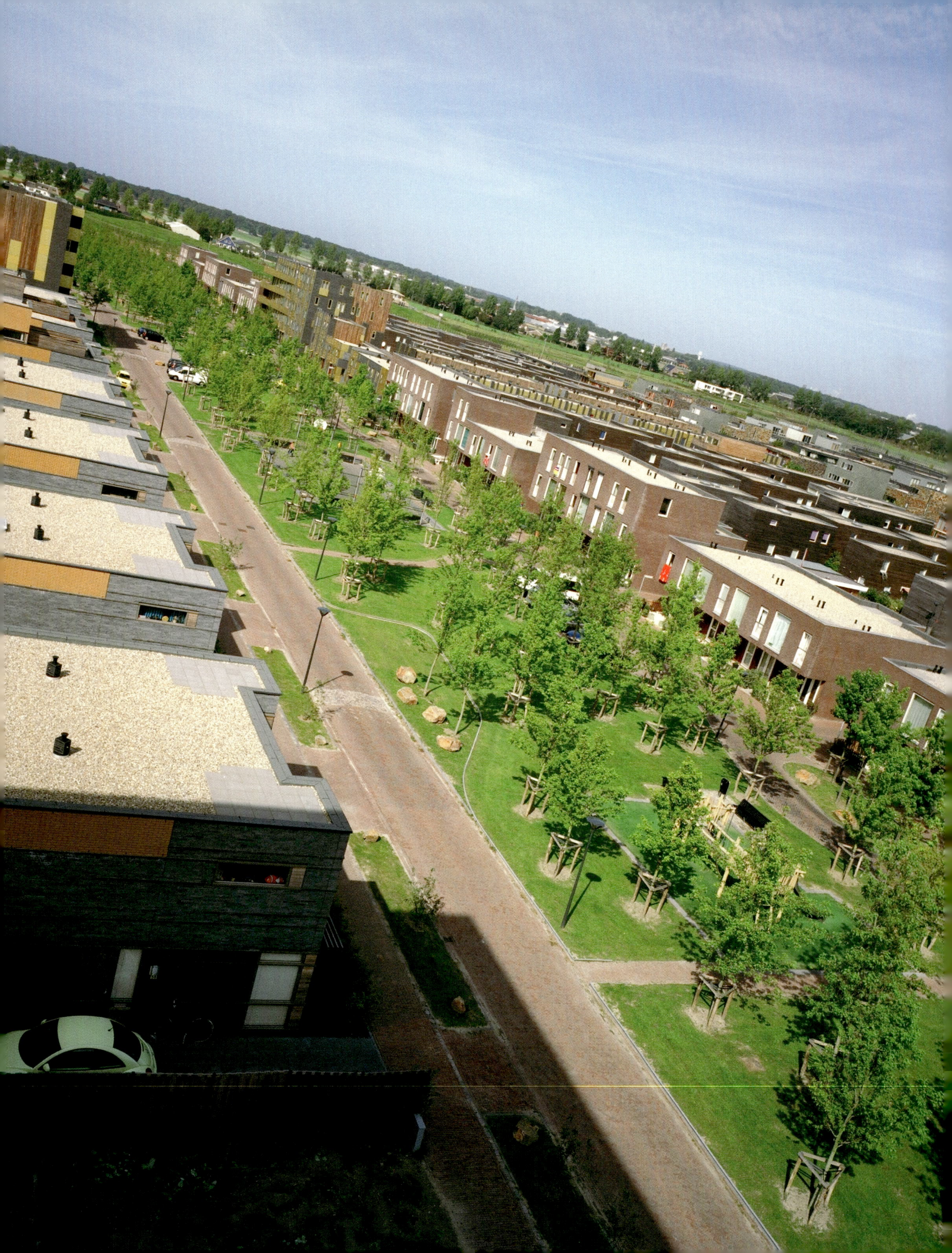

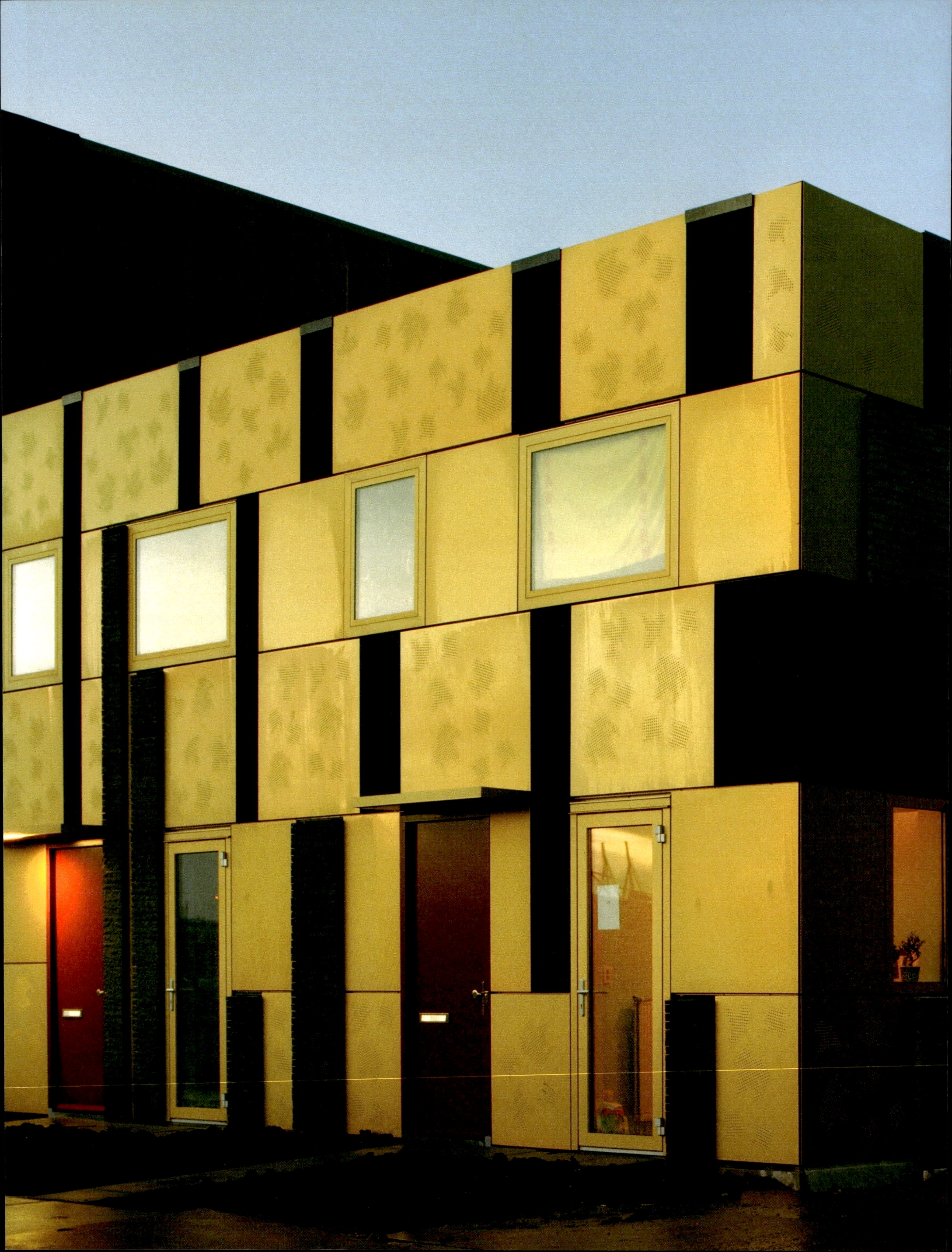

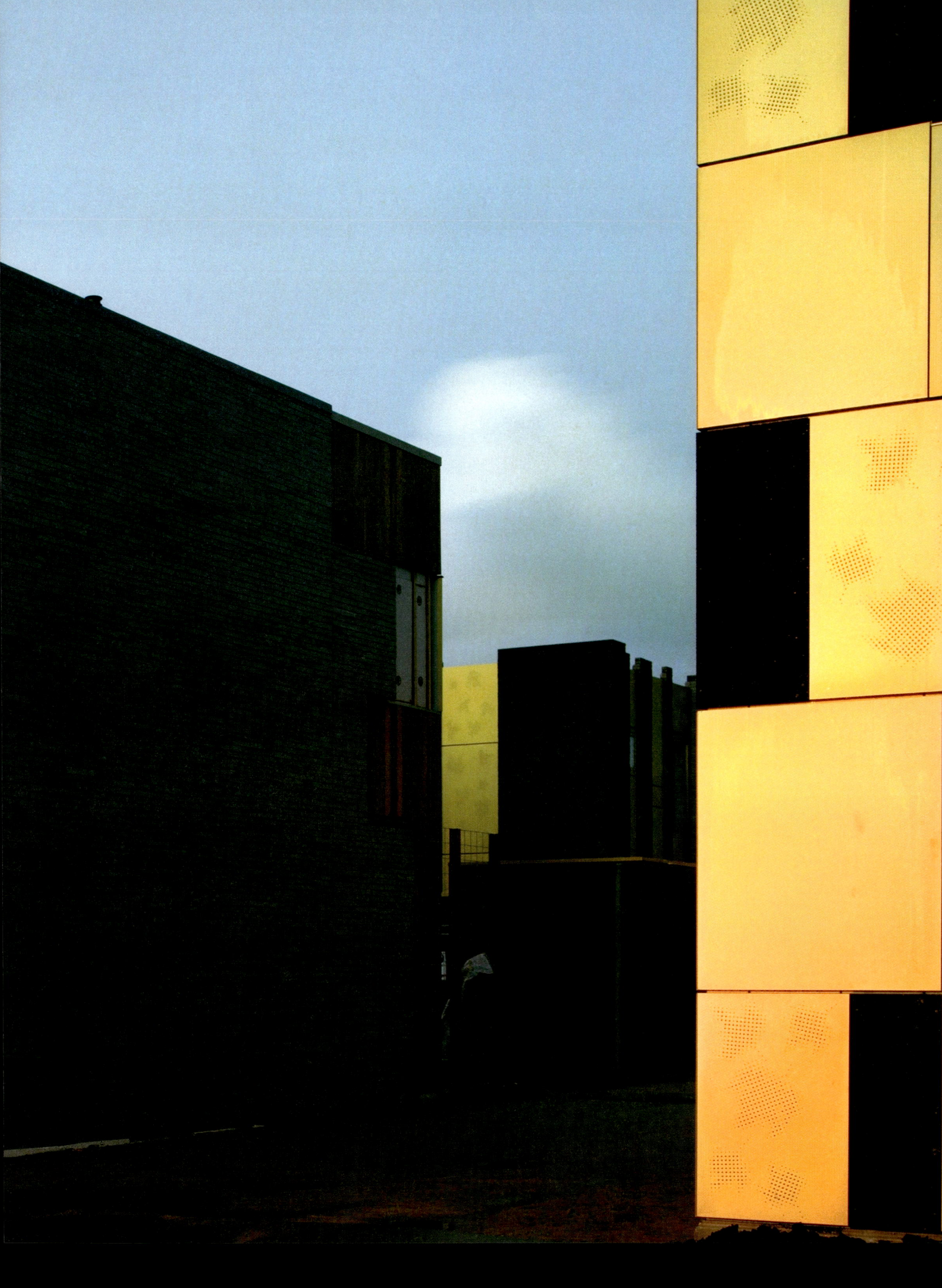

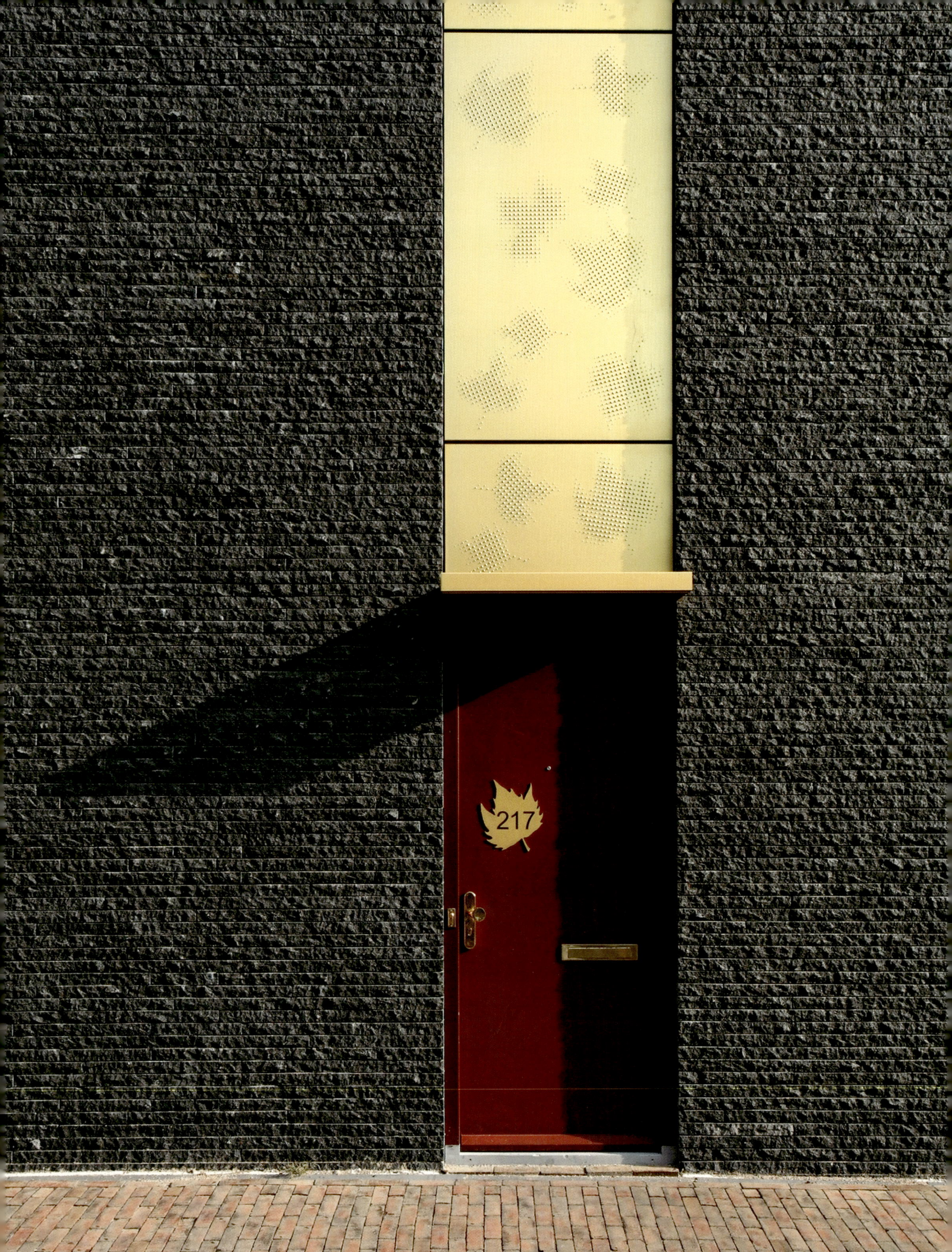
217

How is the value of houses on this island developing? Not a minor issue for those who participate in the pyramid scheme known as the housing market. I make an appointment with Philip de Weerd at the realty firm Schoeman in Hoofddorp. He was granted the assignment of selling part of the newly built homes for the project developer. Sales were down at the time. But the factors involved in the development of the island that led to a slow-down in sales – unusual lots and unusual architecture – no longer play a role. 'We've made up for the dip by now, and prices are consistent with the houses on other islands,' says realtor De Weerd. 'It's remarkable, almost astonishing, to see how well resales are going. The homes now going up for sale are gone like that.' That is to say, the smaller homes up to 100 m²; larger ones haven't been sold yet. A small home, for which the initial buyers paid 200,000 euros and to which they added a level, is now selling for 335,000 euros exclusive of legal costs (which are about 10 percent of the selling price and consist of sales tax as well as notary and sale costs).

The municipality is satisfied, since an anti-speculation condition applies to the smaller inexpensive homes. For the first seven years, the profit is skimmed by the municipality. The idea behind this is that the municipality made a lower (all-inclusive) selling price possible due to a lower land price, thus making some of the homes affordable to buyers with a limited budget. If at all possible, the municipality wants to earn back its subsidy. But who has actually paid for that subsidy? Mainly the buyers of the more expensive homes. With our home's land price alone, we contributed 19,152 euros toward the deficit on the low-income and less expensive homes. The so-called inexpensive homes are resold according to the market. The profit is skimmed by the municipality, by which it profits once again from a rising housing market.

As soon as the seven year term following the completion of the homes has come to an end, a great many 'for sale' signs will be appearing in front yards.

Despite the difficult, yes even painful creative process, there is a striking appreciation of the final result. 'Eiland 7 is, among its kind, one of the better

Vinex neighborhoods,' remarks Maartje Lammers.

The urban plan is durable, says landscape architect Ben Kuipers. 'The houses are almost abstract. You can see that a few people are doing something with that. If they build a shed, then they do it with the material of the house. That's nice to see.'

Urban architect Fred Kaaij looks at the whole of the *Vinex* neighborhood, Floriande, and says that half of the islands have worked out well and the other half not. As far as Eiland 7 is concerned, it's a shame that the original plan wasn't carried out. 'The result is certainly not a reflection of the effort that went into it,' says Kaaij. 'But you could say that Bjarne Mastenbroek's urban plan remained intact with its realization. Residents will be living around a woods one day. It could turn into the most beautiful island of them all.'

Eiland 7, De Muy
Rhea (27), project manager
Gert (40) journalist

Rhea:

I moved in with Gert a few months after his divorce. But both of us wanted to leave that house. It was too big, too bogged down with memories. While looking around for a new place, we drove onto this island. It was still a construction site. The weather was beautiful; things seemed idyllic, like a vacation village. We loved the architecture. There was a house for sale in this hip little street. We knew the original selling price was 199,500 euros. When we heard they were asking 234,500 we thought: this should be fun! Our first offer of 229,500 (plus legal costs) was, to our surprise, accepted right away.

With the furnishings, we kept resale in mind. No ridiculous colors on the wall, no holes in the wall. We bought new furniture and picked out a kitchen that seemed consistent with this type of house: modern, rectangular and simple. The inside should correspond to the outside.

And then I got pregnant. Now we had to think about what we wanted. With a small child, we can still manage here for awhile, but we've decided to buy a larger house that still has to be built. So this place went up for sale. Our goal was to break even, at the very least. We paid 229,500 euros for this house. The bathroom cost 8,000 euros, the garden 5,000; and with all the other furnishing, we came to about 245,000 euros. Our mortgage is for 250,000. So we were asking 274,000 euros and expected the house to be on the market for a good six to nine months. But our realtor had a positive outlook. This is a popular neighborhood, and houses are being sold just under the asking price. People came to look right away, during the first week, and we've been astonished to have sold it twice so far! We accepted the first buyer's bid of 268,000 euros, but within a few days he let us know that the financing wasn't working out. Another interested party, who wanted to bid but came too late, then bid 270,000 euros straight off, and we accepted that. It means that, for the past three years, we'll have lived here for free.

7

Saturday, 22 December 2007: the past few days have been cold. Early this morning, as I lay in bed, my girlfriend calls out, 'Get your camera! Everything's white and the sun is shining – it'll be gone before you know it.' I throw on my clothes and dash out to the street. A neighbor pounds at the window. 'Can you do some pictures of my garden too? It looks so wonderful.' For the rest, nothing but silence. The usual.

Behind us lies the canal that used to define the land parcel. It's frozen over. How strong is the ice? Two small children walk across it. Dad observes from the edge. Could this be a very good idea? Though the canal is shallow, you wonder. Gradually, more people start venturing onto the ice. Not many. Two older people clearly haven't forgotten how to skate. In their streamlined skating garb, they glide away with impressive speed.

Looking at the houses as I walk across the frozen water gives me a strange sensation. Ground level is now at eye level. The houses loom upward like enormous wooden monsters. The scaffolding, normally vacant, now proves useful as a place for putting on skates and getting out to the ice. Also standing on it is a jar of hot chocolate and a big bottle of rum. By the time I get to it, there's no more hot chocolate, only rum. A bit early for me.

Now I get a good look at some neighbors. We're saying hello to each other for the first time. I make acquaintance with a neighbor who bought the last timber-frame house down the street. It had been on the market for a year after its completion. He was living in North Brabant, and when his employer thought it might be more convenient for him to live in the western part of the country, he began to look for houses on the Internet and came up with this one on Eiland 7. Realizing that the project developer would be only too glad to be rid of it, he started bidding. Now he enjoys living here and speaks highly of the acoustics in his house: the piano sounds great. Hans Piek, an island resident from a few streets away, joins in the conversation. He had been living on Park Haagse Weg, in Amsterdam. A nice house, but the bigger your kids get the smaller it seems, he says. Piek has an Internet business; where he lives doesn't matter that much to him. 'Everything is virtual; all I have to do is log in.'

'In Hoofddorp you've got space, and our house has volume. You can't find that anywhere for that kind of money,' remarks Piek. 'But you do have to explain to your friends why you bought a house in Hoofddorp, of all places. It can get comical at times.'

Before buying, Hans Piek took a good look at the subdivision map. At that time, there was still quite a bit of choice. He didn't want to live next to those 'gray areas' on the map: the unspecified parts of the island destined to become low-income housing. 'You never know what'll end up there.' Onto the subdivision map he pasted the volumes, in cardboard, so as to have a three-dimensional impression of the street. How far apart are the houses? He counted the number of homes in every street with timber-frame constructions and selected the street with the fewest: six homes. Then came another consideration: attached or freestanding? Attached it would be. A neighbor's house jutted out slightly, thus sheltering his house from the southwest wind. His lot was large; plans for an extension into the yard are in the making. Piek is content with his place. What he expected he got: value for money. And things are quiet here. We used to go camping, but since we've started living here I prefer my own yard.

When the houses went up for sale, the project developer launched a website 'community' for the buyers. On the website, Eiland 7 was recommended as a neighborhood where cars were condoned. 'Its sense of calm creates a wonderful residential-park feeling.' And that, the copywriter assures us, is 'an extraordinary feeling. Like being on vacation at home.' Meant to attract buyers, this text remained on the website, even in 2002 when the island's redevelopment led to the loss of many original ideas.

The website eventually included a forum where buyers could exchange ideas. Anonymity was not part of this; messages were accompanied by the name and construction number of the buyer. 'Last weekend we were lucky enough to receive, from AM Wonen, a proposal and a list of optional extra work concerning the possible extension. I don't know about the rest of you, but it didn't go over well with me.' Signed by: 'Patrick (angry).' Soon enough, the forum became a depository for every complaint regarding the lack of clarity on the redevelopment. Even before construction began, one buyer

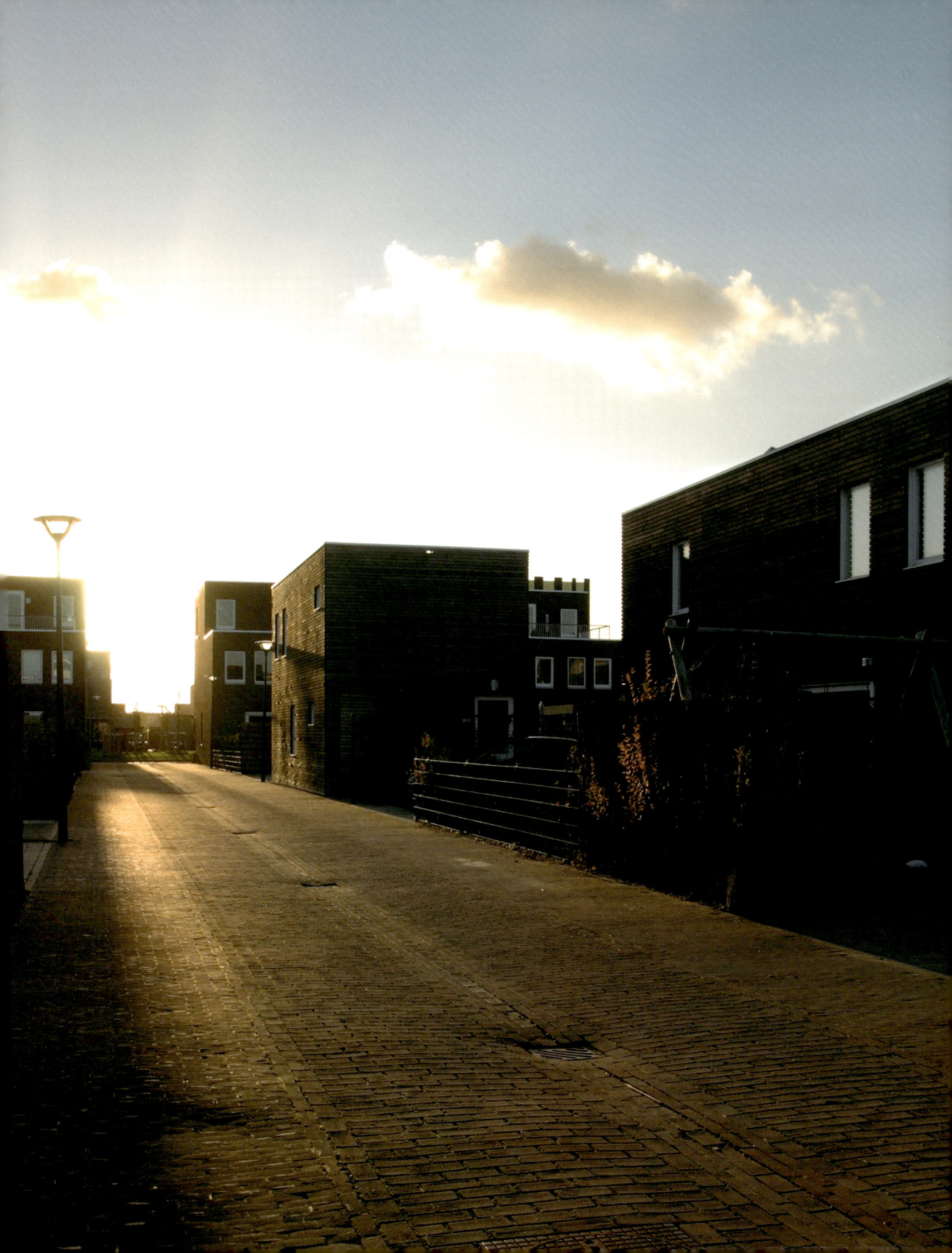

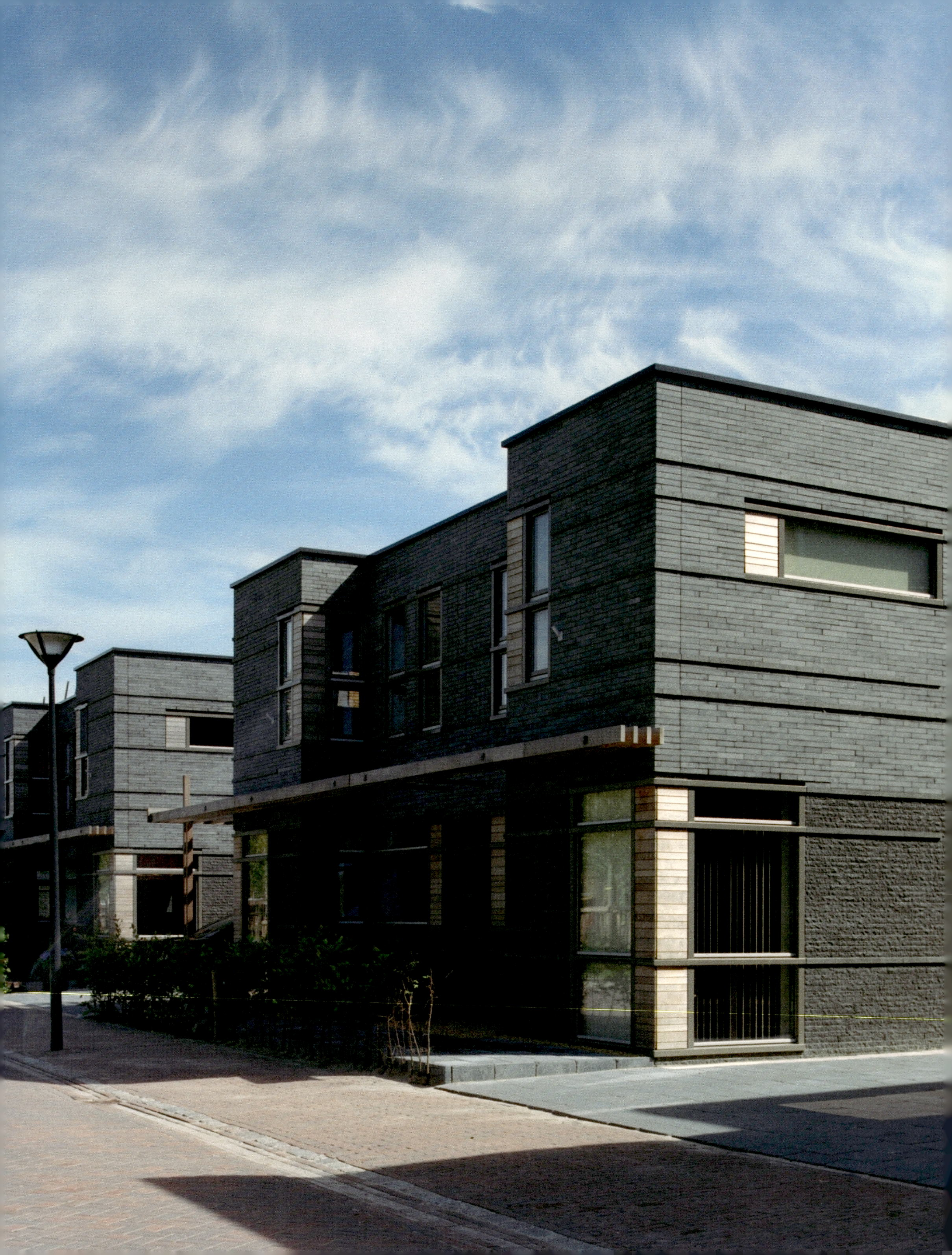

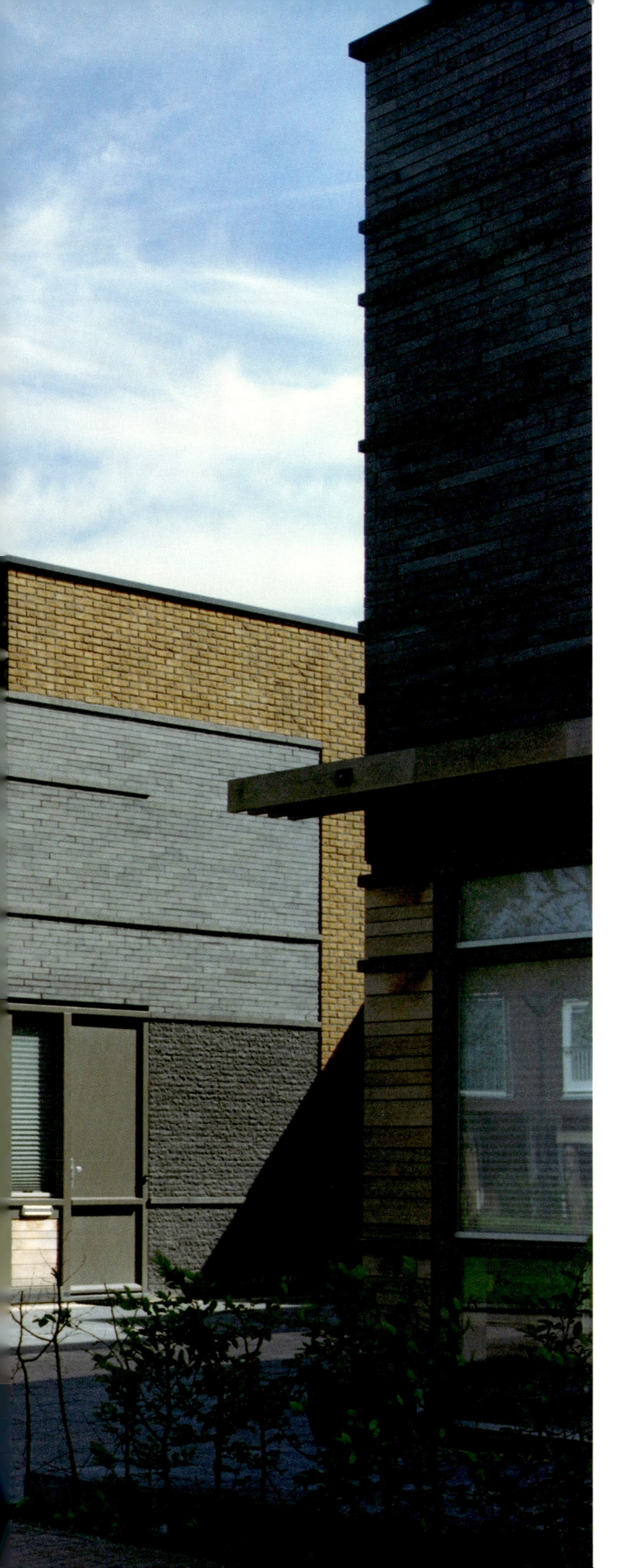

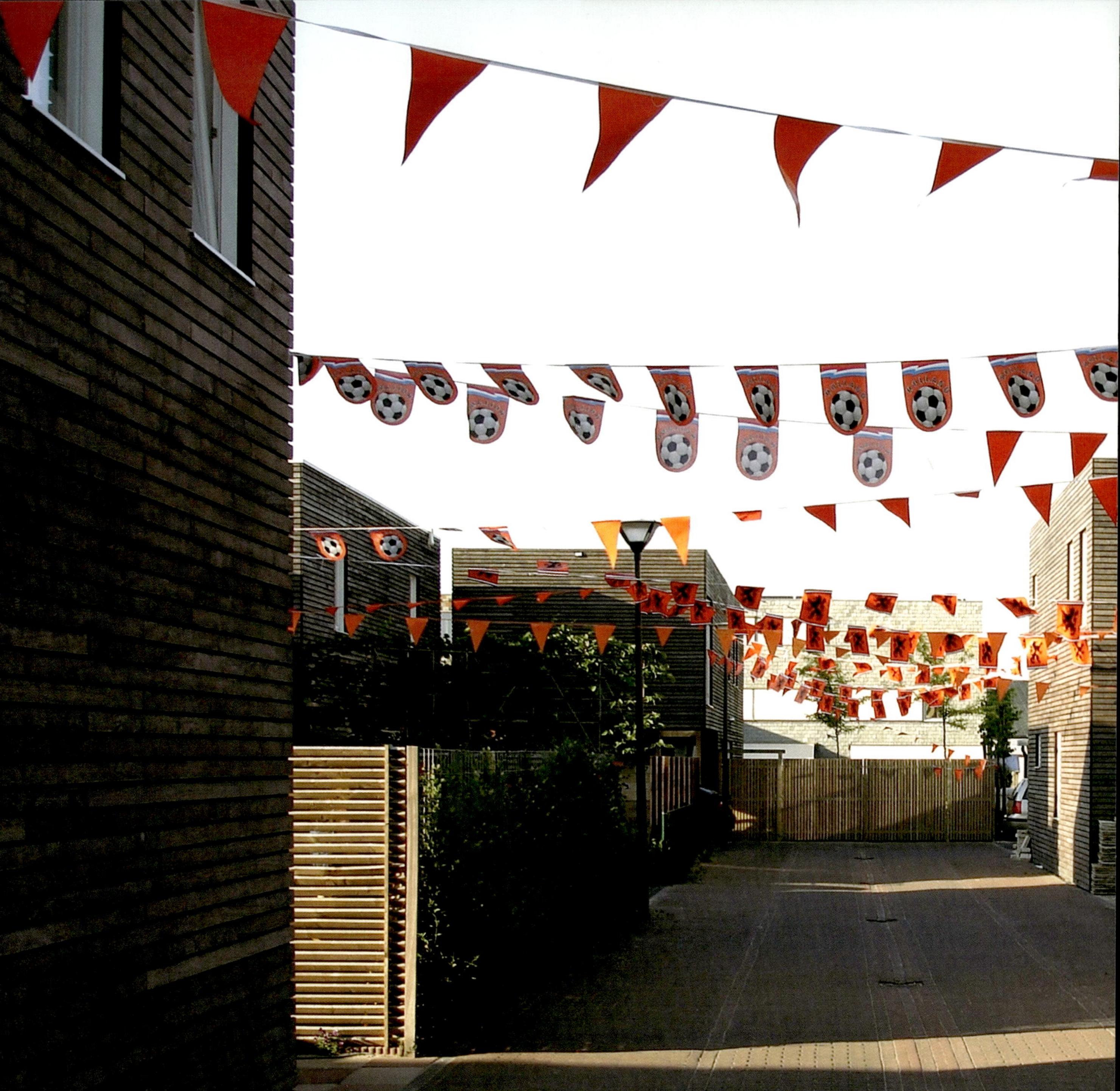

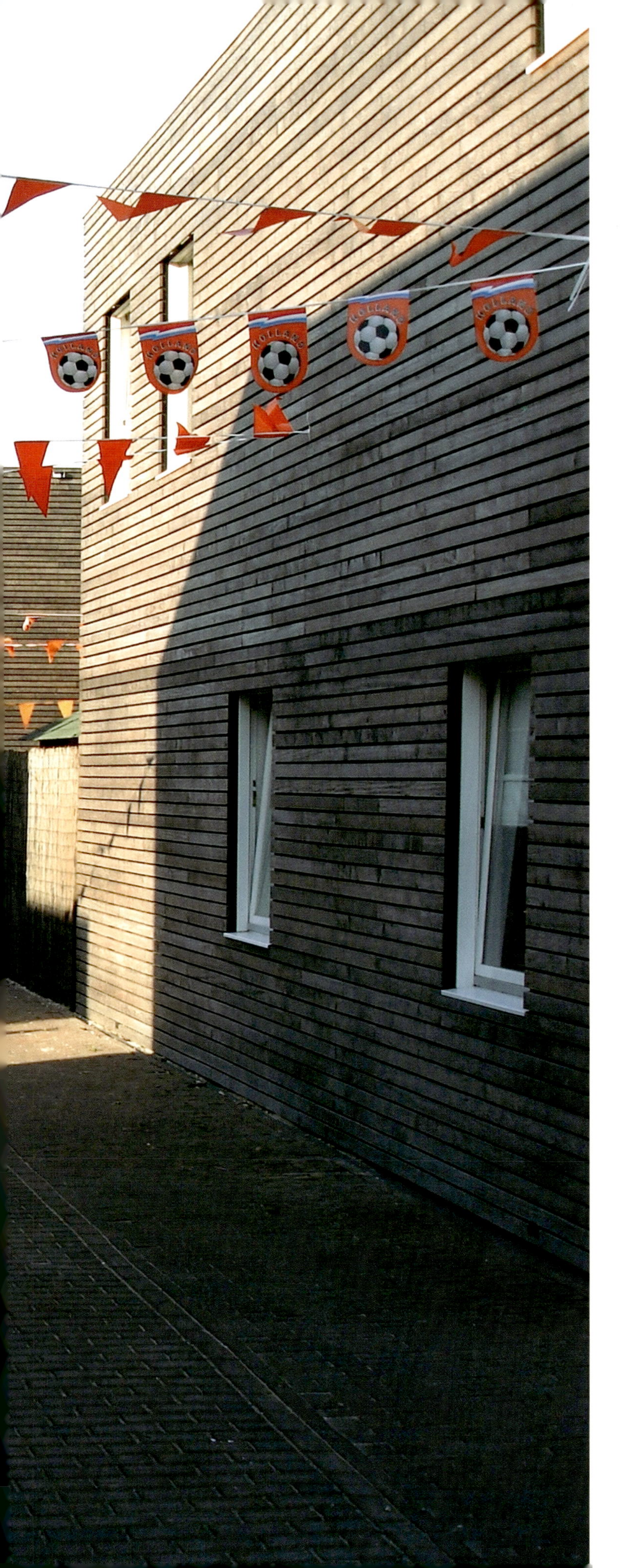

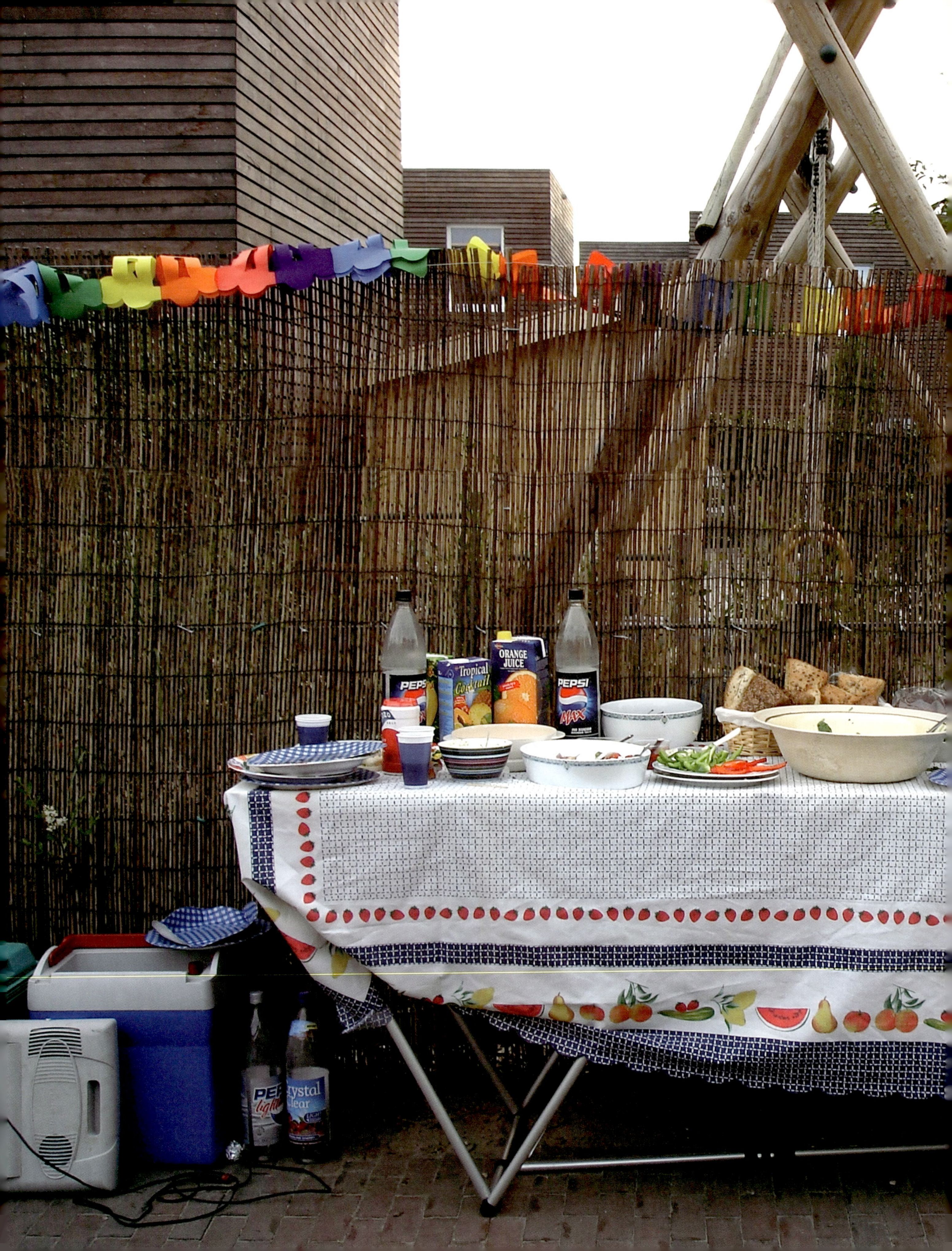

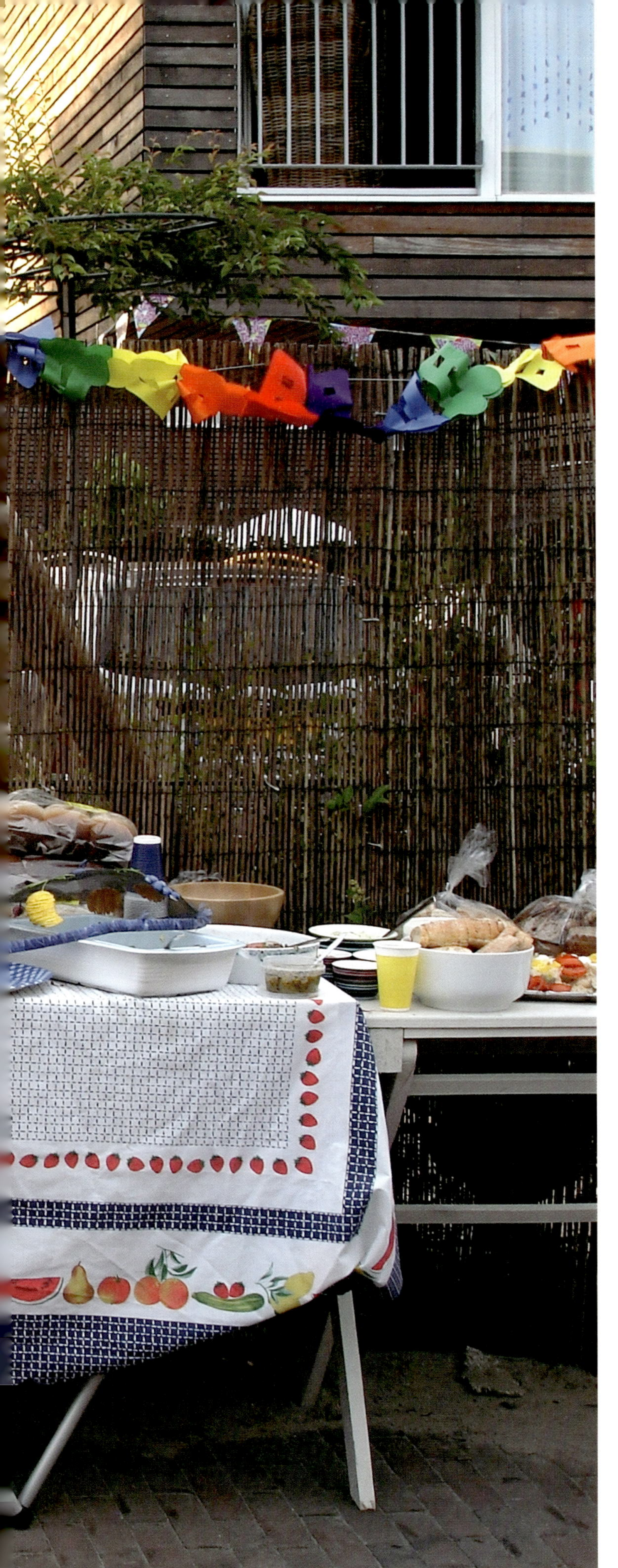

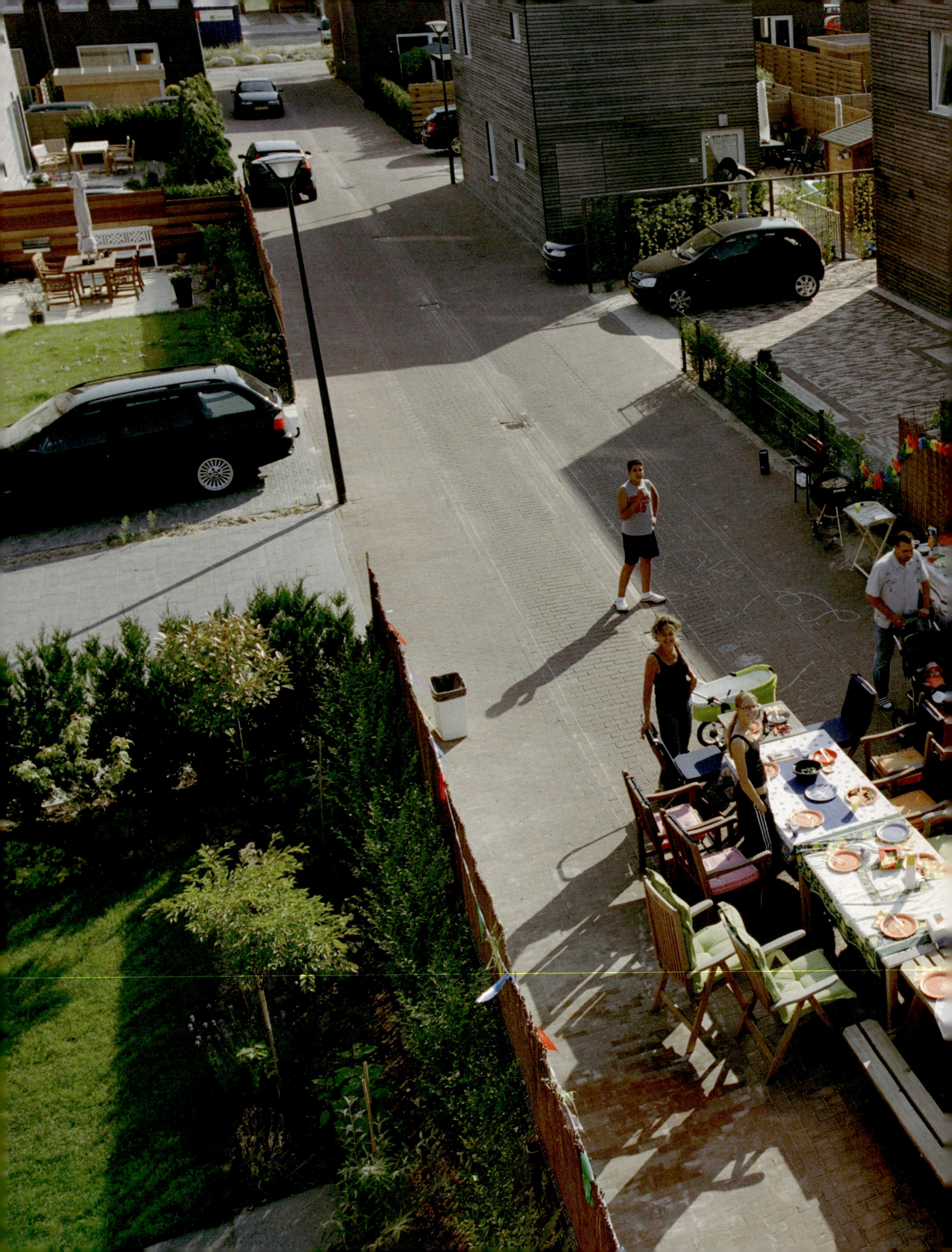

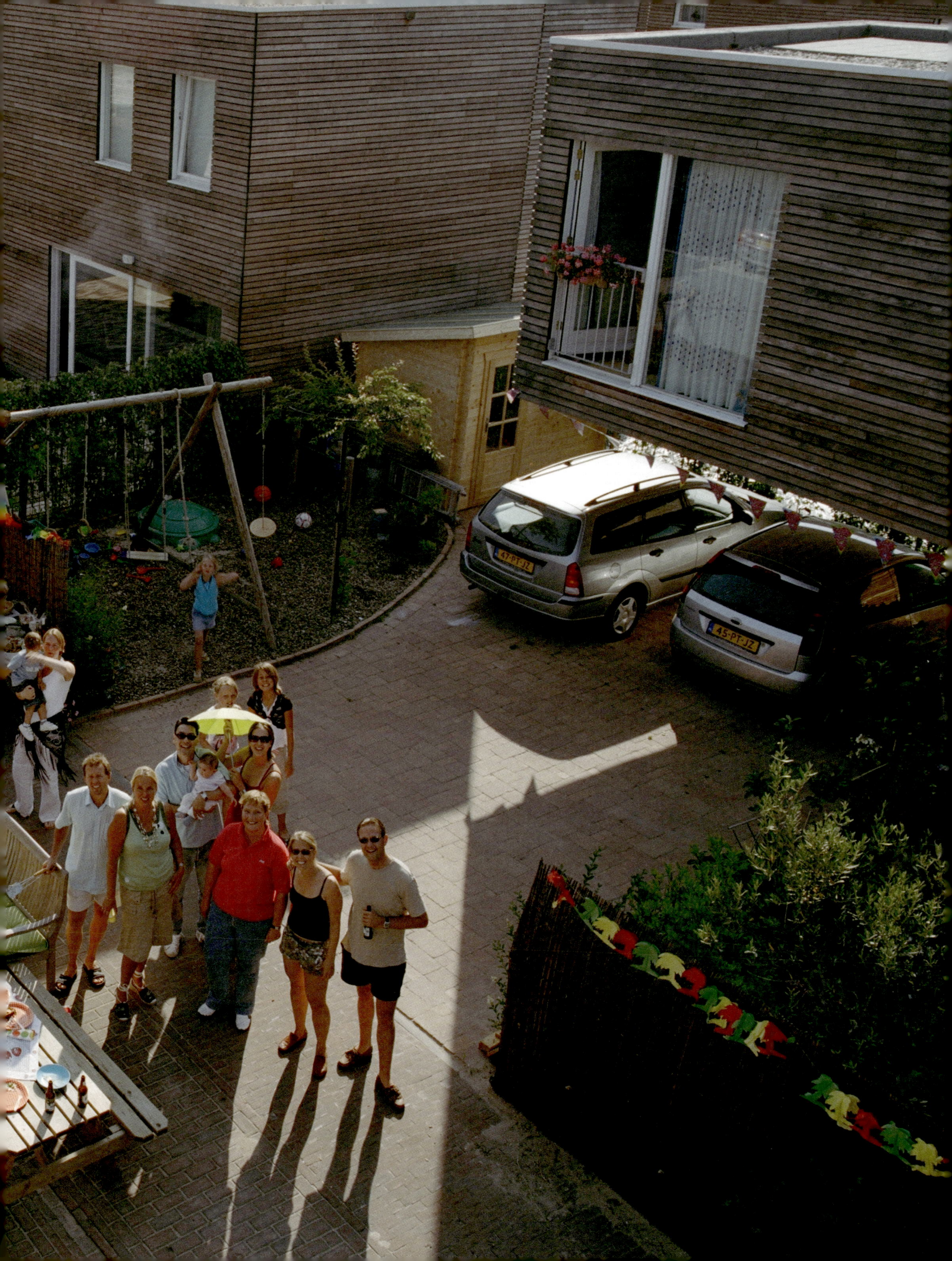

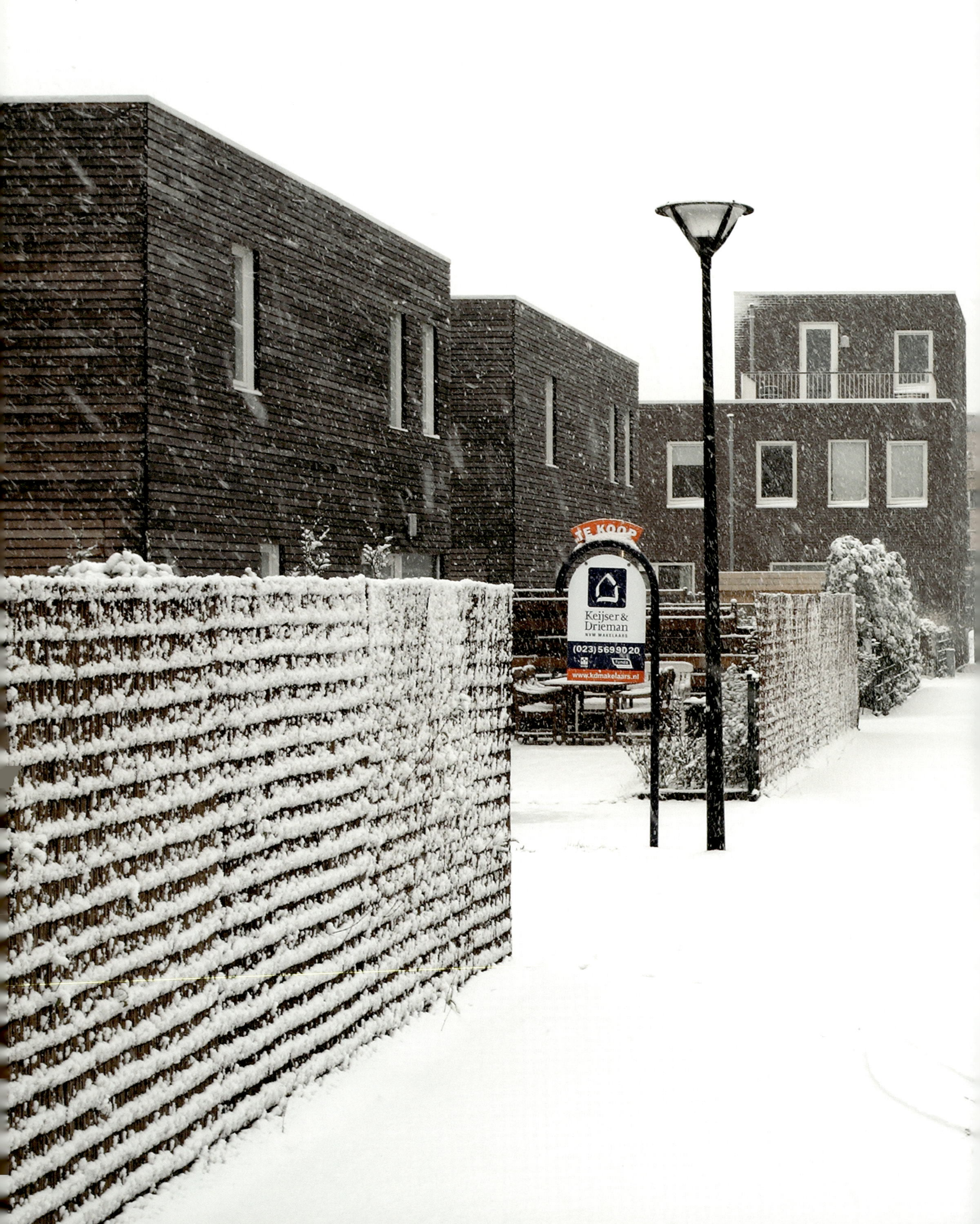
TE KOOP
Keijser &
Drieman
NVM MAKELAARS
(023) 569 90 20
www.kdmakelaars.nl

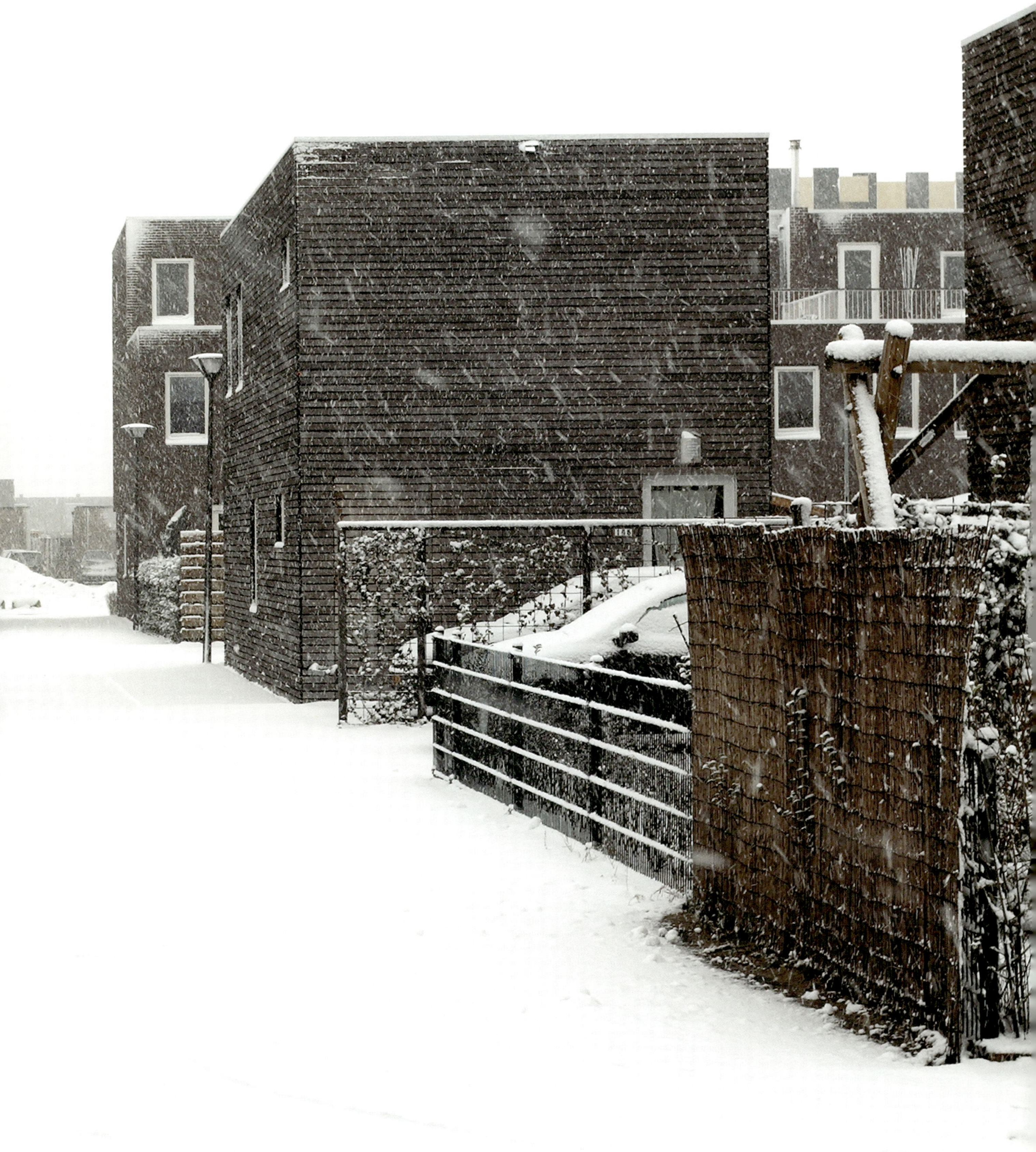

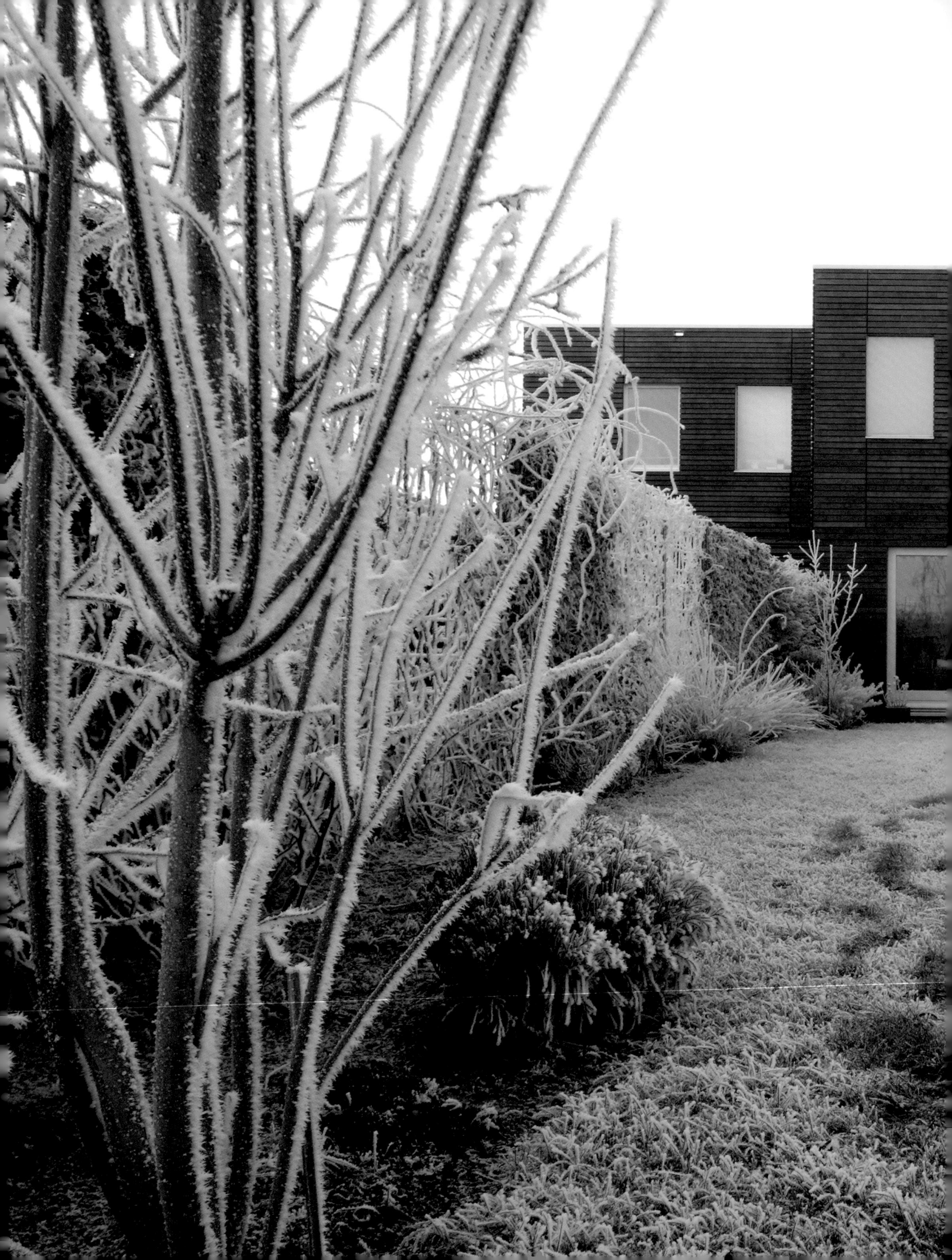

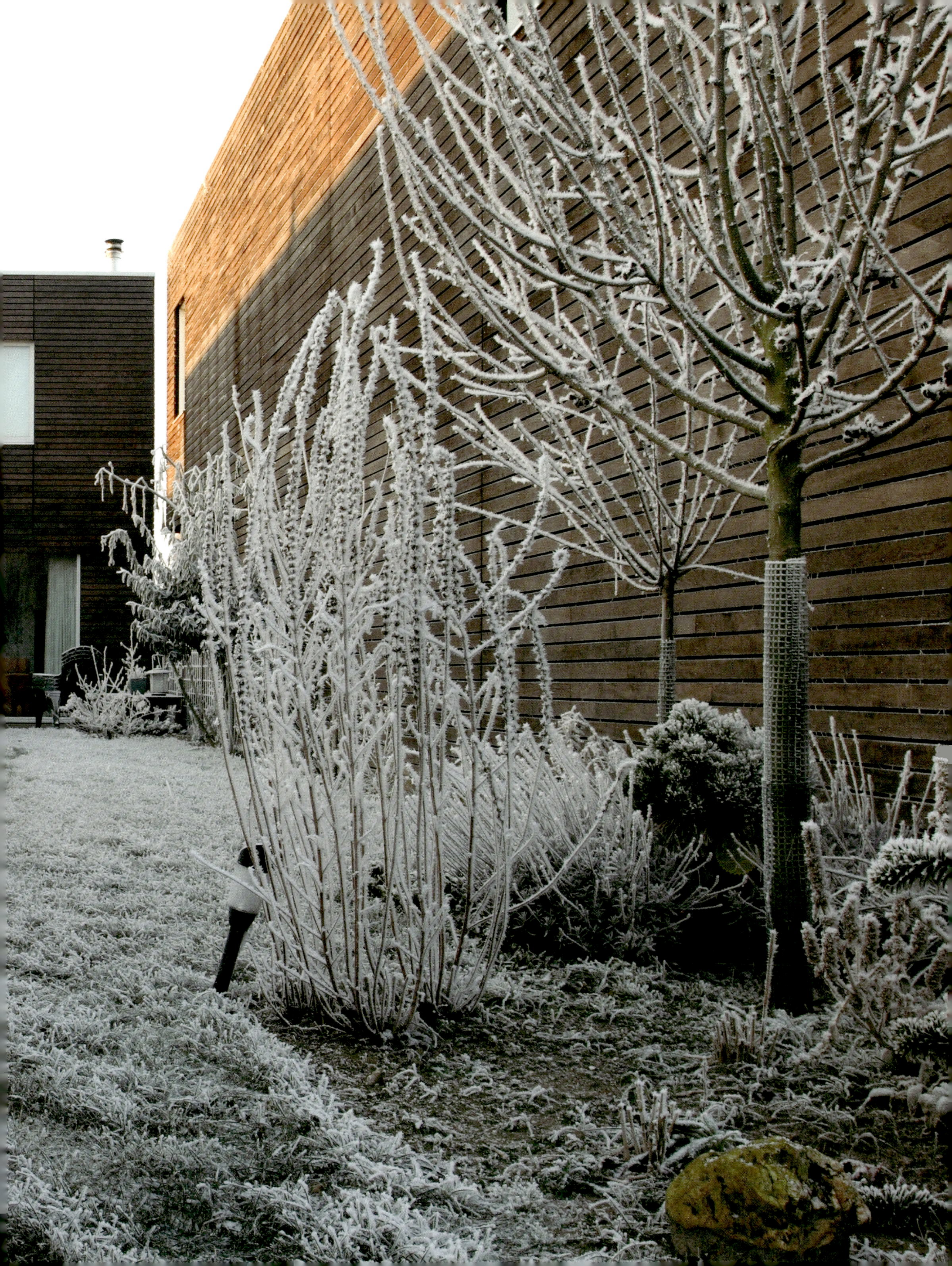

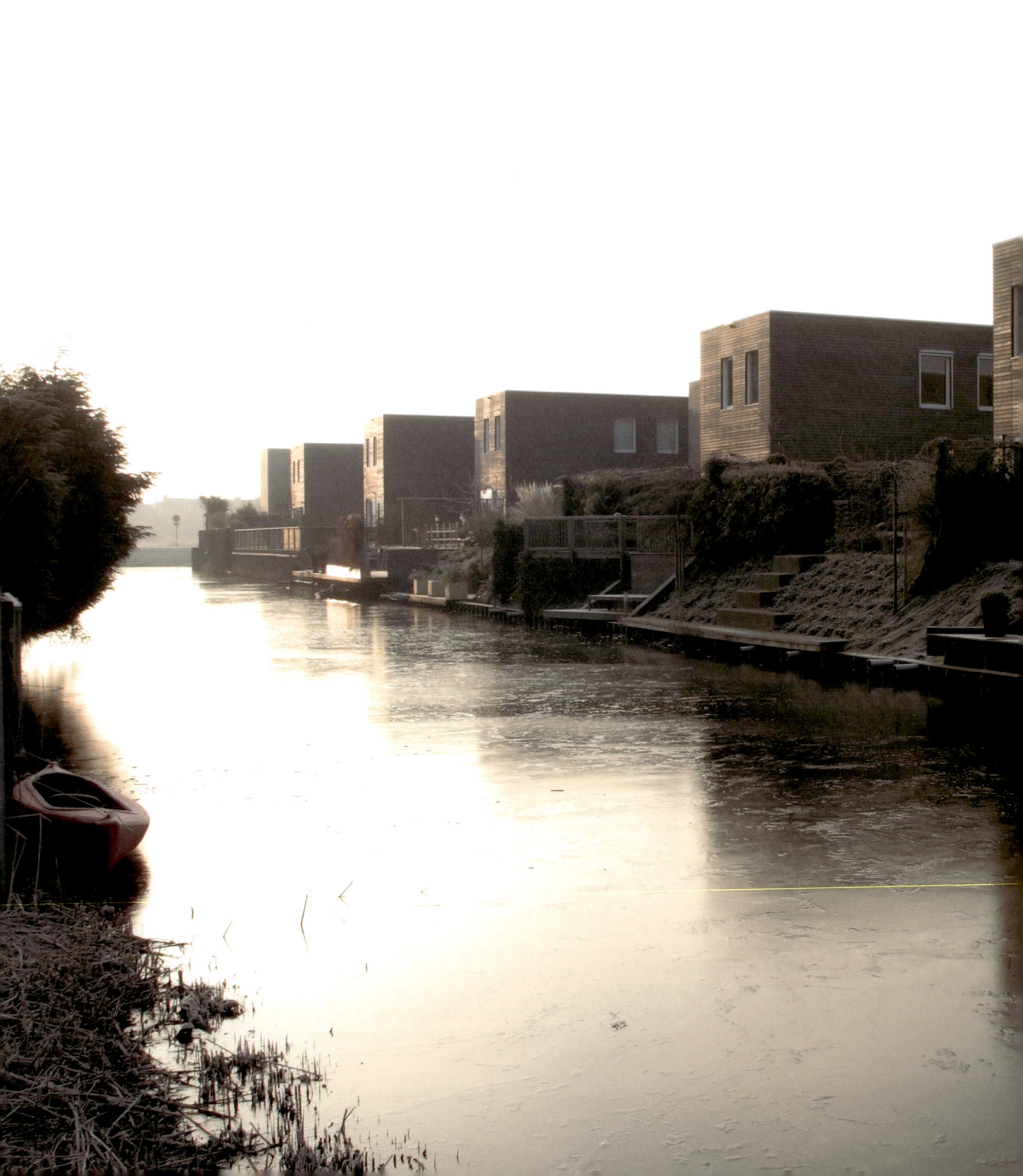

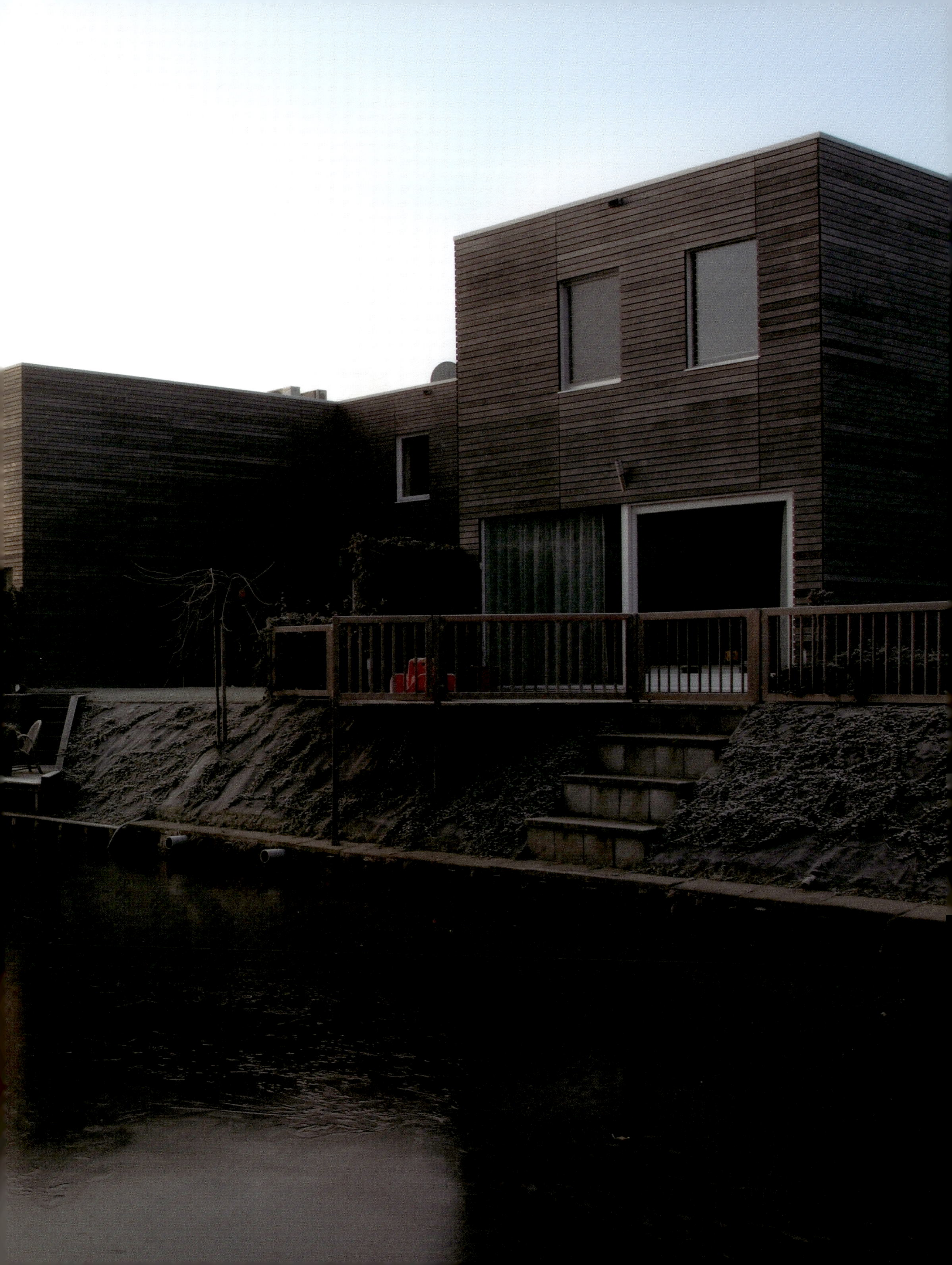

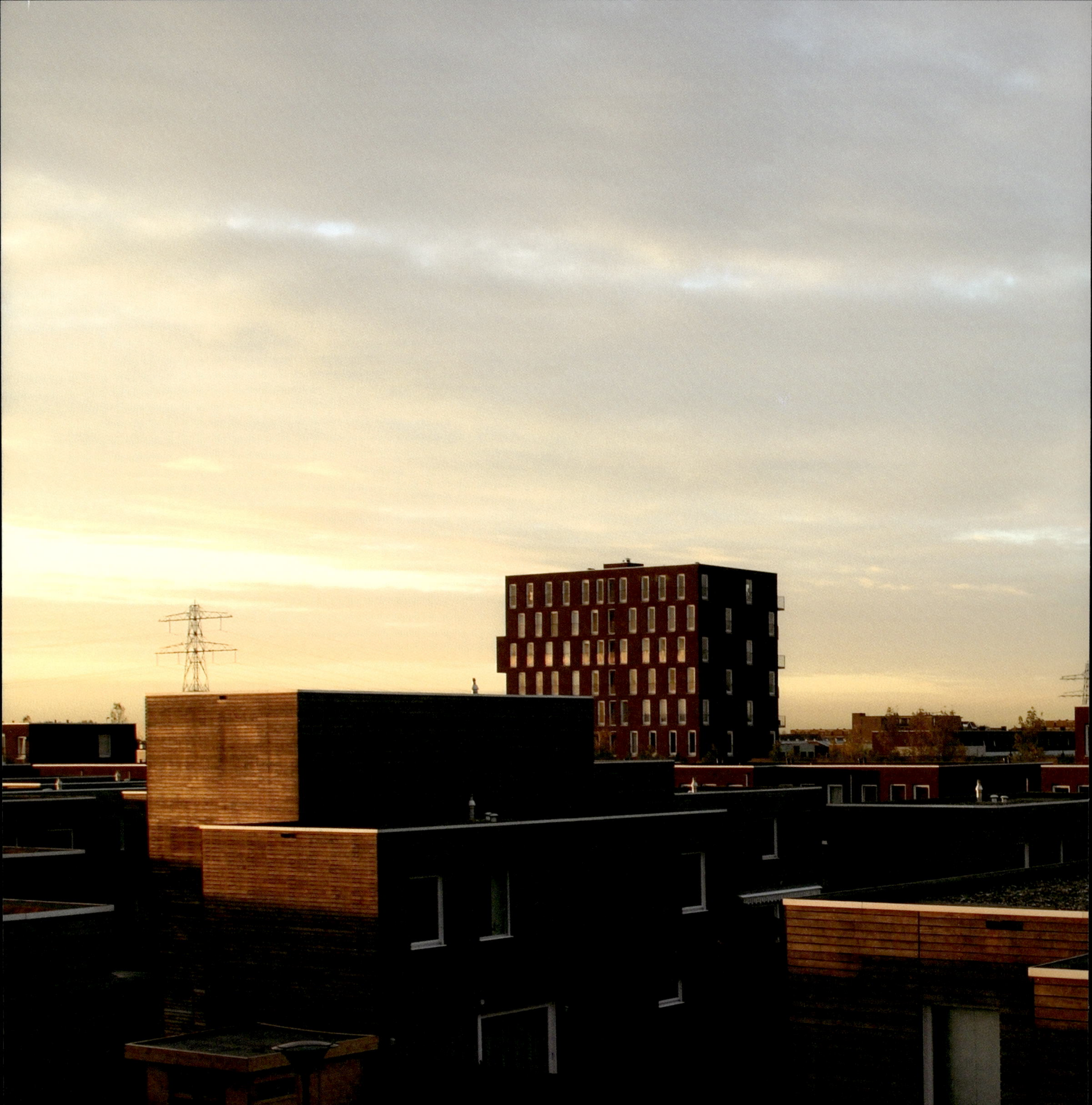

suggested taking a survey with the yes-or-no standpoint: 'Had I known how this project would go, I would never have purchased the house.' Not all of the buyers agreed with this. One fellow buyer struck a more cheerful note with 'Let's look at the future and be positive about it.'

Complaints about insufficient information and feelings of powerlessness among some buyers grew when the first homes were completed. 'If we were looking for a house now, we'd never buy it here. Not because the house doesn't suit us, but because the surroundings have become so shabby.' The project developer's sales advisor became an easy target, being the only recognizable representative in the invisible entity consisting of the project developer, municipality and designers.

According to the forum, quite a few people wanted sunrooms and carports added to their houses. The sales advisor stated, on the forum site, that these were not being offered by the project developer, as they were not consistent with the design. When it appeared that an extra level had been placed on a house (our house) during its construction, astonished responses flooded the forum. How could this happen? Seven buyers made it known that they wanted the same thing. The start of a proliferation of these could already be discerned at this point – but it went unnoticed.

While the duplexes on the south end of Eiland 7 were being built, the buyers set up an association. Almost all of the 34 buyers joined it. Just before the homes were completed, the purchasing committee held an information evening on the landscaping of gardens. Two garden landscapers were invited to present two designs each, plus the corresponding budget. One failed to show up. The remaining landscaper offered special prices on two proposals: a modern stylish garden and a somewhat simpler garden. The ready-made 'standard garden' cost 24,000 euros. A dressed-up version of this could be had for a mere 8,000 euros extra. Thirty buyers ordered one of these two versions from the landscaper.

When construction on our house reached its completion at three o'clock on 15 September 2004, our little street was bustling with people. The houses of our new neighbors had just been finished a few hours before. Much to our surprise, furnishing activities had already begun.

We introduced ourselves to the neighbors on the left, who were in the process of removing radiators from their house. The conversation immediately led to the fence issue. 'Preferably not one from the do-it-yourself store,' we said. 'And what's wrong with that? I happen to work in one of those stores,' quipped my new neighbor. But fortunately he did share our aesthetic viewpoint. Roaring with laughter, that same neighbor told us how he felt when the sales advisor at AM Wonen informed him that he'd be living next to a family with four children. 'I had just finished signing the papers.'

After the completion of our house, we're not given the key right away. Our second mortgage has yet to come through. When it does, a few weeks later, we start our own furnishing activities. The neighbors have already moved in. Those on the west side have even landscaped the garden. What shall we do with ours? It looks like a freshly plowed field – as though the Könst brothers have just driven off with the tractor. We refrain from doing anything; speed isn't our thing. In the spring we still have no idea what to do with the field, now grown over without any help from us. I turn the soil with a shovel. At the advice of a landscape architect, we order 36 euro's worth of floral grass seed. That'll give our garden the look of a blossomy roadside this summer. A year later we still don't know what to do with our field. Should we, like the neighbor on the corner, select a theme? 'We've divided the two patios with the shed. One has a Spanish atmosphere, the other a French. Since we like France . . . and Spain too.'

Our visits to the garden centers that have sprouted up around this *Vinex* neighborhood do me no good. Bring in the steamroller, I keep on thinking, as we walk through the aisles of nonsense.

My girlfriend comes up with a plan: part of it with plants, another part patio. A tradesman who does ornamental pavements for *Vinex* neighborhoods during one half of the year, and goes off to the Philippines for the other half, arrives with his team consisting of two Armenian refugees and a former journalist from Chechnia. They carry out the design. The obligatory parking place on our own property gets done as well; finally, no more dirt. Neighbors across from us, on Eiland 8, are happy: quite a bit of that floral grass seed blew their way and ended up between the patio tiles.

My girlfriend's daughters were already living in Hoofddorp and going to school here. Being settled in, they've also become used to the idea of living on an island. I hear the older one saying, 'I'll bike over to your island' to a friend on the phone.

'One of our neighbors has a Hummer,' observes my oldest son, who lives in the Bijlmermeer half the time. Since day one, he's decided that Hoofddorp has little to offer. A few days later, yet another new car appears on the 'private parking space.' Nor does this one go unnoticed. The cars continue to show up in alternation with a slightly aged Mercedes. This Mercedes seems to be a constant. They must be car dealers, we think, but at the first street get-together, the man with the ever-changing collection proves to be a car journalist.

In the first two summers, some rather cheerful barbecues were held in the middle of our street. It wasn't easy to find a date when everyone could come. But once things were on, the party didn't stop: food and stories lasted deep into the night. And everyone wanted, at some point, to get a view of the neighborhood from our deck. Conversations were about experiences that we shared: about the buying of a house.

And the subject of work came up. Living in the street are an executive secretary, a financial head of a business, an assistant manager of a do-it-yourself store, an account manager, a mortgage advisor for an insurance company and an investment advisor for a large bank. Remarkably, no government employees here. Some of us dared to tell more than we bargained for. One neighbor announced her plan to write a book about what it's like being married to a Dutchman of Moroccan descent. She had already thought of a title: *My Husband Is a Terrorist.* Nice things like this only happen in the summer. Throughout the rest of the year, life goes on indoors and you don't run into anyone. Except when winter hits us like old times: with ice to skate on. Then you see everyone.

I ask the Könst brothers, who bred their varieties of potatoes here, whether they've seen the neighborhood yet. Haven't had the time, they said, since the relocated business is doing well. The potato market is on the move. In addition to their business here in the Haarlemmermeer, they now own a business in Canada, where they distribute specially developed breeds of potatoes, cultivate them and export them to the USA. There these exclusive potatoes are packaged in baskets and marketed as a delicacy.

They cycle over to check out their old property, now referred to as Eiland 7. Dead end streets are considered 'awkward' by them, the houses 'not very beautiful.'

This is suburbia: endless neighborhoods, encircled by roads that lead to large shopping centers and office parks.

Semi-rural, you could say. Here, on this island, the idea was to banish the car from view. That's why cars had to be parked behind the houses. Only a few cars were allowed on the green. But now we have 'parking density,' as our municipal 'area manager' calls it. The solution: create more parking space on the green. 'A percentage of grass will thereby need to be converted.'

The parking lot has become a dominant factor in the Netherlands. Despite every good intention, things are no different on Eiland 7. The green will turn into a parking lot with a grove of trees. In many respects, the car serves as a general indicator of things. Not only where the layout of a newly developed neighborhood is concerned. My girlfriend's younger daughter was knocked off her bike by an automobilist who encouragingly raised his hand and drove on.

Even so, we do like it here. So long as our immediate neighbors don't build any outlandish extensions or oversized huts. To us, the house has a certain appeal and comfort. And you get used to a garden, it seems. Though it was intended for a large part-time family, the oldest children have almost moved out by now. The real *Amsterdammers* among us can't get excited about this place: the city always comes out on top. Soon our house will be a bit large; it was already expensive. But if the mortgage interest stays within reason, who knows, we might just stay a little longer.

Figuring out how a residential area gets built, and how things
look behind its fences, does require a certain amount of
assistance. That was given to me generously, and I thank
everyone who provided me with information about the
development of Eiland 7. I myself am responsible, of course,
for any possible errors.

My neighbors deserve special thanks for allowing me into
their houses and being so frank with me – that nosy guy next
door.

Remarkably, all sorts of funds in the Netherlands make
projects of this type financially possible. Due to that policy,
exceptional photography books can be produced. I should
like to thank the Netherlands Architecture Fund and the
Netherlands Foundation for Visual Arts, Design and Architecture
for having put their trust in me.

By purchasing twenty photographs of mine, the municipality
Haarlemmermeer gave indirect and unconditional support to
this publication.

Cary Markerink and Hans Aarsman provided me with plain
advice, as good friends do. ("Oh right, the photographer
showed up: a bit obvious. Just get rid of that portrait.") Their
criticism was often put to good use. Another friend, Warna
Oosterbaan, undertook the task of editing the text after my
muse and mortgage-sharer Inge Sargentini had made initial
comments on it.

For our children Martijn, Fien, Wouter and Cato, moving to
this house and living in it together was a big step. They hadn't
asked for that, and it wasn't always easy. This book is dedicated
to those four great kids and to my fun parents, Joop and Kees,
who had the bright idea of moving to Hoofddorp in 1960.

Eiland 7 – Tales from suburbia is an initiative of Ideas on Paper and is published in collaboration with NAi Publishers.

Concept, photography and compilation **Theo Baart**
Text **Theo Baart**
Copy editing **Warna Oosterbaan & D'Laine Camp**
Translation **Beth O'Brien**
Design **Joost Grootens**
Lithography and printing **drukkerij Mart.Spruijt bv**
Binding **Epping boekbinders bv**
Paper **Tatami Ivory 150 grs, Royal Print Matt 80 grs**
Project coordinator **Linda Schaefer, NAi Publishers**
Publisher **Eelco van Welie, NAi Publishers**
First print **May 2008 750 copies**

Eiland 7 – Tales from suburbia has been published with financial assistance from the Netherlands Architecture Fund and the Netherlands Foundation for Visual Arts, Design and Architecture

The author would like to thank the municipality Haarlemmermeer

NAi Publishers is an internationally orientated publisher specialized in developing, producing and distributing books on architecture, visual arts and related disciplines.
[www.naipublishers.nl]

Available in North, South and Central America through D.A.P./ Distributed Art Publishers Inc, 155 Sixth Avenue 2nd Floor, New York, NY 10013-1507, Tel 212 6271999, Fax 212 6279484. Available in the United Kingdom and Ireland through Art Data, 12 Bell Industrial Estate, 50 Cunnington Street, London W4 5HB, Tel 208 7471061, Fax 208 7422319.

Ideas on Paper was set up by Theo Baart and Cary Markerink to conduct and publish photography projects.
[www.ideasonpaper.nl]

Printed and bound in the Netherlands

ISBN 978-90-5662-003-5

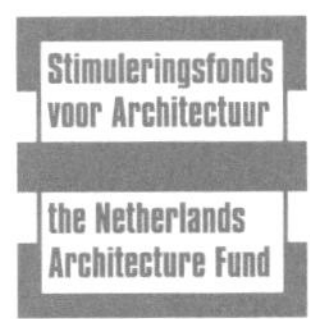

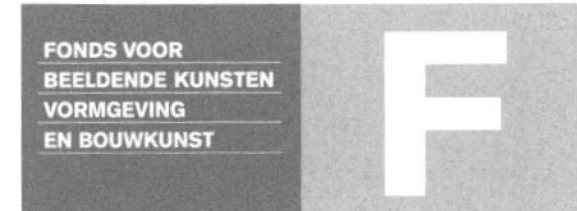

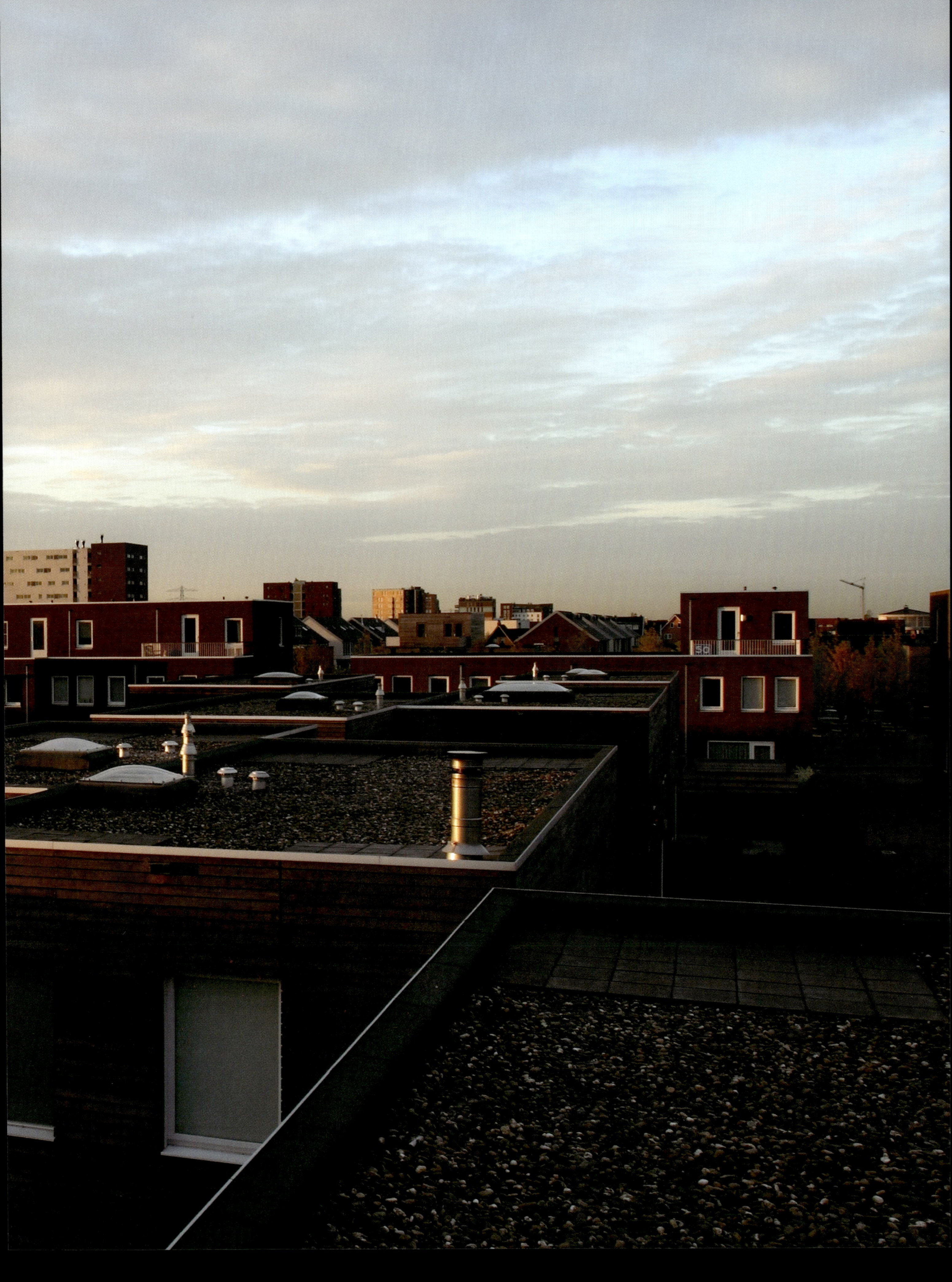

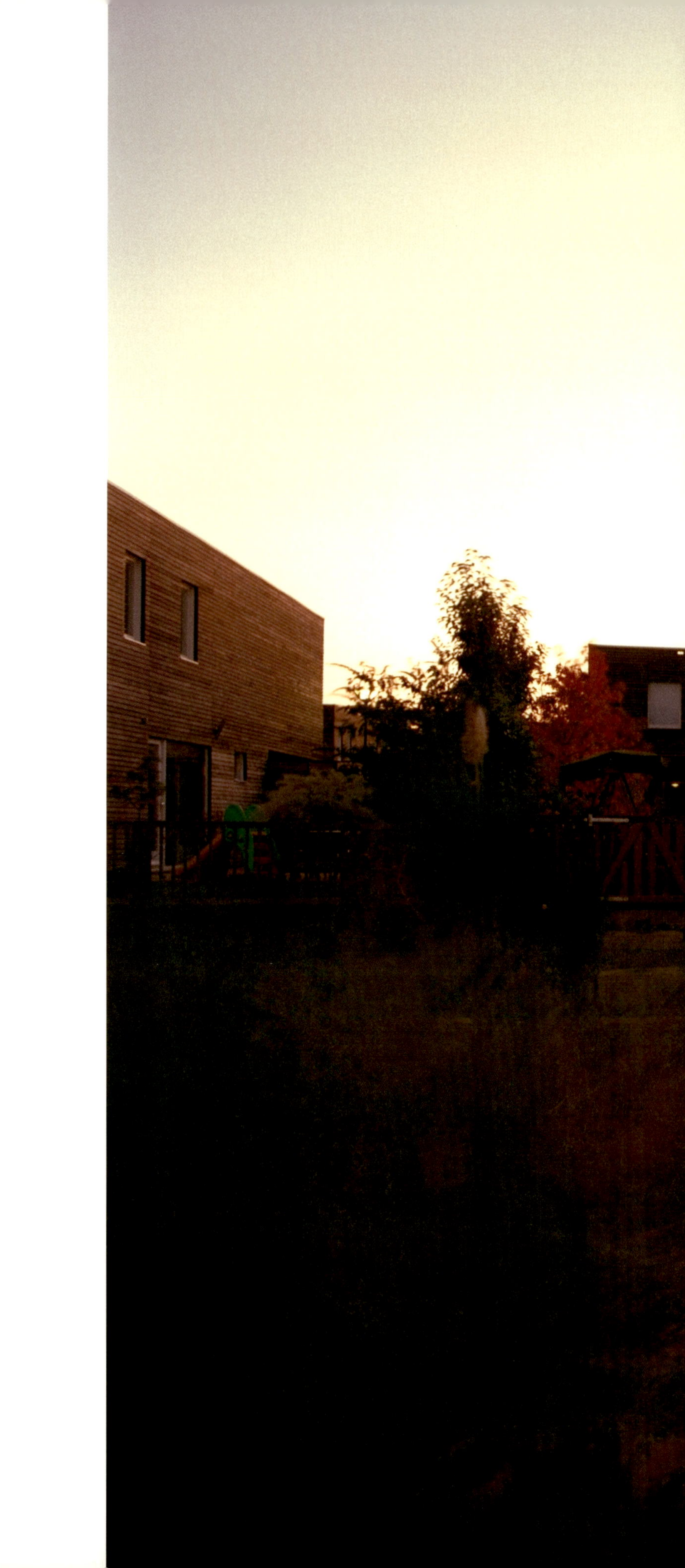

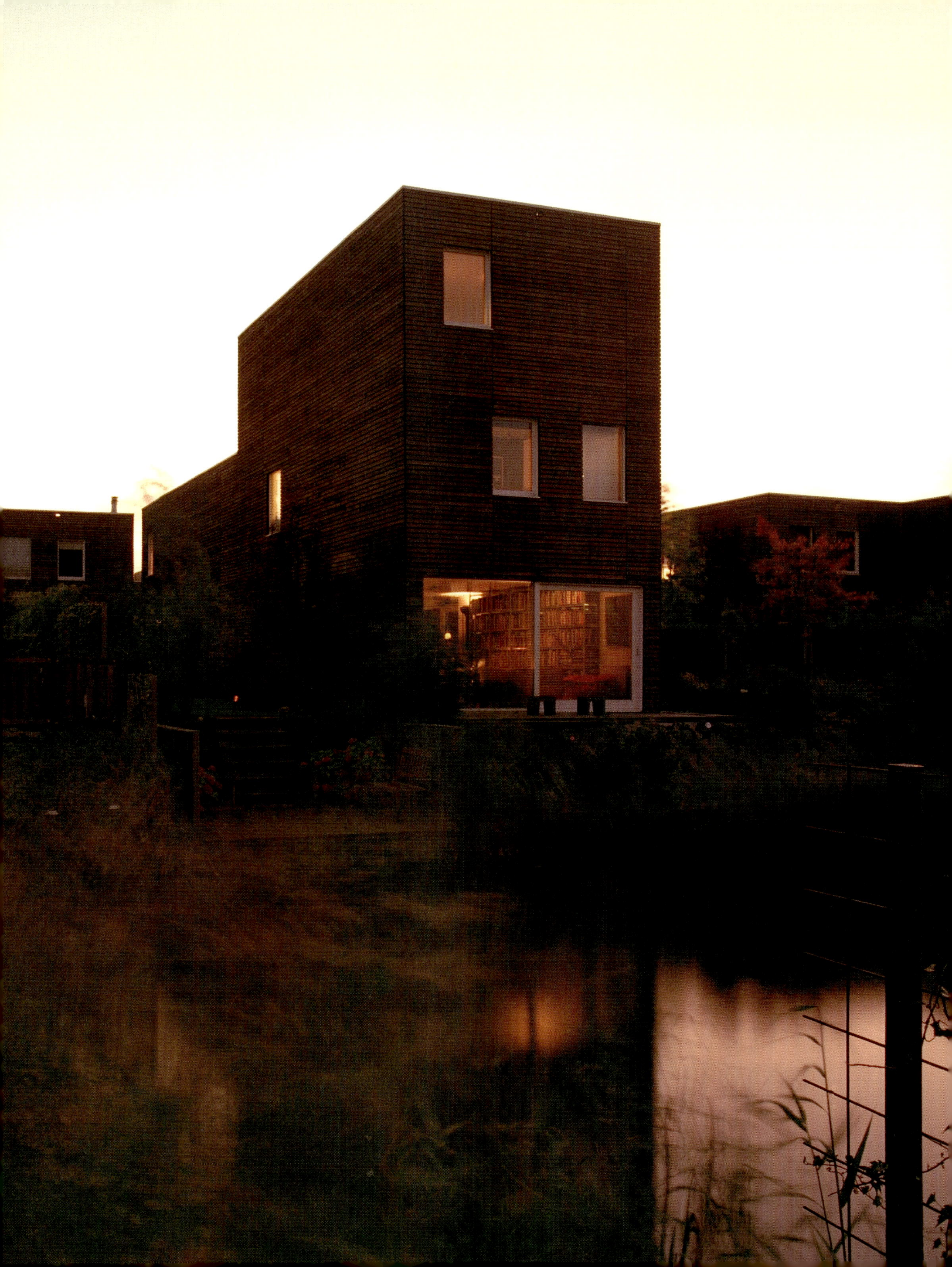

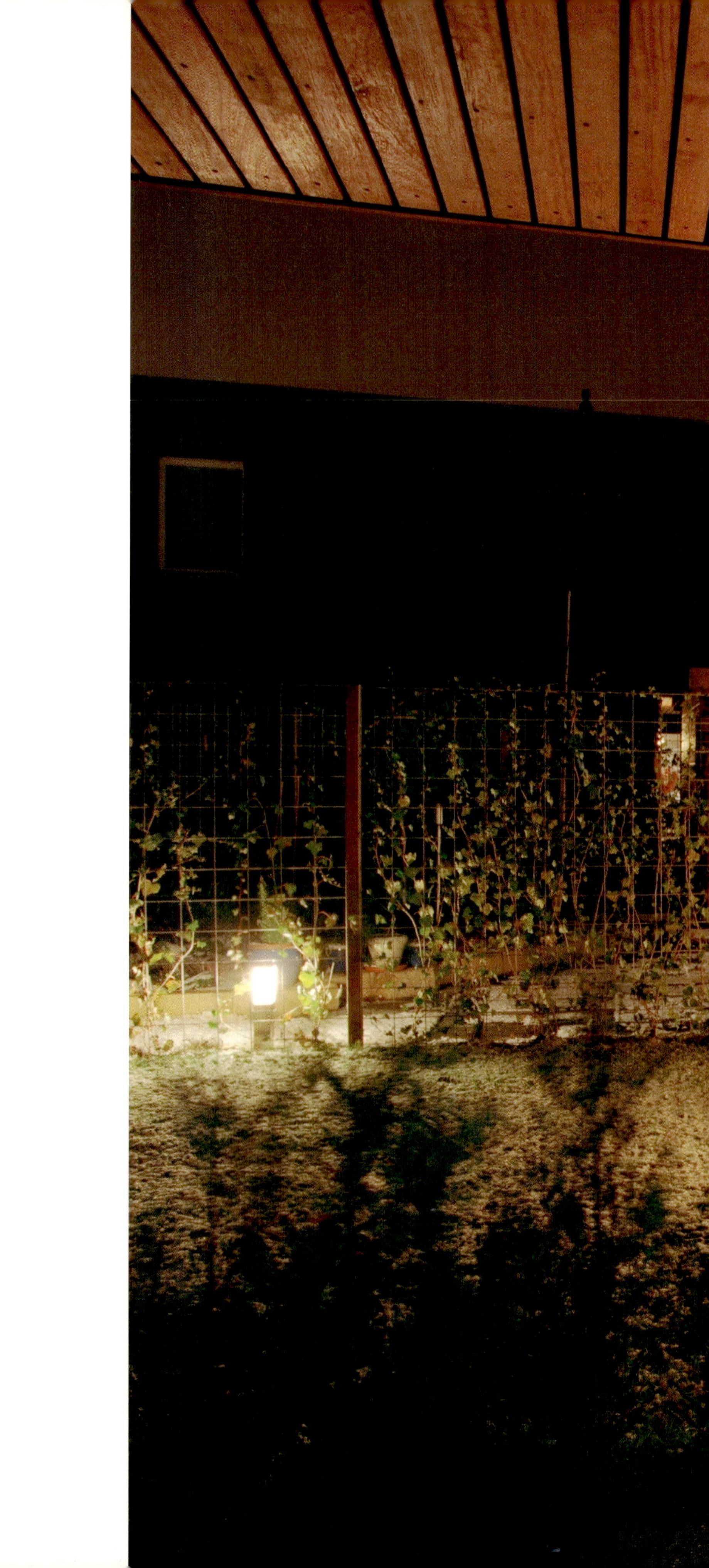

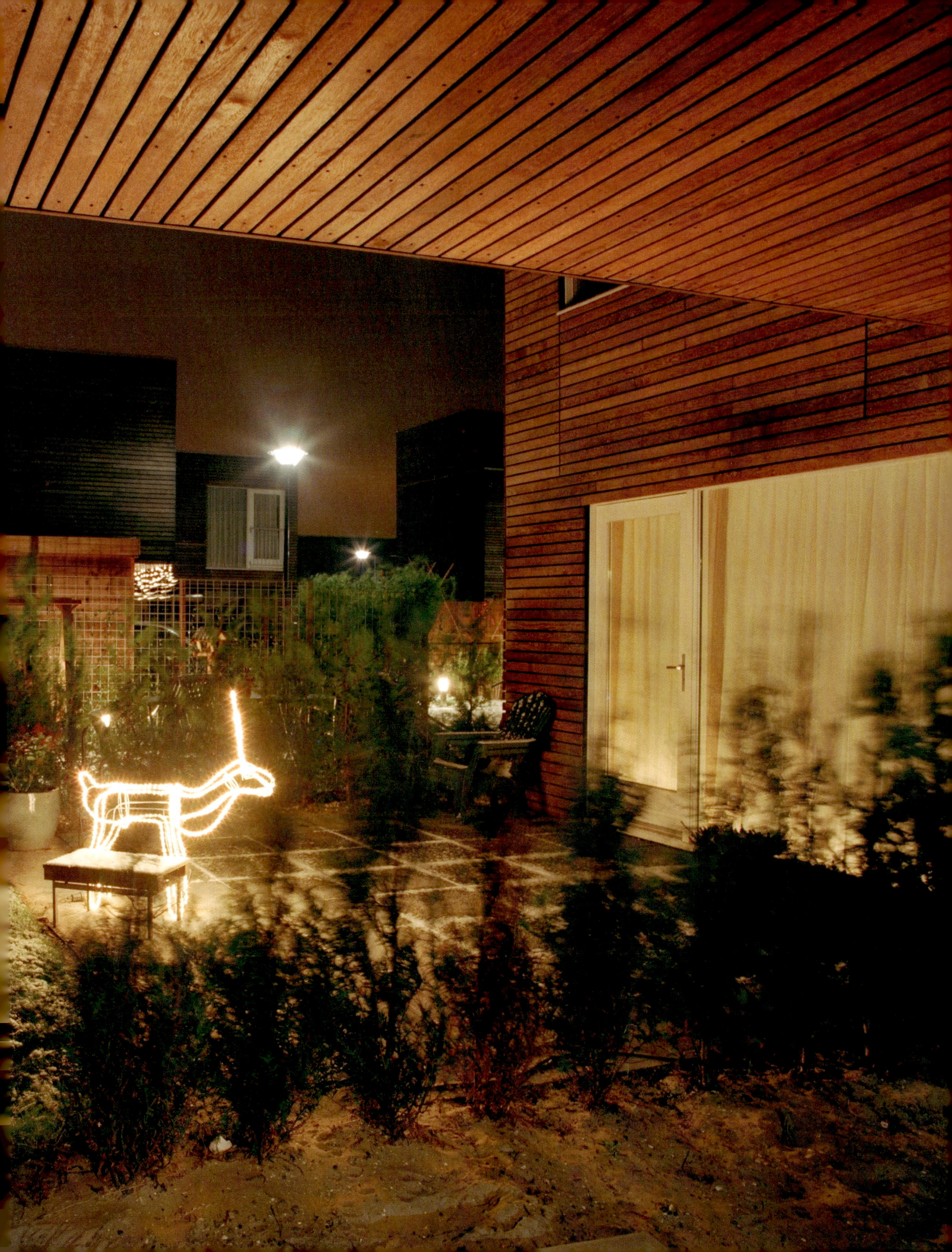

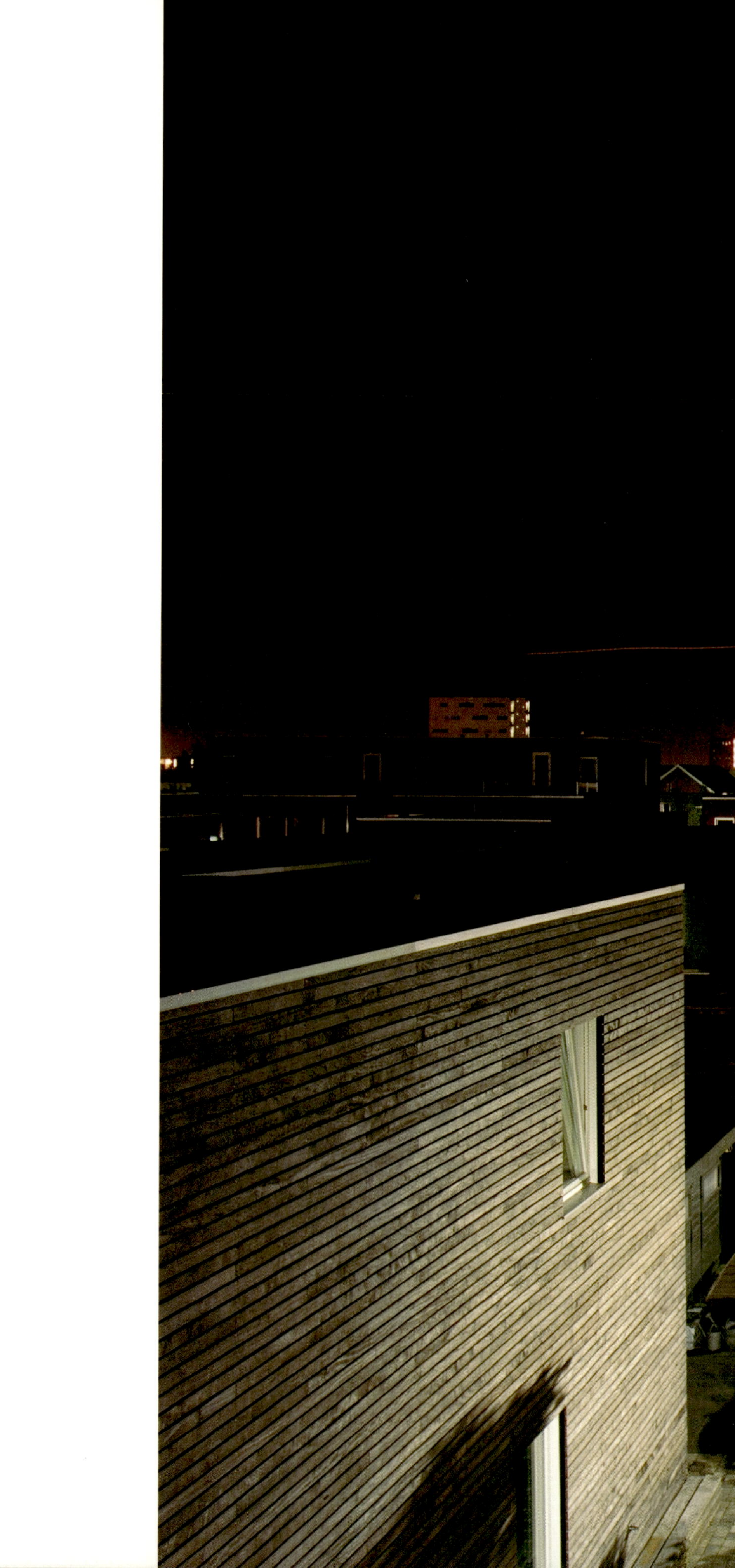

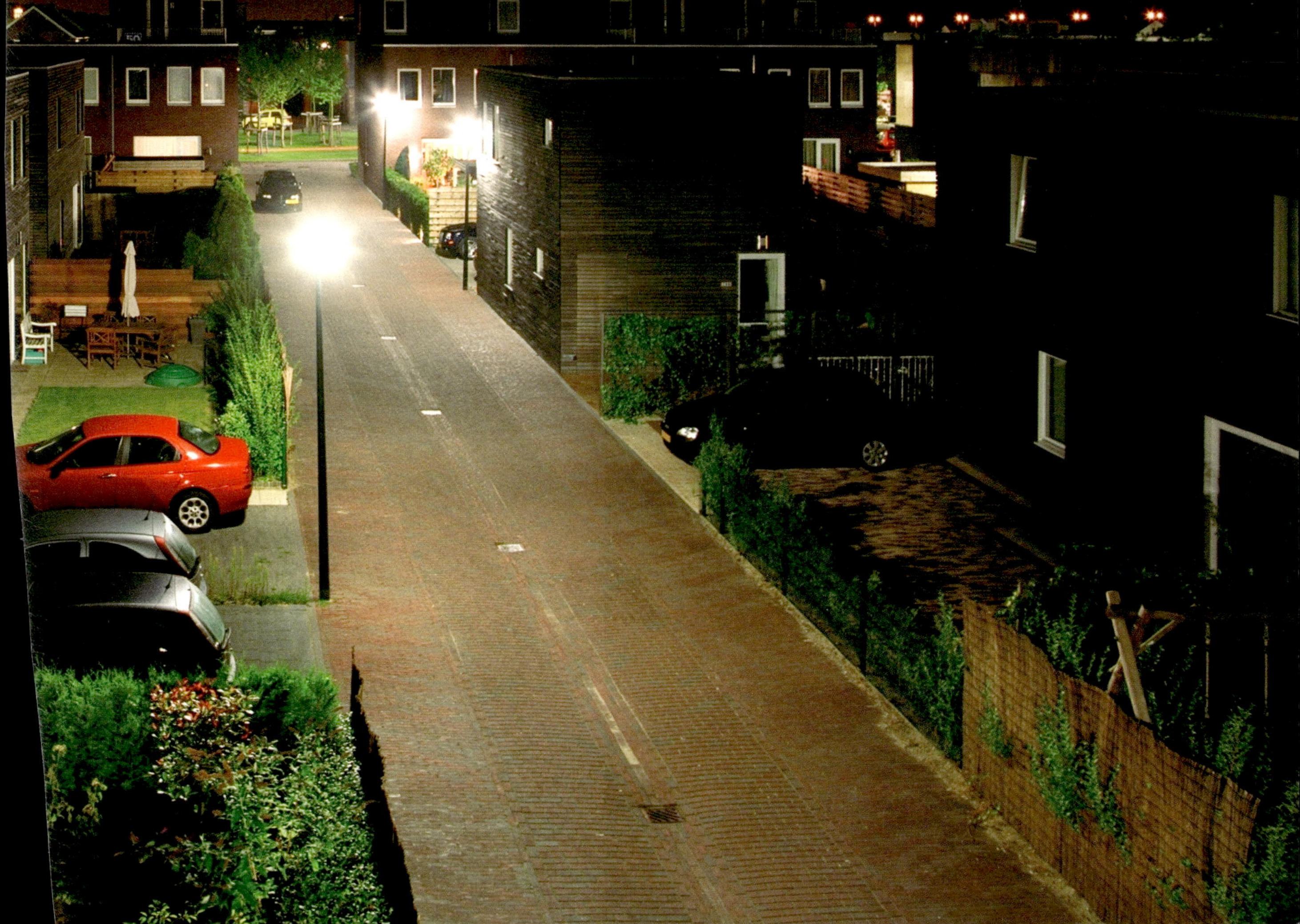

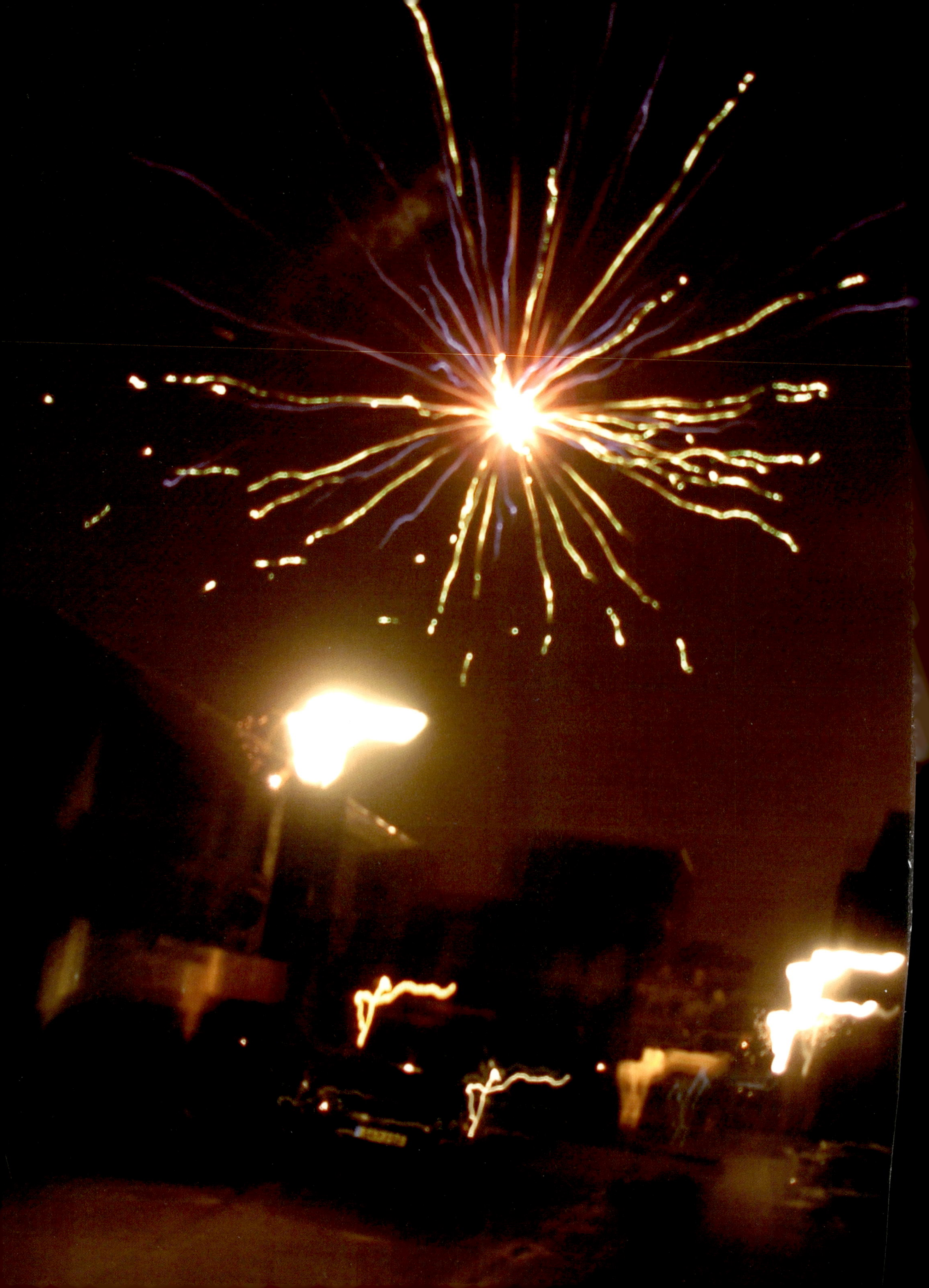